Best Hikes Dallas/Fort Worth

The Greatest Views, Wildlife, and Forest Strolls

Second Edition

Kathryn Hopper

FALCON GUIDES

GUILFORD, CONNECTICUT

FALCONGUIDES®

An imprint of The Rowman & Littlefield Publishing Group, Inc.
4501 Forbes Blvd., Ste. 200
Lanham, MD 20706
www.rowman.com
Falcon and FalconGuides are registered trademarks and Make Adventure Your Story is a trademark of The Rowman & Littlefield Publishing Group, Inc.

Distributed by NATIONAL BOOK NETWORK

Photos by Kathryn Hopper unless otherwise indicated.
Maps by Melissa Baker/The Rowman & Littlefield Publishing Group, Inc.

British Library Cataloguing in Publication Information available

Library of Congress Cataloging-in-Publication Data available

ISBN 978-1-4930-4138-1 (paperback)
ISBN 978-1-4930-4139-8 (e-book)

∞™ The paper used in this publication meets the minimum requirements of American National Standard for Information Sciences—Permanence of Paper for Printed Library Materials, ANSI/NISO Z39.48-1992.

Printed in the United States of America

The author and The Rowman & Littlefield Publishing Group, Inc. assume no liability for accidents happening to, or injuries sustained by, readers who engage in the activities described in this book.

Contents

Overview

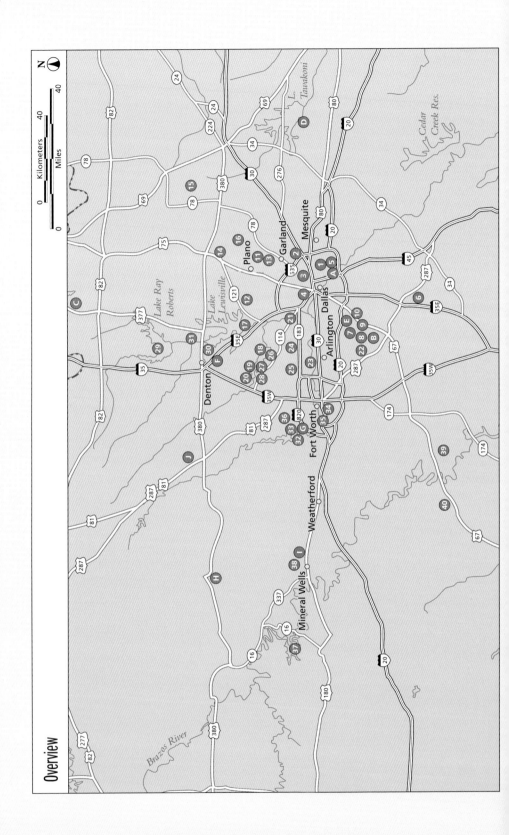

Acknowledgments

Many people helped in researching this book. Thanks to my family—Stuart, James, Henry, Will, and Andrew Tonkinson—for hiking with me. And thanks to the helpful naturalists who aided in my research, including the staff of the Fort Worth Nature Center, River Legacy Nature Center, Bob Jones Nature Center, and Dallas Audubon Society. I would also like to thank everyone who has worked to help preserve and protect what remains of the native Texas landscape so that future generations can enjoy the flora and fauna of this amazing place.

Introduction

North Texas isn't a famous hiking mecca. The region doesn't boast majestic mountain peaks or scenic ocean shorelines that beg to be explored. Indeed, the only hikes some local residents may tackle is trekking from an outer parking lot to AT&T Stadium or strolling from Nordstrom to Neiman Marcus at NorthPark Center. But it doesn't have to be that way. Thanks to the foresight and dedication of civic leaders and outdoor enthusiasts, North Texas has many wonderful parks and preserves that can feel miles away from the region's freeways and massive malls. The purpose of this book is to promote hiking in the Dallas/Fort Worth Metroplex by identifying its natural treasures and adjacent, easily accessible trails suitable for all types of hikers. North Texas has an amazing diversity of plants and animals due to its unique location where several major ecosystems converge. The U.S. Environmental Protection Agency has identified at least six major eco-regions in North Texas, ranging from the Rolling Plains in the far northwest to the wooded glens of the Cross Timbers, and the Blackland Prairie to the Post Oak Savannah in the east. This book includes hikes in all of these regions. Some go through multiple habitats, giving hikers a wide array of flora and fauna to enjoy in just an hour or two.

Catch a glimpse of the Dallas skyline from White Rock Lake (White Rock Lake Trail).

At the center of Dallas and Fort Worth is the Grand Prairie and Plains. This region includes much of the city of Grand Prairie, which reportedly was named when a woman got off the train there in 1873 and remarked, "What a Grand Prairie!" The region has clay soils and limestone rock outcrops that are more resistant to weathering, giving the region a rocky appearance and making the trails here, such as those in the Cedar Ridge Preserve, particularly challenging. The Fort Worth Prairie, home to the Fort Worth Nature Center, has even rockier soils. The region's vegetation includes prairies and upland savannas covered by grasses, such as big bluestem, yellow Indian grass, little bluestem, and sideoats grama scattered with post oaks, blackjack oaks, and mesquite trees. The region also has canyons and low-lying streambeds lined with deciduous forests of pecan, ash, oak, cottonwood, cedar elm, and hackberry trees. Drier upland woodlands contain cedar and juniper trees, which are considered an invasive species capable of taking over the prairie if not cut back or burned out by periodic fires.

Sandwiching the Grand Prairie and Plains are the Eastern and Western Cross Timbers. The Cross Timbers are an ancient line of forests stretching from Kansas south through Texas, dominated by post oaks, blackjack oaks, and understory grasses in a landscape of sandstone ridges. The Eastern Cross Timbers run through Denton

SIDEOATS GRAMA

Sideoats grama is the official state grass of Texas. A perennial prairie grass with a bluish green color, it develops oat-like seeds on its stalk and is considered a good grass for livestock in summer.

Enjoy the view from the tower at Arbor Hills (Arbor Hills Loop).

down through eastern Tarrant County and include Grapevine, Arlington, and Fort Worth down to Mansfield and into Johnson County. As a result, these cities are home to leafy trails that can be enjoyed year-round—even in the heat of summer. The Western Cross Timbers run through Jack County down by Mineral Wells. Compared with the acidic soils of the prairie, the soils here are more neutral to alkaline, making them more hospitable to oaks and other tree species. Streamside areas and riverbeds here contain bottomland forests of pecan, bur oak, and American and slippery elm, as well as ash, cottonwood, sugarberry, and willow.

Much of greater Dallas lies in the Texas Blackland Prairie, which has rich clay soils mixed with chalk, limestone, and shale, giving the soils a dark black color. Soils here have earned the nickname "black velvet" or "black gold" from those who appreciate their rich organic content, and the nickname "black gumbo" from those not as fond of the muddy, mucky texture that can make hiking a challenge for days after a rain. The Blackland Prairie is considered a true grassland dominated by the native grasses and wildflowers that attract birds such as the dickcissel and eastern meadowlark, and butterflies such as the monarch on its annual migration to forests in Mexico and Central America. Before European settlers moved to this region in the 1800s, the prairie was maintained by grazing bison and periodic fires. Agriculture and other human development have greatly diminished the range of this endangered ecosystem, which has been deemed one of the most imperiled in the world. But dedicated naturalists are working to keep what remains and restore vestiges of the Blackland Prairie. Hikes in preserves like the Parkhill Prairie make it possible to see what these landscapes looked like to those first settlers.

Many trails follow or cross creeks (Little Bear Creek Trail).

A sub-ecosystem of the Blackland Prairie is the hardwood forests of the flood-plains, which include the Great Trinity River Forest. Portions of this system can be viewed at the Trinity River Audubon Center and from the L. B. Houston Trail in Irving, which skirts the river. The City of Dallas's Trinity River trail system links trails along the river and its forest of Shumard oak, bur oak, elm, pecan, and eastern cottonwood that provide a home to white-tailed deer, raccoons, possums, and many types of woodland birds.

To the far east of the Dallas area, the Post Oak Savannah is a transitional zone between the Blackland Prairie to the west and the Texas Pineywoods to the east.

It's part of a historic oak belt that extends from Canada south to Central America. Few parts of it remain today, a victim of cattle ranching, hay production, and other development, but it remains an important habitat for endangered species such as the Houston toad, which needs sandier soils.

In searching for the best hikes, I looked for trails that offered a range of scenery, wildlife, topography, and geology. I also looked for hikes suitable for different types of hikers: families with small children, first-time hikers, experienced hikers, and those with limited mobility. Hikes were selected from all over North Texas, from the remote native prairie grasslands of Parkhill Prairie in northeast Collin County to the rocky limestone peaks that ring Dinosaur Valley near Glen Rose. Some hikes are relatively short half-mile jaunts, perfect for a quick lunchtime escape, while others are longer, 6 miles or more, that can stretch over an entire day or provide a weekend getaway. Many of these trails can easily be altered depending on time and energy, and I've outlined options and alternatives where possible.

In North Texas most parks cut off the water to fountains during the months when freezing temps are a possibility, so most water sources are seasonal. The only parks that have water year-round are those that sell water at a gift shop or vending machine or those that have indoor fountains, such as River Legacy, the Heard, Trinity River Audubon, and Fort Worth Nature Center, which have nearby education centers. To be safe, bring your own water.

The Dallas/Fort Worth population continues to grow, meaning each year more land is paved over and hiking trails that were remote paths bordered by fields and forests just a few years ago now feel sandwiched between new subdivisions and strip mall centers. Generally, the trails most accessible to the highest number of people are also the most loved and the most popular. Fort Worth's Trinity Trails and Dallas's Katy Trail and White Rock Lake Trail can get as gridlocked as the North Central Expressway on sunny weekends. I've tried to offer alternatives to these trails that feel worlds away from the Metroplex, including a few favorites located in the Trinity River Audubon Center, Cedar Ridge Preserve, and Walnut Grove Trail along the shores of Lake Grapevine. I hope some of these hikes will become your favorites as well and that this book will encourage you to explore all that North Texas has to offer.

Dallas/Fort Worth Weather

North Texas weather is classified as subtropical, with an average low in January of 31 degrees and an average high in July and August of 97 degrees. Of course, the area is famous for its extreme temperatures. The highest temperature recorded at Dallas/Fort Worth International Airport was 113 degrees, and the coldest was −6 degrees F.

Annual precipitation is around 37 inches, with May typically being the wettest month, averaging around 5 inches. January is the driest, with about 2 inches.

The old North Texas saying, "If you don't like the weather, just wait five minutes and it'll change" is a reminder to be prepared for any and all types of weather when heading out for a hike. Temperatures can drop 50 degrees or more in less than an hour, so check the weather report and layer when appropriate. Current weather forecasts can be found on the National Weather Service's website, www.weather.gov/fwd/.

Powerful storms packing hail and tornadoes can develop any time of the year, but, in general, the spring storm season peaks from mid-March through June. Don't hike if there is a tornado watch when conditions are ripe for tornado formation, or if there's a warning, which means one or more have already been spotted on the ground. Much of the area is equipped with high-pitched sirens that sound an alarm when dangerous weather is approaching. If you hear the sirens, take cover in a nearby building, preferably in a windowless room on the lowest floor. (Remember that cities also periodically test their sirens.) If you are out in the open and cannot make it to a building, find a low-lying area, but avoid culverts or streambeds. Because tornadoes are typically followed or accompanied by heavy rains, creeks can quickly fill with water and flash flooding can occur.

In heavy rains the region's thick clay soils become muddy quagmires, and bubbling streams turn into raging rivers, so consider trail conditions before heading out. Some dirt trails may be closed a day or two after a heavy rain. If you are hiking a trail that's also used by mountain bikers, check the Dallas Off-Road Bicycle Association website, www.dorba.org, to see if the trail is open. You can also contact state and local parks before heading out. Trails that are maintained by equestrian groups are also typically closed after heavy rains, particularly the Trinity Trails at Lake Lavon, whose black soils can stay muddy for several days after a downpour.

Texas State Parks Pass

One of the best deals around is the Texas State Parks Pass, which allows discounted entrance fees for all the state's ninety-plus parks for an entire year. The pass is available at most state parks or by calling the customer service center in Austin at (512) 389-8900.

Flora and Fauna

The trails of North Texas have great biodiversity due to the merging of several ecosystems including the Central Great Plains, the Cross Timbers, and the Blackland Prairie. The region is also part of the Central Flyway, one of the four major bird migration routes in North America. In the winter, migrating bald eagles have been spotted around area lakes, including Possum Kingdom Lake, Cooper Lake, and Lake Worth. The greater roadrunner's habitat extends through North Texas, where the birds can sometimes be seen darting through traffic into the safety of bushes and low trees.

In spring, many bird species migrate north from Mexico and Central America, including the yellow-breasted dickcissel, named for its call—*dick, dick sissel*—and the vibrantly hued indigo bunting. Some of the other colorful birds in the region include

Distantly related to the poinsettia, the wildflower dubbed "snow on the prairie" blooms in the heat of summer along the Talala Trail in Cedar Hill State Park, hike 8.

the northern cardinal, eastern bluebird, great blue heron, and red-tailed hawk. The gray-and-white northern mockingbird, named the state bird of Texas in 1927, can sing up to 200 songs and has even been reported to mimic man-made devices. The region's lakes, rivers, and creeks also draw flocks of wood ducks. Several of the hikes outlined in this book offer great bird-watching opportunities, including those located in the Trinity Audubon Center, Cedar Ridge Preserve, Mineral Wells Trailway, and the Fort Worth Nature Center.

North Texas is also home to a variety of lizards and snakes, including the famous Texas horned lizard, often called a horned frog. To confuse would-be predators, the horned lizard can squirt blood from its eye or mouth up to 5 feet. Unfortunately

Many types of lizards find Texas to be a hospitable home (Dinosaur Valley Trail).

these unique creatures are considered a threatened species, having lost much of their natural habitat in Texas. The state is home to seventy-six species of snakes, including the poisonous varieties such as the coral snake, copperhead, cottonmouth (also called water moccasin), and rattlesnake. Warning signs dot several trails advising hikers to watch their step and not stray off the marked path.

Squirrels are the most common mammals encountered along area trails, but the occasional possum and raccoon can be spotted in early evening and just after sunrise when these nocturnal creatures are out and about. Other mammals found here include white-tailed deer, red foxes, beavers, rabbits, skunks, prairie dogs, porcupines, and those famous Texas armadillos, which can typically be found near a water source where they enjoy wallowing in the mud.

An estimated 2 million feral hogs call Texas home and are increasingly moving into the urban landscape of Dallas/Fort Worth. They are multiplying along the Trinity River and have been known to startle early morning hikers in Arlington's River Legacy Park and on Southlake's Bob Jones Nature Center and Walnut Grove Trails. During times of heavy rains, these animals move out of the Trinity River's floodplains and into suburban neighborhoods, tearing up lawns and other landscaping. While they are generally not considered dangerous and will typically run away from humans, their knife-like tusks can cause serious injury.

Coyotes have also acclimated to city living and are commonly spotted in and around North Texas parks and residential neighborhoods at dawn and dusk when they are most active. Wildlife experts say that coyotes generally want to avoid contact with people, so all it takes is raising your voice and waving your hands to make a skittish coyote head the other direction.

Bobcats are more elusive and rarely seen due to their reclusive nature and nocturnal hunting habits. The urban population of these cats is increasing, and they have been spotted in Arlington, Fort Worth, and even downtown Dallas in the early morning and around sunset. Although some people may mistake it for either a domestic cat or mountain lion, the bobcat has a distinct shape—its shortened, bobbed tail and its back legs that are disproportionately larger than its front legs. Bobcats weigh anywhere from 15 to 40 pounds and have large, tufted ears. Trees bearing deep scratch marks could be evidence that bobcats are in the area, as they use the bark to sharpen their claws. The

DFW Wildlife Coalition, a nonprofit group that protects native wildlife in the Metro-plex, notes that bobcat attacks on humans are virtually unknown, but cautions not to attempt to touch or handle a bobcat, noting that it is especially important to stay away from female bobcats and their young kittens.

Some of the most commonly spotted animals on North Texas trails are dogs and horses. Most trails welcome dogs, provided you pick up their waste, but a few trails in wildlife sanctuaries restrict dogs because their presence tends to disrupt wildlife in the area. Be sure to check on the status of a trail before heading out with dogs in tow.

Hikers in North Texas share several trails with horseback riders, who generally enjoy the right-of-way. When you see a horse or a group of horses on the trail, don't feel shy about speaking up. Many riders will say a friendly hello, in part to get you to speak up so the horse can recognize you as a human and not be spooked as it tries to figure you out. Once a horse hears a human voice, it typically moves on by without incident. Of course it's not smart to run up or suddenly approach a horse from behind, and remember that wherever horses have traveled, it's important to watch your step.

The region draws a colorful array of butterflies that float above the trails. The Dal-las County Lepidopterists' Society offers a comprehensive list of area species at www .dallasbutterflies.com and organizes periodic field trips that include great butterfly-watching trails such as the Black Creek Trail in the LBJ National Grasslands.

On sunny summer days North Texas hikers appreciate shade provided by the region's tree species, including oak, evergreens, and pecan, the state tree. Rivers and creeks are lined with hackberry, bald cypress, and cottonwood, named for the fluffy

The Spring Creek Preserve Trail winds through a bottomland forest of chinquapin, bur, and Shumard oaks.

white seeds produced by female trees in early summer. Some trails, including the Bob Eden Park Trail in Euless and the Cottonwood Nature Trail at the Lewisville Lake Environmental Learning Center, have informative signs identifying tree species. The Texas Tree Trails organization tracks the region's noteworthy trees and offers a guide to champion and historic trees plus virtual tree tours online at www.texastreetrails.org.

In spring and summer, wildflowers form a carpet of blooms throughout much of North Texas, particularly the Blackland Prairie region, making hiking a special treat from March through May. Some common species include coreopsis, red firewheel, Mexican hat, purple winecup, and bluestem grass. Prickly pear cactus sports yellow and red blooms in spring through summer. North Texas is also home to unique types of summer-blooming maroon and brown orchids that feed on forest fungi found in the Cedar Ridge Preserve. The state's famous bluebonnet typically peaks in late March through April, along with the vibrant orange of Indian paintbrush.

Even the heat of summer brings out vibrant blooms from wildflowers, such as snow on the prairie, which blankets the fields of Cedar Mountain State Park in late July and August, while fall brings the yellow blooms of goldenrod. Although North Texas isn't known as a great spot for fall foliage, the leaves here can offer a colorful and relatively long show. Depending on fall temperatures, North Texas leaves typically don't begin changing until November, and it may be Christmastime before deciduous trees are bare. In fall the red leaves of crape myrtle and Shumard oak contrast with the gold of cedar elm and bur oak.

Another source of fall color is the poison ivy that climbs tree trunks of oak and other species. Although the plant's berries can be toxic to people, they provide an important food source for many species of birds.

With so much plant and animal diversity, the area's ever-changing landscape makes hiking here a true pleasure. Enjoy the experience of hiking in North Texas.

Wildlife and Bird-Watching Trails

The Texas Parks and Wildlife Department has developed a comprehensive guide that outlines parks and trails that offer prime bird and wildlife viewing. North Texas is covered by the Prairie and Pineywoods Trail, which is divided into east and west regions. Maps are available at many state parks, or online at the TPWD website at www.tpwd.texas.gov.

Wilderness Restrictions/Regulations

Trails in this guide are located in city parks, state parks, federal lands, wildlife refuges, and lands managed by the U.S. Army Corps of Engineers. Most trails are in city parks and do not require special-use permits or fees. Texas state parks charge a per person, per entrance fee. The state offers an annual pass that's good for a year's worth of park entries and covers everyone in the car or up to five people entering on foot or bike. Passes are sold at most parks or are available by calling (512) 389-8900.

Due to tightening budgets, some parks' hours are being reduced and, in extreme cases, some parks are being permanently closed. Check with the park's operating agency before heading out for a hike.

Enjoy and Respect This Beautiful Landscape

As you take advantage of the spectacular scenery offered in North Texas, remember that our planet is very dear, very special, and very fragile. All of us should do everything we can to keep it clean, beautiful, and healthy, including following the Green Tips you'll find throughout this book.

Getting Around

Area Codes

The Dallas/Fort Worth area has a growing number of area codes—traditionally 214 was the area code for Dallas, but in 1996 the 972 area code was added for the city's growing suburbs. Since then, the 469 area code has also been added. Tarrant County's area code is 817, and area code 682 was recently added. To the south the 254 area code covers Glen Rose down to Waco, and the 940 area code covers Denton and points west such as Mineral Springs.

Roads

For current information on North Texas road conditions and closures, call the Texas Department of Transportation at (817) 370-6500 in Tarrant County and points west, (214) 320-6100 in Dallas County and points east, or visit www .transguide.dot.state.tx.us, which has maps of current accidents and lane closures. For those using a mobile device, visit the site www.daltrans.org.

By Air

The Dallas/Fort Worth International Airport (DFW) is located midway between downtown Fort Worth and downtown Dallas and is the home base of American Airlines. For a complete list of airlines serving the airport, call (972) 973-8888 or visit www.dfwairport.com. Dallas Love Field (DAL) is located northwest of downtown Dallas and is the home of Southwest Airlines. Call (214) 670-6073 or visit www .dallas-lovefield.com.

To book reservations online, check out your favorite airline's website or search one of the following travel sites for the best price: www.travelocity.com, www.expedia .com, www.orbitz.com, www.priceline.com, or www.kayak.com, just to name a few.

By Rail

Dallas and Fort Worth are served by AMTRAK. Schedules and pricing are available at www.amtrak.com or by calling (800) 872-7245. Dallas Area Rapid Transit (known as DART) operates rail and bus service throughout Dallas and its suburbs. Visit www .dart.org or call (214) 979-1111. The Fort Worth Transit Authority (now known as

Trinity Metro) serves Tarrant County. For more information, visit www.ridetrinity
metro.com or call (817) 215-8600. The Trinity Railway Express links downtown
Dallas and Fort Worth and the Dallas/Fort Worth International Airport. For more
information visit www.trinityrailwayexpress.org or call (817) 215-8600.

By Bus
In addition to DART and Trinity Metro, Dallas-based Greyhound serves many towns
in the region; call (800) 231-2222 or visit www.greyhound.com for more information. Megabus offers transportation from Dallas to Austin and other cities, www.us
.megabus.com.

Visitor Information
For general information about Texas, visit the Texas State Travel Guide website at
www.traveltex.com or call (800) 888-8839 to order a hard copy of the guide.

For information about visiting Dallas, visit the Dallas Convention and Visitors
Bureau at 325 N. Paul St., Ste. 700, Dallas; call (800) CDALLAS (232-5527); or visit
www.visitdallas.com. For information about Fort Worth, visit the Fort Worth Convention and Visitors Bureau at 508 Main St., Fort Worth; call (800) 433-5747; or visit
www.fortworth.com.

*This Loyd Park Trail meanders through a dense bottomland forest as it heads toward Joe Pool Lake
(Loyd Park Trail).*

How to Use This Guide

Take a close-enough look and you'll find that this guide contains just about everything you'll ever need to choose, plan for, enjoy, and survive a hike in North Texas. Packed with useful area information, *Best Hikes Dallas/Fort Worth* features forty mapped and cued hikes. Here's an outline of the book's major components:

Each section begins with an **introduction to the region,** in which you're given a sweeping look at the lay of the land. Each hike then starts with a short **summary** of the hike's highlights. These quick overviews give you a taste of the hiking adventures to follow. You'll learn about the trail terrain and what surprises each route has to offer. A few chapters also include a Kid Appeal recommendation that provides parents with a quick reference for keeping their youngster engaged.

Following the overview you'll find the **hike specs:** quick, nitty-gritty details of the hike. Most are self-explanatory, but here are some details on others:

Distance: The total distance of the recommended route—one-way for loop hikes, the round-trip on an out-and-back or balloon hike, point-to-point for a shuttle. Options are additional.

Approximate hiking time: The average time it will take to cover the route. It is based on the total distance, elevation gain, and condition and difficulty of the trail. Your fitness level will also affect your time.

Difficulty: Each hike has been assigned a level of difficulty. The rating system was developed from several sources and personal experience. These levels are meant to be a guideline only and may prove easier or harder for different people depending on ability and physical fitness.

- Easy—3 miles or less total trip distance in one day, with minimal elevation gain, and paved or smooth-surface dirt trail.
- Moderate—Up to 7 miles total trip distance, with moderate elevation gain and challenging terrain.
- Difficult—More than 7 miles total trip distance in one day, strenuous elevation gains, and rough and/or rocky terrain.

Trail surface: General information about what to expect underfoot.

Seasons: General information on the best time of year to hike.

Water availability: Whether potable water can be found or you need to bring your own.

Other trail users: Such as horseback riders, mountain bikers, in-line skaters, and so on.

Canine compatibility: Know the trail regulations before you take your dog hiking with you. Dogs are not allowed on several trails in this book.

Land status: National forest, county open space, national park wilderness, and so on.

Fees and permits: Whether you need to carry any money with you for park entrance fees and permits.

The Bob Jones Nature Center's butterfly garden includes scarlet milkweed, also known as Mexican butterfly weed (Bob Jones Nature Center Trail).

Schedule: The days and times the area is open for hiking.

Maps: This is a list of other maps to supplement the maps in this book. USGS maps are the best source for accurate topographical information, but the local park map may show more recent trails. Use both.

Trail contact(s): This is the location, phone number, and URL for the local land manager(s) in charge of all the trails within the selected hike. Before you head out get trail access information, or contact the land manager after your visit if you see problems with trail erosion, damage, or misuse.

Other: Other information that will enhance your hike.

Special considerations: This section calls your attention to specific trail hazards, like a lack of water or hunting seasons.

The **Finding the trailhead** section gives you dependable driving directions to where you'll want to park. **The Hike** is the core of the chapter. Detailed and honest, it's a carefully researched impression of the trail. It also often includes lots of area history, both natural and human. Under **Miles and Directions,** mileage cues identify all turns and trail name changes, as well as points of interest. **Options** are also given for many hikes to make your journey shorter or longer depending on the amount of time you have. The **Hike Information** section provides information on local events and attractions, restaurants, hiking tours, and hiking organizations.

Don't feel restricted to the routes and trails that are mapped here. Be adventurous and use this guide as a platform to discover new routes for yourself. One of the simplest ways to begin this is to just turn the map upside down and hike any route in reverse. The change in perspective is often fantastic, and the hike should feel quite different. With this in mind, it'll be like getting two distinctly different hikes on each map. For your own purposes, you may wish to copy the route directions onto a small sheet of paper to help you while hiking, or photocopy the map and cue sheet to take with you. Otherwise, just slip the whole book in your backpack and take it all with you. Enjoy your time in the outdoors and remember to pack out what you pack in.

How to Use the Maps

Overview map: This map shows the location of each hike in the area by hike number.

Route map: This is your primary guide to each hike. It shows accessible roads and trails, points of interest, water, landmarks, and geographical features. It also distinguishes trails from roads. The selected route is highlighted, and directional arrows point the way.

Map Legend

TRANSPORTATION

═╛35╘═	Freeway/Interstate Highway
═╛82╘═	U.S. Highway
═╛78╘═	State Highway
= = = =	Unpaved Road
├──┼──┤	Railroad

TRAILS

▪▪▪▪▪▪	Selected Route
------	Trail or Fire Road
———	Paved Trail
⟶	Direction of Travel

WATER FEATURES

⬭	Body of Water
∿	River or Creek
▭	Wetland or Meadow
⋙	Waterfall

LAND FEATURES

▭	Local and State Parks

SYMBOLS

⑳	Trailhead
🛋	Bench
▥	Boardwalk/Steps
≍	Bridge
■	Building/Point of Interest
▲	Campground
⚑	Gate
🅿	Parking
🅿	Picnic Area
🛈	Ranger Station
🚻	Restroom
🏞	Scenic View
🗼	Tower
○	Towns and Cities

Trail Finder

Hike No.	Hike Name	Best Hikes for Water Lovers	Best Hikes for Dogs	Best Hikes for Children	Best Hikes for Views	Best Hikes for Wildflowers	Best Hikes for Wildlife	Best Hikes for Wheelchairs	Best Hikes for Birding	Best Hikes for History Lovers	Best Hikes for Meeting People
1	Piedmont Ridge Trail			•	•						
2	Duck Creek Trail							•			
3	White Rock Lake Trail	•	•								
4	Katy Trail										•
5	Trinity River Audubon Center Trail			•					•		
6	Waxahachie Creek Trail							•	•		
7	Cedar Hill State Park Duck Pond Trail						•				
8	Cedar Hill State Park Talala Trail					•				•	
9	Cattail Pond Trail—Cedar Ridge Preserve				•				•		
10	Cedar Breaks Trail—Cedar Ridge Preserve								•		
11	Breckenridge Park Trail			•	•	•					
12	Arbor Hills Loop										
13	Spring Creek Preserve Trail							•			
14	Heard Sanctuary Wood Duck Trail			•		•	•				
15	Parkhill Prairie Trail					•					
16	Trinity Trail at Lake Lavon	•									
17	Cottonwood Nature Trail								•	•	

	1	2	3	4	5	6	7	8	9	10
18 North Shore Trail	●									●
19 Rocky Point Trail	●							●		
20 Knob Hills Trail						●				
21 L. B. Houston Trail	●									
22 Loyd Park Trail	●									
23 River Legacy Park Trail	●	●				●	●			
24 Little Bear Creek Trail	●	●	●							
25 Colleyville Nature Center Trail			●					●		
26 Lake Grapevine Horseshoe Trails		●								
27 Bob Jones Nature Center Trail		●	●							
28 Walnut Grove Trail						●				
29 Lake Ray Roberts Johnson Branch Trail	●	●								
30 Lake Ray Roberts Greenbelt Trail		●				●				
31 Lake Ray Roberts Elm Fork Trail	●								●	
32 Fort Worth Nature Center Canyon Ridge Trail				●						
33 Fort Worth Nature Center Shoreline and Forked Creek Trails	●		●			●		●		
34 Trinity Trails	●	●					●			●
35 Airfield Falls Trail	●	●	●							
36 Eagle Mountain Park Trails				●	●	●				
37 Possum Kingdom Lake Trail	●			●		●		●		
38 Lake Mineral Wells Trailway					●				●	
39 Cleburne State Park Spillway Trail	●			●						
40 Dinosaur Valley Trail						●			●	

The Piedmont Ridge Trail offers a peekaboo view of downtown Dallas (Piedmont Ridge Trail).

Dallas, Collin County, and Points East

The eastern portion of the Metroplex is home to Dallas and its burgeoning suburbs, including Plano, Richardson, and Garland. This area was once covered with Blackland Prairie, but early settlers cleared the land for crops and discovered that its rich black soils, sometimes called black gold or black gumbo, proved both a blessing and a curse. Today much of the prairie has been paved over, but portions remain in places such as the Parkhill Prairie and Heard Wildlife Sanctuary.

The area is also home to the Great Trinity Forest, one of the nation's largest urban forests, containing dense hardwoods that border the river as it makes its way to the Gulf of Mexico. Hikers can enjoy portions of this riparian forest at places such as the Trinity River Audubon Nature Center, an example of reclaiming land that once served as a dumping ground for trash.

Despite the urban setting, the area has many places to commune with nature nestled amid the corporate headquarters and residential neighborhoods. Places such as Spring Creek Nature Preserve, Arbor Hills, and White Rock Lake offer easy escapes from city living.

Even inside the city, a hike can make you feel miles away (Arbor Hills Loop).

1 Piedmont Ridge Trail

Located at the intersection of the White Rock Escarpment and the Great Trinity Forest, this trail just south of downtown Dallas starts with a series of switchbacks as it heads up a hill then levels out as it winds along a forested ridge. Butterflies and dragonflies float over wildflowers, grasses, and shrubs along the trail including American beautyberry, popular with birds and deer. At the top of the ridge, there's a peekaboo view of the Dallas skyline, and a pair of west-facing rustic cedar benches provide prime sunset views.

Start: Trailhead south of Kelton Golf Course
Distance: 1.3-mile out-and-back
Approximate hiking time: 40 minutes
Difficulty: Moderate
Trail surface: Dirt trail
Season: Sept through Dec
Other trail users: Birders

Canine compatibility: Dogs must be on leash
Land status: Operated by City of Dallas
Fees and permits: None
Schedule: Open daily sunrise to sunset
Map: National Geographic TOPO! Texas
Trail contact: Dallas Parks and Recreation;
(214) 670-4100; www.dallasparks.org

Finding the trailhead: The trail is located adjacent to city-owned Grover C. Keeton Golf Course, 2323 Jim Miller Rd., Dallas. Park in the golf course lot or the nearby gravel lot on Jim Miller Road by the soccer fields. Walk toward the tall power tower and look for the sign and small shelter marking the beginning of the trail. GPS: N 32 75.739' / W 96 70.145'

The Hike

Dallas isn't known for its hilltop vistas, but just a few miles southeast of downtown, there are several peaks along the White Rock Escarpment near the confluence of White Rock Creek and the Trinity River. Hikers can tackle these elevations through a series of trails called the Gateway Trails that wind through Gateway Park, the Grover C. Keeton Golf Course, and Devon Anderson Park, home to the Comanche Storytelling Place, a natural limestone bowl recognized as a sacred place to the Comanche Nation. The Piedmont Ridge Trail winds through the Great Trinity Forest, a 6,000-acre wooded bottomland considered the largest urban forest in the United States. The trail is best enjoyed on a late fall day when the forest of largely deciduous trees' leaves—oaks, maples, and hackberries—are vibrant crimson, amber, and gold. In spring, there's flowering dogwood and prairie wildflowers sprinkled along the trail. At the top of the ridge, a pair of rough-hewn cedar benches provide an ideal picnic or photo opportunity and a prime perch to catch the Texas sunset. It's easy to feel worlds away from the urban bustle, but just below the ridge lie busy DART Rail tracks. Every so often, a passing train whirrs by, bringing the sounds of the city. During spring and summer, tall grasses, briars, and low branches can make the trail difficult to navigate; wearing long pants and sturdy shoes is advised. The trail has grown in popularity in recent years, but its location can be tricky to find. To access the trail, head south from the entrance of the Keeton Golf Course toward a large electrical tower and look for the primitive shelter and small sign that mark the trailhead.

The trail begins at the edge of the forest and at the 0.2-mile mark begins winding up a series of switchbacks as it heads up the ridge. At the 0.4-mile mark, the trail levels out and the forest canopy opens up as the trail goes through a series of small grassy areas dotted with wildflowers, which draw dragonflies and butterflies. At the 0.6-mile mark, turn right on a short turnoff to reach two cedar benches under a pair of gnarled live oak trees. Keep going another 50 yards past the lookout to just before the trail reaches a point overlooking Bruton Road. Here it's possible to catch a partial view of downtown Dallas. The view is better during the winter months when the leaf canopy isn't obscuring the lower half of the skyline. After taking in the view, head back down the ridge to the trailhead. (**Option:** After completing this trail, take in the nearby Scyene Overlook Trail, which starts just north of the baseball field in Gateway Park, across Jim Miller Road. Head across a large field to where the trail begins, passing through a stand of walnut trees. The trail climbs through a cedar forest before leading to a viewing spot at the top of the ridge overlooking the Great Trinity Forest.)

The trailhead is marked by a rustic signpost and covered bench.

The highlight of the trail is a cedar bench that overlooks part of the Great Trinity Forest.

Miles and Directions

0.0 Begin trail south of the Keeton Golf Course, where a small sign and primitive shelter mark the trailhead.

0.2 The trail begins an uphill climb through a series of switchbacks.

0.6 Go right at the fork to where rustic cedar benches provide a resting spot to enjoy vistas of points west.

0.65 The trail reaches the end of the ridge at a point where it's possible to view the Dallas skyline. Turn around and head back down the trail.

1.3 Arrive back at trailhead.

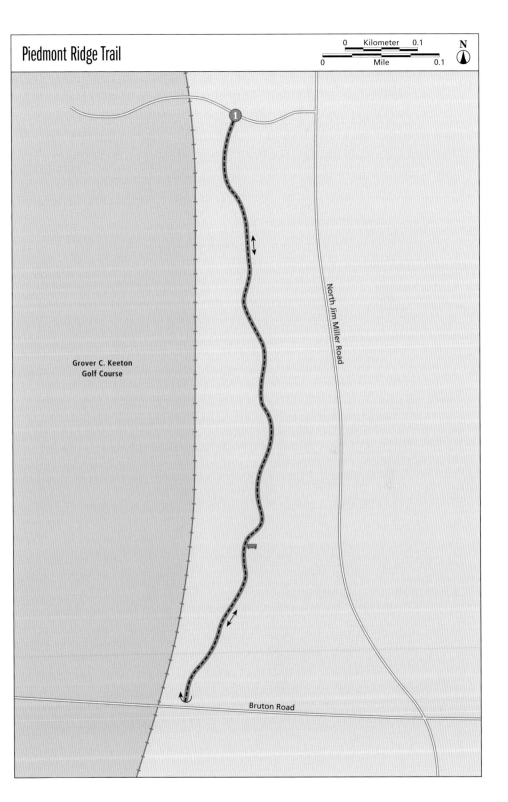

Piedmont Ridge Trail

0   Kilometer   0.1

0   Mile   0.1

N

Grover C. Keeton
Golf Course

North Jim Miller Road

Bruton Road

ROGERS WILDLIFE REHABILITATION CENTER

Kathy Rogers spent eight years rehabilitating injured birds out of her home before she obtained official status as a nonprofit wildlife organization. Once that was granted, she moved her organization and its many volunteers to work out of Samuell Farm in Garland. In 1999, Browning-Ferris Industries donated 20 acres of restored wetland habitat to serve as the permanent home of Rogers Wildlife Rehabilitation Center. Now located in Hutchins near the I-45 and I-20 interchange, the center has grown to be the largest all-species avian rehabilitation center of its kind in North Texas.

The wildlife center includes a critical care clinic, the George and Fay Young Clinic Annex, the Stemmons Foundation native Texas owl exhibit, and a museum and classroom. Visitors at any given time can find more than 600 birds of all types residing at the center and its avian-care facilities, which include more than twenty-five rehabilitation flight cages. Located at the edge of the Trinity River, bordering the Great Trinity Forest, the center also provides wonderful opportunities for visitors to view migratory birds.

A peacock recuperates at the Rogers Wildlife Rehabilitation Center.

Over the last decade, the center has provided medical treatment and care for more than 35,000 birds, most of which came with life-threatening injuries from abuse, bird strikes, animal attacks, nest displacement, or natural and man-made disasters. The center's staff provides almost all the medical treatment, from treating infections and wounds to mending broken legs and wings. Only surgeries that require anesthesia are handled off-site. Recovery time, depending on the injury, ranges from three days to six months.

In addition to its wildlife rehabilitation efforts, the center also serves as an environmental educational facility, teaching about Texas wildlife, natural history, and conservation. Rogers Wildlife offers a variety of educational programs from pre-K through 12th grade to encourage the protection and preservation of wildlife and natural habitats. The center is entirely dependent on private donations and relies heavily on volunteers. To check on operating hours and to learn more about the center and some of the birds it has served, visit www.rogerswildife.org or call (972) 225-4000. Rogers Wildlife is located at 1430 E. Cleveland Rd., Hutchins.

The Rogers Wildlife Rehabilitation Center offers some general tips for those who find an injured bird:

- Always exercise caution when rescuing wild birds. It's easier to catch a bird on the ground if you subdue the bird by throwing a towel or cloth over it and gently picking it up.
- Place the bird on a towel or T-shirt in a ventilated box with a secure lid.
- Place the box on a heating pad set at the lowest setting.
- Keep the box inside in a quiet, dark area away from children and pets.
- If the bird can stand on its own, you can provide a bowl of water. Otherwise, do not attempt to force-feed or give water to the bird.
- Contact the Rogers Wildlife Rehabilitation Center's hotline at (972) 225-4000 to arrange life-saving medical care.

Hike Information

Local information: Dallas Convention and Visitors Bureau, Dallas; (214) 571-1000; (800) 232-5527; www.visitdallas.com

City of Mesquite; (972) 288-7711; www.cityofmesquite.com

Attractions/events: In this city known as the "Rodeo Capital of Texas," the Mesquite Rodeo has rodeo competitions every Friday and Saturday night through the summer months; the popular Resistol Arena is also home to a variety of concerts and other athletic events throughout the year; 1818 Rodeo Dr., Mesquite; (972) 285-8777; www.mesquiterodeo.com

The Sunnyvale Pecan Harvest Festival is held at nearby Sunnyvale High School in November, complete with pony rides, hayrides, and lots of pecan products; (972) 226-8984; www.sunnyvalechamber.com

Good eats: Cheese's Pizza serves up New York–style thin-crust pies and a variety of pastas in a family-friendly atmosphere; 1925 Towne Center Dr., Mesquite; (972) 682-9262

Organizations: Friends of Samuell Farm; (972) 289-3276

GREEN TIP
Wash and reuse zip-top bags.

2 Duck Creek Trail

The shaded trail winds alongside the brackish Duck Creek and provides an easy escape from the nearby urban neighborhoods of Garland and Mesquite. Its wide, flat-paved surface makes it an easy hike for those in wheelchairs and families with young kids, who can also play in adjacent playgrounds and a nearby water park, the Surf & Swim. The trail is also popular with area runners and dog walkers. A disc golf course draws players of all skill levels from throughout the metro area.

Start: Audubon Park parking lot
Distance: 3.1-mile balloon
Approximate hiking time: 1 hour
Difficulty: Easy
Trail surface: Concrete
Season: Mar through Oct
Other trail users: Birders, cyclists, in-line skaters, dog walkers

Canine compatibility: Dogs must be on leash
Land status: City park
Fees and permits: None
Schedule: Open daily 6 a.m. to midnight
Map: National Geographic TOPO! Texas
Trail contact: Garland Parks and Recreation; (972) 205-2750

Finding the trailhead: Take I-30 east onto I-635 north. Go 1 mile and take exit 9A, turning right onto Oates Road. Drive approximately 1 mile eastward to the entrance of Audubon Park on the right at 440 W. Oates Rd. GPS: N 32 51.183' / W 96 36.43'

The Hike

The creek and its many springs attracted early settlers to the area back in the 1840s. By 1884 the Duck Creek community had grown to include a corn mill, post office, and one-room schoolhouse for its population of over 100 residents. In 1886 railroad lines bypassed the town, but a small depot was built about a mile north of the settlement and became known as New Duck Creek. Then, both Duck Creek and New Duck Creek began a rivalry with the nearby community of Embree (named after the local postmaster and doctor Kelley Embree), located on the other main rail line established by the Santa Fe Railroad. The two communities even worked to prevent each other from incorporating until Congressman Joseph Abbott intervened in the dispute and moved the train depot midway between the two settlements, naming the combined communities Garland after US attorney general Augustus H. Garland, who was reportedly one of Abbott's friends. In 1891 Garland officially annexed both Duck Creeks and Embree.

This 8-foot-wide trail is part of a longer trail that runs through Audubon, Gatewood, and Greenbrook Parks in Garland. The lush canopy of tall hardwoods located along the green waters of Duck Creek provides a welcome retreat from the area's urban sprawl. It's also a haven for wildlife, including woodland birds, a resident owl

A cool creek and shade make this a pleasant walk.

or two, and frogs, salamanders, and lizards. The heavy shade makes this trail a great choice during the heat of summer, when families can also enjoy an après-hike dip in the nearby Surf & Swim Pool located in Audubon Park. The trail is lined with picnic tables and benches, offering plenty of resting places. The trail begins on the north side of the parking area and heads northwest, coming close to Duck Creek at the 0.75-mile mark. The creek is down a steep gulley, so be careful if hiking with children.

COTTONWOOD TREES

If you see what appears to be cotton tufts covering a tree limb, there's a good reason why—it's a cottonwood tree.

Cottonwood trees produce seeds borne on a cotton-like mass that allows them to fly long distances on the breeze. The seeds typically appear in late spring to early summer. Cottonwoods prefer moist soils near creeks, rivers, and springs and so were a welcome sign to early pioneers and cowboys looking for a shaded place to water their animals. Arborists generally discourage planting cottonwoods because, while they are fast growing, their wood is weak and their roots can be invasive, growing into water and sewer lines.

A 79-foot-tall cottonwood in Davis County, Texas, is listed in the American Forest's National Register as the biggest Meseta cottonwood in the United States.

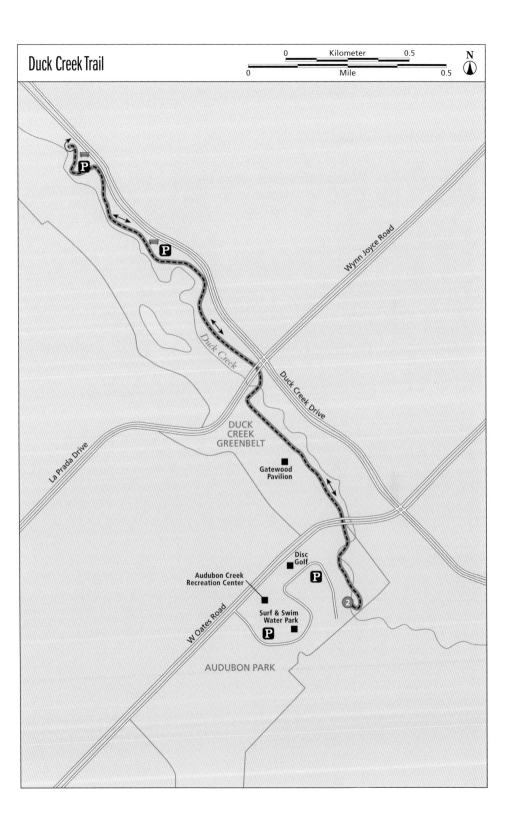

Duck Creek Trail

0 — Kilometer — 0.5

0 — Mile — 0.5

N

Wynn Joyce Road

Duck Creek

Duck Creek Drive

DUCK
CREEK
GREENBELT

La Prada Drive

Gatewood
Pavilion

Disc
Golf

Audubon Creek
Recreation Center

Surf & Swim
Water Park

W Oates Road

AUDUBON PARK

2

At 1.65 miles, bear right where the trail crosses over a small bridge above the creek. After the bridge, turnaround and retrace your steps to the trailhead. In winter it's easier to spot the nest of birds high in the trees here, and in summer and early fall butterflies float under the canopy of cottonwood trees, elms, and oaks.

Miles and Directions

0.0 Trail begins on north side of parking lot. Look for paved sidewalk and head north into the forested area where trees may separate you from the creek.

0.2 Cross under Oates Drive.

0.35 After moving away from Duck Creek, a tributary that feeds into the Trinity River, the trail again follows the creek bank.

0.5 Cross La Prada Drive.

1.65 Bear right as the trail crosses over the creek. Retrace steps back to the trailhead.

3.3 Arrive back at trailhead.

Hike Information

Local information: Garland Chamber of Commerce; (972) 272-7551; www.garland chamber.com

Attractions/events: The adjacent Surf & Swim is a popular spot to cool off for area families looking to escape the Texas heat. With a large wave pool and plenty of splash-pad areas, the facilities can get crowded on summer days, so call ahead if coming later in the day. The park is located off I-635, exit Oates Road and travel east for 1 mile to 440 W. Oates Rd., Garland; (972) 205-3993; www.surfandswim.org

The Garland Parks and Recreation Department sponsors periodic family camp-outs, called Garland's Gone Camping, at Audubon Park, which include a night hike, games, campfire, and outdoor movie. For more information contact the parks department at (972) 205-2750, or access www.ci.garland.tx.us and click on the parks and recreation link.

Good eats: Soul Man's Barbecue serves up traditional Texas brisket, ham, pork, sausage, hot links, and turkey with the slogan "We're not stingy with our meat!" 3410 Broadway Blvd., Garland; (972) 271-6885; www.soulmans.com

3 White Rock Lake Trail

Before air-conditioning, White Rock Lake was where Dallasites went to cool off and where teens went to cruise along winding Lawther Drive. But after city officials banned swimming and disconnected the scenic waterside byway in four places, the park slowly went into decline. Now joggers, cyclists, and hikers have made the 1,000-acre park and its 9.3-mile hiking and biking loop a recreational mecca. In some parts the trail feels isolated, making it easy to forget it's just a few miles from downtown Dallas—that is until the trail rounds a corner and provides a stunning view of the skyline. While it's only about 15 feet deep, White Rock Lake is home to bass, crappie, and catfish, and more than 200 species of birds have been spotted here, including swans, seagulls, loons, and, of course, ducks. There are plenty of picnicking spots, a popular dog park, and a cultural center with an intimate theater, art gallery, and museum highlighting the lake's colorful past.

Start: Fishing dock
Distance: 5-mile out-and-back
Approximate hiking time: 2 to 3 hours
Difficulty: Moderate—relatively flat terrain, but winds off the lake can add to the workout
Trail surface: Paved road
Season: Mar through Oct
Other trail users: Cyclists
Canine compatibility: Dogs must be on leash
Land status: Owned and operated by the City of Dallas
Fees and permits: None

Schedule: Open daily 5 a.m. to 11 p.m
Map: National Geographic TOPO! Texas
Trail contact: Dallas Parks and Recreation; (214) 670-4100; www .dallasparks.org/235/White-Rock-Lake
Special considerations: Coyotes have been spotted at dawn and dusk by the lake, particularly when mating season peaks around Valentine's Day. Break-ins have occurred at parking lots so lock your vehicle, hiding valuables inside.

Finding the trailhead: About 4 miles north of downtown Dallas, take the Mockingbird Lane exit off US 75; travel east, exiting at West Lawther Drive. Follow the winding road south, around the lake. Lawther meets White Rock Road in a tight corner; look for a railroad bed overhead. Bear left onto White Rock Road, passing the pumping station on the right and continuing to a large parking lot next to a fishing dock at 2920 White Rock Lake Rd. The trail begins just behind the parking lot. GPS: N 32 49.384' / W 096 43.803'

The Hike

Created in 1911 as the main water source for the growing city of Dallas, White Rock Lake no longer quenches thirst, but has evolved to become the primary recreational outlet for the city's west side. The area surrounding the lake has an interesting history, having once housed 200 or so Civilian Conservation Corps workers in the 1930s at a campsite on Winfrey Point. Their handiwork is evident in many of the area's art deco

Top: The bridge over the spillway runs by Garland Road.
Bottom: Lake water pours over the spillway.

THE LADY OF THE LAKE

White Rock Lake is home to one of Dallas's most famous ghosts—the Lady of the Lake, an apparition of a young woman occasionally spotted along the roads and paths circling the lake. The first published account of her was in 1945, when she was described as a young girl in a sheer, dripping-wet white dress who flagged down a driver and asked for a ride to her home on nearby Gaston Avenue. When she entered the car, she vanished; but the spot where she sat was wet. For more about the Lady of the Lake and other lore, check out the White Rock Lake Museum, located in the Bath House Cultural Center at 521 E. Lawther Dr.

buildings and monuments. The lake is bounded by the quiet Lakewood neighborhood to the west and Garland Road on the east side, where you'll also find the Dallas Arboretum and the Bath House Cultural Center.

This out-and-back hike turns around at Winfrey Point after a panoramic view of downtown, but it's easy to modify or continue to circle the 9-mile loop around the lake to arrive back at the trailhead. Start from the parking lot just north of the pumping station, built in 1911 and now available for party rentals. At 0.5 mile, the trail straightens out as it heads toward the spillway; a bridge crosses over the spillway, with warnings not to walk on the concrete spillway. The trail turns left, running alongside busy Garland Road for 0.3 mile, then follows the lakeshore along East Lawther Drive, where the trail passes the Dallas Arboretum on the right. A fence separates the trail from the gorgeous gardens, but it's possible to steal a few glimpses of the flowers and Rancho Encinal, the Spanish colonial home built by pioneering geophysicist Everette Lee DeGolyer and his wife Nell in 1940. The DeGolyers willed the estate to Southern Methodist University, and it eventually became the property of the City of Dallas, now housing parties and other events at the arboretum. At 2.25 miles, the trail continues to Winfrey Point, where a side trail winds up the hill offering a great view of the lake and downtown Dallas. If you want to extend your hike, continue around the lake's 9-mile loop.

Miles and Directions

0.0 Begin trail by the fishing boardwalk, bearing left out of the parking lot.

0.1 Take paved trail to the left when the trail splits and passes by a pumping station.

0.5 Head down the hill on the straight path as it approaches the spillway area, now a collection of several smaller ponds.

0.8 Cross over the bridge; turn left as the trail runs alongside busy Garland Road.

1.1 Bear left as the trail follows East Lawther Drive, passing Dallas Arboretum on the right.

2.25 Bear right, taking the side trail up to Winfrey Point.

2.5 Take in the view from the shore or head up to the highest point for a view of the Dallas city skyline. Then retrace your steps back to the trailhead.

5.0 Arrive back at trailhead.

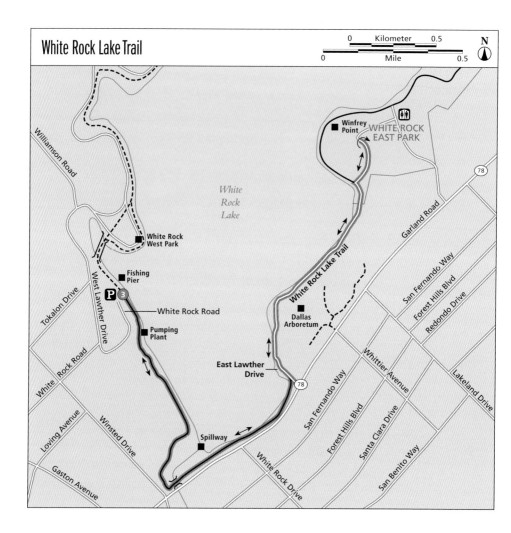

Hike Information

Local information: Dallas Convention and Visitors Bureau, Dallas; (214) 571-1000; (800) 232-5527; www.visitdallas.com

Attractions/events: The annual BMW Dallas Marathon draws more than 22,000 racers each December; www.bmwdallasmarathon.com

Good eats: Located in east Dallas on Northeast Highway, Keller's Drive-In dates back to the 1950s and has an authentic feel complete with car hops. It draws motorcyclists and classic car enthusiasts, as well as cheeseburger lovers; 6537 E. Northwest Highway; (214) 368-1209

Hypnotic Doughnuts offers creative concoctions such as the "Evil Elvis," a doughnut topped with honey, bacon and bananas; 9007 Garland Rd., Dallas; (214) 668-6999

Barbec's offers some of the best biscuits in town. Bring cash because they don't take credit cards; 8949 Garland Rd., Dallas; (214) 321-5597

Organizations: For the Love of the Lake monitors the water and stages periodic shoreline cleanups and special events; (214) 660-1100; www.whiterocklake.org

White Rock Conservancy works to enhance the safety and serenity of the park; www.whiterockdallas.org

The Dallas Trekkers Walking Club has a White Rock Lake walk most Sunday mornings; (972) 489-3072; www.dallastrekkers.org

Other resources: Rodriguez, Sally. 2010. *Images of America, White Rock Lake*. Charleston, SC: Arcadia Publishing.

GREEN TIP
Pass it down—the best way to instill good green habits
in your children is to set a good example.

4 Katy Trail

The trail runs along the site formerly occupied by the tracks of the Missouri–Kansas–Texas Railroad, called the Katy for short. The tracks were taken up long ago, and the old right-of-way of the railroad has evolved from a neighborhood eyesore to become the place to see and be seen in uptown Dallas. It's the closest thing North Texas hiking has to a singles bar, as the city's buff and beautiful come to see and be seen. Some couples have even married on the trail. But don't feel put off if you're not in the market; the trail welcomes all ages as long as you don't wander into the adjacent private homes and apartment complexes. It's also the only Dallas area trail with a logoed dog leash and bandanna—available on the website of Friends of the Katy Trail, the non-profit group that promotes and protects this ever-popular pathway.

Start: Reverchon Park
Distance: 4-mile out-and-back
Approximate hiking time: 1.5 to 2 hours
Difficulty: Easy
Trail surface: Concrete with pedestrian-friendly, soft-surface side trails
Seasons: Mar through June; Oct through Dec
Other trail users: Cyclists, joggers, in-line skaters, dog walkers
Canine compatibility: Dogs must be on leash

Land status: Maintained by the City of Dallas
Fees and permits: None
Schedule: Open daily 5 a.m. to midnight
Maps: National Geographic TOPO! Texas; Friends of the Katy Trail map
Trail contact: Operated by the Dallas Parks and Recreation Department; (214) 670-4100
Special considerations: There are a few portable potties in Reverchon Park, but no facilities along the densely populated trail.

Finding the trailhead: Exit Woodall Rogers onto North Pearl Street; go north on Pearl to Maple Avenue. Follow Maple Avenue to entrance of Reverchon Park at 3535 Maple Ave. From the parking lot, walk toward Turtle Creek, exiting at a stone bridge, and bear right on the trail, passing playgrounds on the right. The trail winds up a hill, by a stone pavilion, to the Katy Trail. GPS: N 32 48.090' / W 096 48.576'

The Hike

Located on the old rail bed of the Missouri–Kansas–Texas or MKT Railroad, this trail was born in 1997 to preserve the narrow greenbelt and create an urban path traveling north from downtown Dallas to posh Highland Park and beyond. The 12-foot-wide concrete path is supplemented by an 8-foot-wide soft-surface trail for pedestrians in many, but not all, areas. The trail is largely maintained and improved by the very active Friends of the Katy Trail, a volunteer organization that has raised more than $1 million to maintain and improve the trail. One of the easiest places to access the trail is from Reverchon Park, where the Friends of the Katy Trail raised more than $1.5 million to construct an elaborate stone entrance. The trail actually begins 0.5 mile to the south, and if time permits, you can take a right at the trailhead and hike the short distance to enjoy a view of downtown Dallas and American Airlines Center.

From the Reverchon trail entrance, simply bear left and start heading north, walking between upscale apartment and office buildings on the right and leafy Turtle Creek on the left. The trail is a straight shot with no street crossings up to Knox Street, the border of Highland Park. Mileage markers are embedded in the trail every quarter mile, beginning at American Airlines Center from the south, and go up to 3.5 miles, then return to zero.

Dallas police officers patrol the trail on bikes, and the Friends of the Katy Trail can be spotted making the rounds on a golf cart. In 2008 the city added 911 markers every eighth of a mile along a 3.5-mile stretch of the trail. At the bottom of these markers, labeled KT-100 through KT-125, are numbers indicating the GPS coordinates to help determine a location in an emergency—the Katy Trail doesn't have an official address.

The trail's length continues to grow, spreading from Highland Park to Southern Methodist University and connecting to East Dallas and White Rock Lake. In 2017, Dallas voters approved a $1.05-billion bond package that includes construction of the Dallas Circuit Trail, a 50-mile loop that includes the Katy Trail. The trail is great for

A park-like atmosphere appeals to many city dwellers.

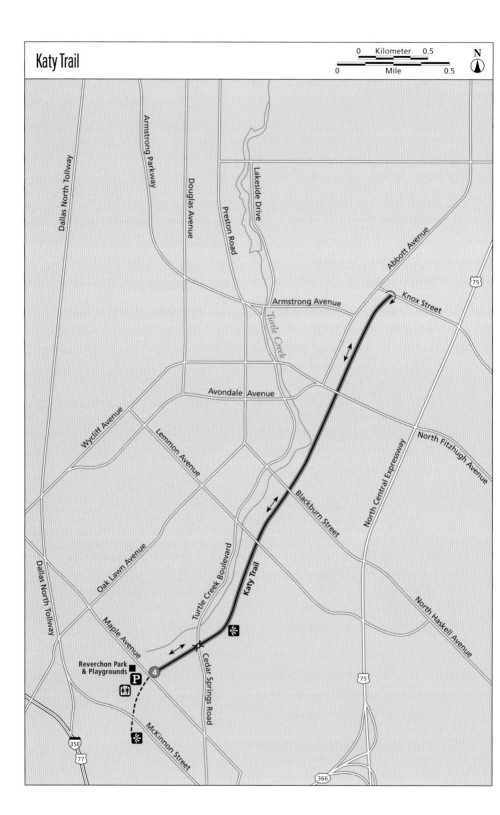

Katy Trail

Kilometer
0   0.5

Mile
0   0.5

N

Dallas North Tollway

Armstrong Parkway

Douglas Avenue

Preston Road

Lakeside Drive

Abbott Avenue

75

Armstrong Avenue

Knox Street

Turtle Creek

Avondale Avenue

North Fitzhugh Avenue

Wycliff Avenue

Lemmon Avenue

North Central Expressway

Blackburn Street

Katy Trail

Oak Lawn Avenue

Turtle Creek Boulevard

North Haskell Avenue

Dallas North Tollway

Maple Avenue

Cedar Springs Road

75

Reverchon Park
& Playgrounds

P

4

35E

77

McKinnon Street

366

SAFE PASSAGE

Each year more than a million people walk or run on the Katy Trail along with another 200,000-plus cyclists. As the Katy Trail has grown in popularity, so has the need to keep it safe. The 2010 death of Dallas jogger Lauren Huddleston, who was fatally injured by a cyclist, raised awareness of the trail's safety issues. The accident caused some to swear off the trail, at least at peak-use times, and avoid it altogether if they have pets or small children. In 2018, 10 mph speed limit signs were posted along the trail by supporters, but the limits are just a suggestion since Dallas doesn't have laws limiting trail speeds. A list of safety guidelines for the trail is posted on the Friends of the Katy Trail website, including:

- Keep to the right and announce "passing on left" when passing someone.
- Always look both ways before moving across the trail.
- Watch children carefully.
- Keep pets on a short leash.
- Walkers and runners should use the soft surface designated for pedestrians when possible.
- Stop and look for traffic before crossing Knox Street.

people-watching—both fellow hikers and cyclists on the trail, and residents perched on patios overlooking the trail. Some upscale developments now use the trail as an amenity to boost adjacent property prices. As you cross over Cedar Springs Road at 0.75 mile, take a look to your left at the pinkish building styled like a sixteenth-century Italian Renaissance villa—that's the luxurious Mansion on Turtle Creek Hotel where rock stars and other celebrities routinely hang their hats—and perhaps hit the trail.

Pass over Hall Street and Lemmon Avenue, then at 2 miles, turn around at Knox Street to return to the trailhead, but be sure to go all the way to the intersection—otherwise you might miss Christopher Janney's soundscape titled *Parking in Color* that creates what he calls "urban musical instruments" for passersby. Take a break to grab some food or drink in one of the area's trendy eateries, or simply turn around and head back down the line to the trailhead.

Miles and Directions

0.0 Begin trail at Reverchon Park, heading uphill through a stone plaza to the entrance of the trail.

0.2 Enter Katy Trail and bear left. Due to the sometimes crowded conditions on the trail, runners and walkers are advised to stay on the softer-surface trail to the right, leaving cyclists the harder, asphalt trail area whenever possible.

0.75 Cross the bridge over Cedar Springs Road.

2.0 Turn around at Knox Street, taking a break to enjoy shops and restaurants on the trendy street before retracing your steps to return to the trailhead.

4.0 Arrive back at trailhead.

Hike Information

Local information: Dallas Convention and Visitors Bureau, Dallas; (214) 571-1000; (800) 232-5527; www.visitdallas.com

Attractions/events: The Friends of the Katy Trail organizes an annual 5K run; (214) 303-1180; www.katytraildallas.org

The Sixth Floor Museum at Dealey Plaza examines the life and legacy of President John F. Kennedy as well as the events that led up to his assassination and the aftermath of that fateful day in November 1963; 411 Elm St., Dallas; (214) 747-6660; www.jfk.org

Good eats: Chuy's offers casual Mexican dining and an annual Elvis Birthday Bash every January 8, complete with impersonators of The King; 4544 McKinney Ave., Dallas; (214) 559-2489; www.chuys.com

Organization: Friends of the Katy Trail; (214) 303-1180; www.katytraildallas.org

Other resources: Katy Railroad Historical Society; www.katyrailroad.org

GREEN TIP
Carpool or take public transportation to the trailhead.

5 Trinity River Audubon Center Trail

Opened in 2008, this LEED-certified education center and the surrounding nature preserve is popular with schoolchildren and birders drawn by informative programs and abundant wildlife. This trail takes in an expansive view of the Trinity River, then heads through a prairie and adjacent woodland before circling back to the education center. The center offers several miles of trails through varying terrain and makes a great day trip with a picnic lunch.

Start: Trailhead Point
Distance: 1-mile balloon
Approximate hiking time: 30 minutes
Difficulty: Easy
Trail surface: Boardwalk and packed dirt
Season: Late Mar through Nov
Other trail users: Birders, school field trips, scout groups
Canine compatibility: No dogs permitted except for companion service dogs
Land status: Operated and maintained by the Dallas Audubon Society
Fees and permits: Small entrance fee charged

Schedule: Mon to Fri 9 a.m. to 4 p.m., Sat 7 a.m. to 3 p.m., Sun 11 a.m. to 5 p.m.; open third Thurs of each month 9 a.m. to 4 p.m. with free admission
Maps: National Geographic TOPO! Texas; maps also available at education center
Trail contact: Dallas Audubon Society; (214) 398-TRAC (8722); www.tx.audubon.org
Other: The center provides a handy checklist of commonly spotted birds at www.trinityriver audubon.org, including "birds of conservation concern," such as the eastern meadowlark, green heron, and chimney swift.

Finding the trailhead: Take I-45 south from downtown Dallas to Loop 12. Go east on Loop 12, approximately 2 miles. Look for the entrance sign on the right side of the highway at 6500 Great Trinity Forest Way, formerly known as South Loop 12. Cross the boardwalk from the Education Center to reach the start at Trailhead Point. GPS: N 32 38.283' / W 96 57.549'

The Hike

The Trinity River Audubon Center is designed to be green—minimizing adverse effects on the environment. It's located on a closed landfill, part of the reclamation of more than 120 acres on the Great Trinity River Corridor. The landfill was the site of more than 1.5 million tons of construction debris dumped illegally here over more than a decade. Now the land is reemerging to its natural state thanks to the replanting of tallgrass prairie and hardwood trees that dominate this area of Blackland Prairie. Note that collecting any plant is prohibited, as is attempting to touch, befriend, feed, or help any wildlife encountered in the preserve.

At the park's solar-powered education center, there's a large informative map detailing the various trails. This hike combines the 0.3-mile Trinity River Trail with the 0.65-mile Forest Trail for a stroll through riparian woodland. You can easily add on the interconnecting 0.4 mile Overlook Trail, hiking up a small hill to take in a

Tallgrass prairie has been reintroduced at Trinity River Audubon Center.

bluff-top view from the preserve's tallest point, and the 0.9-mile Wetland and 0.5 mile Prairie Trails, which together wind through several ponds frequented by a variety of ducks and egrets.

Enter the education center, where you'll pass an information desk and classrooms plus a large open lecture room, and go through to the rear exit glass doors.

The trailhead begins on the boardwalk over the appropriately named Trailhead Pond, the junction of several trails. Bear right onto the Trinity River Trail, away from the pond and into the open prairie. At 0.15 mile the trail splits; bear left into the forest where you'll wind under the dense canopy of ancient oaks to a rustic wooden fence where you can take in the view of a bend in the Trinity River. Turn around and head back to the spot where the trail splits, this time going straight to enter the Forest Trail at 0.5 mile and pass by three large ponds in an open prairie where birders like to stop and spot birds resting on tree limbs above the grasses.

▶ **KID APPEAL**
Trinity River Audubon Center offers a variety of kids' activities including camps and classes on fishing, birding, butterfly migration, and survival skills. A complete listing is available at www .trinityriveraudubon.org.

The trail continues on toward a wooded area and loops around two smaller ponds. Snakes have been known to rest on and alongside the trails, so keep an eye on the trail even as you look up to spot birds. It's also unwise to wander off the well-marked trail because poison ivy grows rampantly in these woods.

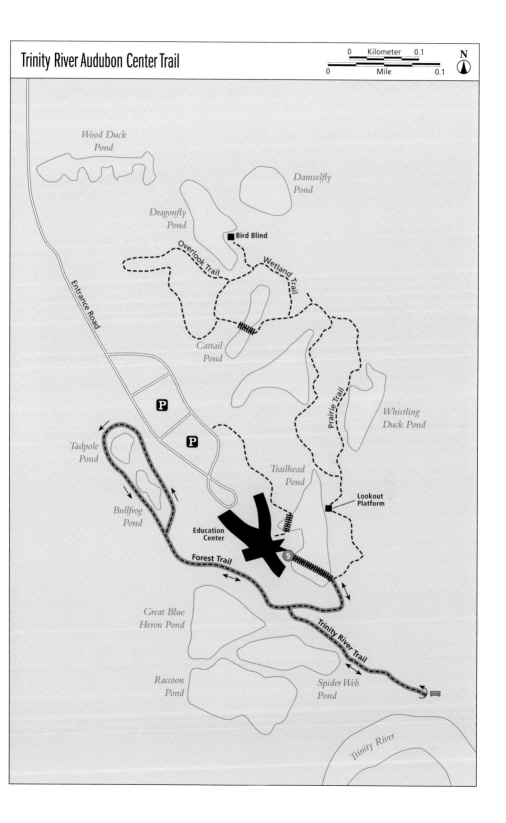

Trinity River Audubon Center Trail

Wood Duck
Pond

Damselfly
Pond

Dragonfly
Pond

Bird Blind

Overlook Trail

Wetland Trail

Entrance Road

Cattail
Pond

Prairie Trail

Whistling
Duck Pond

Tadpole
Pond

Trailhead
Pond

Lookout
Platform

Bullfrog
Pond

Education
Center

Forest Trail

Great Blue
Heron Pond

Trinity River Trail

Raccoon
Pond

Spider Web
Pond

Trinity River

N

EASTERN FOX SQUIRREL

The eastern fox squirrel is the biggest tree-dwelling squirrel in the United States. Their tendency to bury acorns and pecans and store them for the winter, but then forget to dig them up, is a major contributor to forest regeneration.

At 0.7 mile, the Forest Trail loops around back to the junction with the Trinity River Trail, so simply wind back to Trailhead Pond. If time permits, head over to the lookout platform across from the center and check out some of the other trails. Otherwise, head back through the center and exit to the parking lot. On the south side of the building, a large bank of solar cells helps power the preserve's utilities, and educational markers explain various ways to minimize human impact on the earth's resources.

Miles and Directions

0.0 Walk through education center and exit the rear of the building to the boardwalk area over Trailhead Pond. After crossing the boardwalk, go right to follow the sign for Trinity River Trail and head into the open prairie.

0.15 Bear left at the split, heading into forest toward the Trinity River.

0.3 The trail ends at the Trinity River where there's an overlook and small bench. Turn around and head back toward the education center.

0.5 At the trail junction, head straight, entering Forest Trail, passing by three ponds on the left. Be careful to look for snakes, which have been spotted sunning themselves on the sunny portions of this trail in colder times of the year.

0.7 Enter forest and loop around back to the three ponds.

0.8 At the trail junction, bear left and head back to Trailhead Pond and the education center.

1.0 Arrive back at trailhead.

Hike Information

Local information: Dallas Convention and Visitors Bureau, Dallas; (214) 571-1000; (800) 232-5527; www.visitdallas.com

Attractions/events: The center hosts Celebrate Birds, a free family-oriented festival held in the spring, and Owl-O-Ween, in the fall.

Good eats: Norma's Café is a small Oak Cliff diner with Texas favorites such as chicken-fried steak and mashed potatoes served in vinyl booths or at the counter; 1123 W. Davis St., Dallas; (214) 946-4711

Organizations: Dallas Chapter of the National Audubon Society; (214) 398-8722; www.trinityriver.audubon.org

Hikes/workshops: The center offers an extensive array of guided hikes and nature workshops on topics such as nature journaling, beginning bird watching, camping, and survival skills; (214) 398-8722; www.trinityriveraudubon.org

GREEN TIP
Hiking is a great carbon-free winter activity!

6 Waxahachie Creek Trail

This relatively flat, 5-mile out-and-back trail winds along a creek by horse pastures and features remnants of an abandoned railway. Its smooth, wide surface makes it a great choice for families with strollers or people in wheelchairs. The trail also features a peek at the elaborate pink granite and Pecos red sandstone turrets of the Ellis County Courthouse. Because much of the trail is shaded, it's suitable even on sweltering summer days.

Start: Parking lot by Lion's Park
Distance: 5-mile out-and-back
Approximate hiking time: 2 hours
Difficulty: Easy
Trail surface: Concrete
Season: Spring through fall
Other trail users: Birders, joggers, in-line skaters, cyclists

Canine compatibility: Dogs must be on leash
Fees and permits: None
Schedule: Open daily 6 a.m. to 10 p.m.
Map: National Geographic TOPO! Texas
Trail contact: Waxahachie Parks and Recreation; (972) 937-7330; www.waxahachie.com/departments/parks_and_recreation/index.php

Finding the trailhead: From Dallas take I-35 south to Waxahachie and take exit 408 onto US 77 south. Go approximately 9 miles, then turn left onto Howard Road / FM 877. Lion's Park is 1.3 miles on the left just past the rodeo center and wastewater treatment plant. Park in the lot adjacent to the small playground and concrete marker by the trail entrance. GPS: N 32 22.115' / W 96 49.943'

The Hike

Waxahachie was the bustling hub of this region's cotton farming industry back in the late nineteenth and early twentieth centuries. Today the city retains a historical charm with its vast collection of vintage Victorian homes that earned it the nickname "Gingerbread City," a nod to the detailed trims that decorate porch and roof lines. Its well-preserved architecture has also made the city a magnet for moviemakers, who have used it as a backdrop for the Academy Award–winning films, *Bonnie and Clyde* and *Places in the Heart*.

This trail captures the city's agrarian past as it winds by the Waxahachie Rodeo Center along Waxahachie Creek before coming to the edge of downtown. The entire paved trail runs more than 6 miles from Lion's Park to Getzendaner Park, but this hike is the more scenic section along the creek. The trail begins at Lion's Park and ends before crossing US 77 and entering the downtown area. There's a small playground with a shaded, wooden swing by the parking lot, and the trailhead is well marked on the east side. The trail begins with woods to the right and an open field to the left where bird boxes are posted. Because the trail straddles open fields and woodlands, a variety of birds can be spotted, from crows to cardinals. The trail winds by the field, coming to the edge of the creek before turning left as it follows along the creek bank.

Enjoy the pastoral setting.

The trail then winds by several pastures where horses amble under the shade of large oaks and pecans. Eventually the sounds of the country, horses neighing and birds chirping, fade away as the trail gets closer to downtown Waxahachie.

At the 1.5-mile mark, the trail passes the city's rodeo arena to the left, and there are restrooms and a water fountain. The trail crosses a two-lane road, and a glance to the left provides a nice view of the Ellis County Courthouse, constructed in 1897 in the Romanesque revival architectural style. The trail also briefly passes over two steel rails embedded in the concrete—the remnants of the Interurban Rail Line, a 97-mile line that ran from Waco to Dallas from 1913 through 1948.

Waxahachie is also home to the annual Scarborough Renaissance Festival held each spring, featuring costumed performers and artisans re-creating a sixteenth-century village. The grounds are located at 2511 FM Road 66 southwest of Waxahachie. For more information go to www.srfestival.com.

The longest bridge on the system was here in Waxahachie, stretching 1,454 feet long and standing 40 feet high. The cement supports are all that remain of the old trestle for the line, which also had a 400-kilowatt motor generator substation designed to deliver 1,200 watts of direct current to power the passenger cars. The line eventually closed, a victim of the rise of the American automobile and the advent of improved federal roads, including the interstate highway system.

As it approaches downtown, the trail gets a bit less scenic, with a junkyard and several barking dogs on the left. The turnaround spot at the 2.5-mile mark offers a view of the creek and several historical markers detailing the history of the railway. It's possible to cross Rogers Street and continue the hike into downtown for a meal at one of the eateries on the historic courthouse square.

Miles and Directions

0.0 Enter trail in Lion's Park by a marker adjacent to the parking lot.

0.15 Bear left as the trail turns and begins to follow Waxahachie Creek.

1.5 Cross over the street and follow the trail as it winds by a rodeo complex, restrooms, and a small butterfly garden.

2.5 Trail reaches downtown Waxahachie; turn around and return to trailhead. (**Option:** You can continue the trail, crossing South College and South Rogers Streets, heading downtown.)

5.0 Arrive back at the trailhead.

FACE TIME

Once dubbed "The Pink Extravagance," the ornate Ellis County Courthouse symbolizes the wealth of Waxahachie and the surrounding area during the cotton-farming boom that fueled growth a century ago. While the building is stunning when viewed from afar, it's even more amazing close-up because it features hundreds of elaborately carved gargoyles. As it was being constructed, locals looked at the creatures and tried to guess their real-life identities. One local legend has it that one of the carvers fell in love with the daughter of the owner of the boardinghouse where he stayed. He lovingly re-created her image in the stone he carved until one day she made it clear that she didn't return his affection. Spurned, he took to creating her image in progressively grotesque and demonic ways as his heart hardened. While historians have little evidence that the tale is true, it's fun for careful spectators to try to trace the rise and fall of his failed courtship.

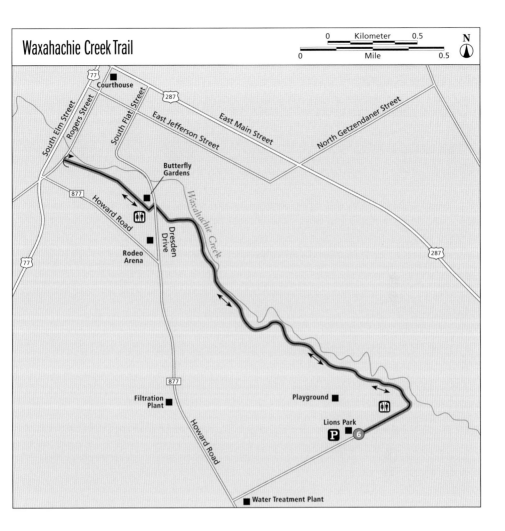

Hike Information

Local information: City of Waxahachie; (972) 937-7330; www.waxahachie.com

Attractions/events: Waxahachie is the designated Crape Myrtle Capital of Texas, and each July the city holds the Crape Myrtle Festival to celebrate the downtown's hundreds of pink crape myrtles as they reach full bloom; (972) 937-2390; www .waxahachiecvb.com

Good eats: The College Street Pub brings a bit of the United Kingdom to Texas, serving up British faves such as fish-and-chips plus sandwiches and burgers; 210 N. College St., Waxahachie; (972) 938-2062; www.collegestreetpub.com

Organizations: Ellis County Museum; 201 S. College St., Waxahachie; (972) 937-0681

7 Cedar Hill State Park Duck Pond Trail

This popular state park combines limestone bluffs and forests of dark green cedars along the shores of Joe Pool Lake. It's only minutes from downtown Dallas, making it a popular weekend retreat. This 1-mile hike is an easy jaunt through the woods and along a tranquil pond. It's also a great way to introduce young children to hiking and to please those eager to enjoy nature without tackling a long, arduous trail. In late spring and early summer, the trail can get overgrown with grasses and weeds, so wear long pants. The pond attracts wildlife, including possums, bobcats, coyotes, and foxes, and features a series of informative markers describing the various tracks these animals leave on the muddy bottoms. The trail can be combined with the nearby Talala Trail for a more challenging full day of hiking, or simply add the 1-mile side trail up the hill to take in a panoramic view of the park. Combined with a picnic, this trail is hard to beat.

Start: Duck Pond parking lot
Distance: 1-mile loop
Approximate hiking time: 30 minutes
Difficulty: Easy
Trail surface: Packed dirt, some packed gravel, wooden bridges
Season: Nov through Apr
Other trail users: Campers, birders
Canine compatibility: Dogs must be on leash
Land status: State park
Fees and permits: Day-use fee

Schedule: Open daily 8 a.m. to 10 p.m.
Maps: National Geographic TOPO! Texas; entrance gate has park maps with designated trails
Trail contact: Texas Parks and Wildlife; (972) 291-3900; www.tpwd.texas.gov/state-parks/cedar-hill
Other: Texas Parks and Recreation periodically conducts guided hikes and child-friendly talks about the park's animal residents; (972) 291-5940; www.cedarhillstatepark.org

Finding the trailhead: From US 67, take exit 1382 and go 2.5 miles north; the park is on the left. From I-20, exit FM 1382, go 4 miles south and the park is on the right. From the park entrance, turn left onto South Spine Road and look for the Duck Pond parking lot, about a mile on the left. The trailhead is adjacent to the parking lot, by the information sign. GPS: N 32 36.705' / W 96 59.377'

The Hike

This 1-mile, well-maintained trail offers wide steps of railroad ties set into slightly hilly landscape for a fun, easy ascent under a shaded canopy of trees. Halfway into the walk you pass the duck pond, then continue on to a fork in the trail where you can bear left back to the parking area and your vehicle, or right toward the primitive campground and connecting path to the Talala Trail. The Duck Pond and the Talala Trails may be hiked together if you have time for the 5.5-mile trek.

Cedar Hill State Park is one of the few places in the Dallas/Fort Worth area where the native tallgrass prairie that once covered the region still remains. Located just 10

ANIMAL CROSSINGS

It's not uncommon to spot the occasional animal track while hiking the trails of North Texas. While many times the tracks are simply dogs accompanying hikers or horse hooves on equestrian trails, there are other animals that leave traces of their paths. The best times to spot tracks are after rains and in the morning, before other hikers have tromped over them. Of course soft dirt trails provide the best place to see tracks, but the Duck Pond Trail offers an alternative—concrete markers with examples of common animal tracks in North Texas. It's relatively easy and very fun to become familiar with the various animal tracks you might find on a trail, particularly for families with children. Many, but not all, state parks offer a free, one-page leaflet identifying various animal tracks, and it's worth asking at the front gate when entering the park. The leaflet is also available online at www.tpwd.state.tx .us/publications/pwdpubs/media/pwd_lf_k0700_0001.pdf.

A coyote left this sandy pawprint.

miles southwest of downtown Dallas, the park is a popular weekend camping getaway. Its trails also draw avid mountain bikers, but this trail is only for hikers.

From the parking lot, the trail begins by the information sign, heading down a slight incline over a footbridge that crosses a small creek. At about 0.15 mile, the trail divides; turn right and wind counterclockwise around the forest of oaks and elms toward the pond, which appears on your right. The trail follows the shoreline of the pond briefly, crosses another wooden bridge, then splits again. If you want a more arduous trek, you can bear right to hike up a hill that offers a view of the park and surrounding suburban neighborhood. But this easier hike bears left, then comes to a series of markers that give concrete examples of various animal tracks commonly spotted in the park. At 0.75 mile, just past the coyote track marker, the trail splits. Bear right to return across the bridge and back to the trailhead.

Miles and Directions

0.0 Start at the rear of the Duck Pond parking lot then bear right as the trail winds into the woods.

0.15 Cross over a footbridge then bear right at the trail split and head to Duck Pond, which appears to the right.

0.85 The trail winds back to the junction; this time, bear right and return over the footbridge to the parking lot.

1.0 Arrive back at trailhead.

The pond provides a source of water that draws local wildlife.

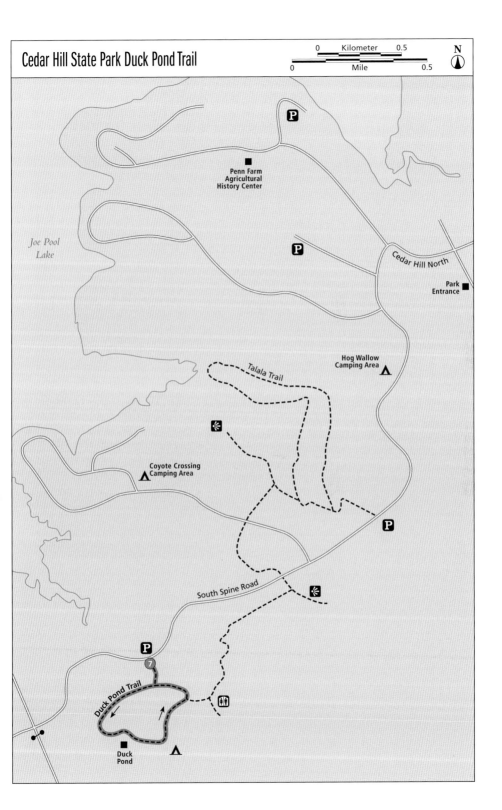

Cedar Hill State Park Duck Pond Trail

0   Kilometer   0.5

0   Mile   0.5

N

Penn Farm
Agricultural
History Center

Joe Pool
Lake

Cedar Hill North

Park
Entrance

Hog Wallow
Camping Area

Talala Trail

Coyote Crossing
Camping Area

South Spine Road

7

Duck Pond Trail

Duck
Pond

Wander the wooded paths.

Hike Information

Local information: Cedar Hill Chamber of Commerce; (972) 291-7817; www
.cedarhillchamber.org

Dallas Convention and Visitors Bureau, Dallas; (214) 571-1000; (800) 232-5527;
www.visitdallas.com

Good eats: The Cedar Hill outpost of Babe's Chicken Dinner House offers homey
comfort food; 200 S. Main St., Cedar Hill; (469) 272-4500; www.babeschicken.com

Guided walks: Cedar Hill State Park conducts periodic nature walks with park
rangers on the Duck Pond Trail. Walks are subject to cancellation due to trail conditions or weather; (972) 291-5940.

8 Cedar Hill State Park Talala Trail

Located only 10 miles southwest of downtown Dallas, this trail feels worlds away as it winds through the westernmost vestiges of Blackland Prairie on the way to Joe Pool Lake. While it can often be difficult to follow in places where grasses can overtake the trail, the payoff is a nice overlook of the lake before heading back to the trailhead. The nearby Penn Farm Agricultural History Center provides a hands-on history lesson for children.

Start: Talala Trail parking lot
Distance: 1.8-mile balloon
Approximate hiking time: 1 hour
Difficulty: Moderate
Trail surface: Packed dirt and grass
Season: Feb through May
Other trail users: Campers, birders
Canine compatibility: Dogs must be on leash
Land status: State park
Fees and permits: Day-use fee

Schedule: Open daily 8 a.m. to 10 p.m.
Maps: National Geographic TOPO! Texas; entrance gate has park maps with designated trails
Trail contact: Texas Parks and Wildlife; (972) 291-3900; www.tpwd.texas.gov/state-parks/cedar-hill
Special considerations: Much of the trail is in open fields, so wear a hat and sunscreen.

Finding the trailhead: From US 67, take exit 1382 and go 2.5 miles north; the park is on the left. From I-20, exit FM 1382, go 4 miles south and the park is on the right. From the park entrance, turn left onto South Spine Road and look for the Talala Trail parking lot, 0.5 mile on the left. The trailhead is adjacent to the parking lot, by the information sign. GPS: N 32 36.987'/W 96 58.879'

The Hike

The Cedar Hill area's unique landscape combines Texas Blackland Prairie with Dallas's own miniature mountain range. The Cedar Mountains are a mix of Austin chalk limestone and Eagle Ford shale, which, after millions of years of erosion, have created a tight series of craggy hills and valleys covered in upland forests of cedars, scrubby oaks, and elms. For hikers, that means lots of up-and-down trails, a departure from the typically smooth or gradually rising and falling trails in the region.

SNOW IN AUGUST

Temperatures in North Texas commonly top 100 degrees F in August, and that's just fine for snow on the prairie, a native wildflower that cools down the hot, dry landscape with its cool, airy white blooms. Distantly related to the poinsettia, the plant's white sap can be irritating to the skin and even toxic to some people.

▶ KID APPEAL

In 1854 John Anderson Penn and his wife, Lucinda, migrated from Illinois to settle in the rugged Cedar Mountains, and the land here largely remained in family hands until the 1980s. The 1,826 acres eventually became a state park officially opening in 1991, but the Penn family farm has been restored, and the nearby Penn Farm Agricultural History Center offers a glimpse back at what farm life was like a hundred years ago. There's a 1-mile, self-guided hike that includes historic buildings from the late nineteenth century and an array of antique farm machinery.

The park is located on the western edge of the Blackland Prairie, which once covered a great swath of the midsection of America and into Canada, but was plowed over for farmland and development. Today only 1 percent of this tallgrass prairie remains. It's home to a diverse ecosystem with more than 250 plant species including wildflowers such as Maximilian sunflower, celestial ghost iris, and purple coneflower. The black soil is heavy and turns to thick muck after a heavy rain. When it dries, it creates mounds of what some early settlers called hogwallow for its resemblance to mud pies made by wild hogs. The trails are closed after heavy rains to prevent human traffic from turning them into hogwallows, so call ahead to check on the trail's status.

This trail is largely through open prairie, making it hot on a warm day, so bring sun protection and plenty of water. The trail begins in the parking lot by a large sign. At about the 0.15 mark, bear left, continuing on through the tallgrass prairie. Cross over a small bridge and bear right, traveling down a short hill. At 0.8 mile the trail winds down toward the banks of the lake, eventually reaching a primitive camping area and chemical toilet, which serve as the turnaround point. At 1.3 miles, bear left at a trail split and continue back to the trailhead.

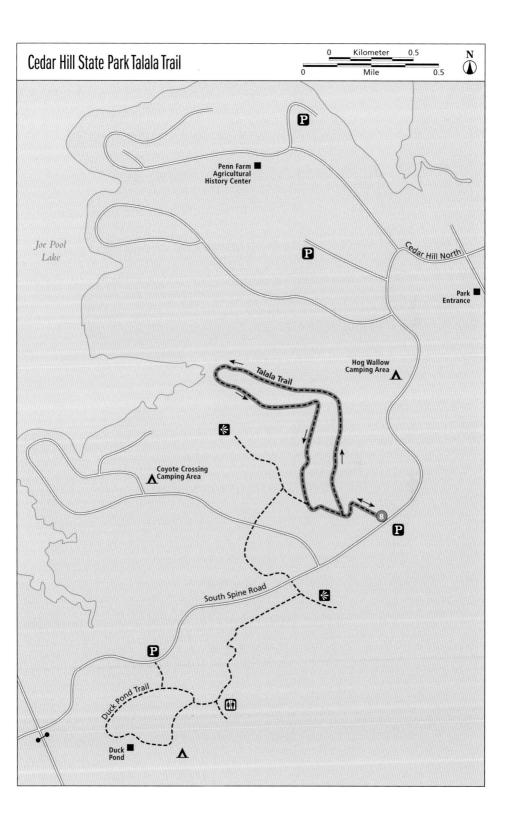

Cedar Hill State Park Talala Trail

0   Kilometer   0.5

0   Mile   0.5

N

Penn Farm
Agricultural
History Center

Joe Pool
Lake

Cedar Hill North

Park
Entrance

Hog Wallow
Camping Area

Talala Trail

Coyote Crossing
Camping Area

8

South Spine Road

Duck Pond Trail

Duck
Pond

Miles and Directions

0.0   Enter trail by marker adjacent to parking lot.

0.15 Bear left, continuing through tallgrass prairie. Here the trail can be tricky to follow depending on the height of the grass.

0.25 Cross wooden bridge over the creek; creek may be dry in the summer and in periods of drought. Turn right onto the loop portion of the hike, which you'll walk counterclockwise. Head down the hill toward the treed areas and lake.

0.8   The trail skirts the treed area as it makes its way to the shore of the lake. Bear left as the trail comes to a primitive camping area.

1.0   The trail passes through the primitive campground area with chemical latrines and areas for tent campers.

1.3   Bear left where trail splits, heading uphill as the trail winds back through the tallgrass prairie toward the parking lot.

1.8   Arrive back at trailhead.

Hike Information

Local information: Cedar Hill Chamber of Commerce; (972) 291-7817; www .cedarhillchamber.org

Dallas Convention and Visitors Bureau, Dallas; (214) 571-1000; (800) 232-5527; www.visitdallas.com

Attractions/events: Cedar Hill's annual Country Day on the Hill is held the second Sat in Oct and features a parade, arts and crafts, a chili cook-off, and other contests.

Hike tours: Cedar Hill State Park conducts periodic nature walks with park rangers. Walks are subject to cancellation due to trail conditions or weather; (972) 291-3900

Texas Parks and Recreation offers guided hikes and child-friendly talks about the park's animal residents; (972) 291-5940

◀ *Here you'll find "original" native tallgrass prairie.*

9 Cattail Pond Trail–Cedar Ridge Preserve

This challenging hike to one of the area's tallest peaks feels like it belongs in the Texas Hill Country and, given its central location in the Dallas/Fort Worth Metroplex, can be surprisingly secluded. Unlike other area trails that have little change in elevation, this one moves up and down like a roller coaster, offering thrilling views of Joe Pool Lake to the west and a calming moment or two by a cattail pond before winding back up to the trailhead.

Start: Butterfly garden
Distance: 1.2-mile out-and-back
Approximate hiking time: 45 minutes
Difficulty: Moderate
Trail surface: Packed dirt
Season: Oct through Dec
Other trail users: Birders
Canine compatibility: Dogs must be on leash
Land status: Operated and maintained by the Dallas Chapter of the National Audubon Society
Fees and permits: The Audubon Society accepts donations online at www.audubon dallas.org.

Schedule: Open 6:30 a.m. to dusk; closed Mon
Maps: National Geographic TOPO! Texas; Dallas Audubon Society
Trail contacts: Dallas Audubon Society; (972) 709-7784; www. audubondallas.org
Other: On the third Sat of every month, the preserve has workdays with volunteers, including many Boy Scout troops, doing trail maintenance and plant restoration. No bicycles permitted on the trails.
Special considerations: Signs warn *not* to leave the marked trail due to poisonous snakes in the area.

Finding the trailhead: From I-20, take exit 458 to Mountain Creek Parkway and drive 2.8 miles to Cedar Ridge Preserve on the right. A short, paved drive leads to a gravel parking lot. After parking, bear left by the building with restrooms, heading toward the butterfly garden. Follow the main trail about 500 yards to the woods where the Cattail Pond Trail begins by a large sign showing a map of the center's trails. GPS: N 32 38.276'/W 96 57.531'

The Hike

Cedar Ridge Preserve is a natural habitat of 633 acres owned by the City of Dallas and managed by Audubon Dallas, with about 9 miles of hiking trails. There's also a butterfly garden and picnic area. Depending on the weekend, the preserve can feel either crowded or blissfully remote. The preserve has ten trails ranging from the Little Bluestem Trail, a 0.25-mile wheelchair-accessible trail through a garden, to the Cedar Break Trail, a 1.7-mile up-and-down trek. It's easy to vary the trails at different visits, taking advantage of the time of year. The 1-mile Bluebonnet Trail is a perfect spring-time pick, while the challenging Escarpment Trail is a great winter escape.

The Cattail Pond Trail is a great introduction to the preserve, moving through scrubby woods with prickly pear cacti up to a prime peak where hikers can take in views to the west. The trail then travels down to the peaceful pond where benches provide a midpoint picnicking spot. It's also one of the best-marked trails in the preserve.

The trail begins next to the preserve's restrooms, by the butterfly garden, bearing right as the Possumhaw Trail splits off to the left near the beginning. These two trails rejoin just 0.3 mile from here, making for an interesting detour if time permits. Signs on the left side of the trail warn of the dangers of poisonous snakes, occasionally spotted on and along the trail, so keep an eye out. At about 0.3 mile, the Cedar Break Trail branches to the left; bear right to stay on Cattail Pond Trail. The trail begins to descend gradually as it passes by rocky outcrops. The Cedar Break Trail also loops back to Cattail Pond farther along the trail, for another detour option, but it is more challenging and may be too difficult for families with young children.

About 0.5 mile into the hike, stay right when Cedar Break Trail rejoins the trail, and enjoy a nice view of Joe Pool Lake through the cedar trees. At 0.6 mile the trail winds down a steep ravine to the Cattail Pond and a view of the pond. Turn around and retrace your steps uphill and back to the trailhead.

Relax at Cattail Pond before finishing your hike.

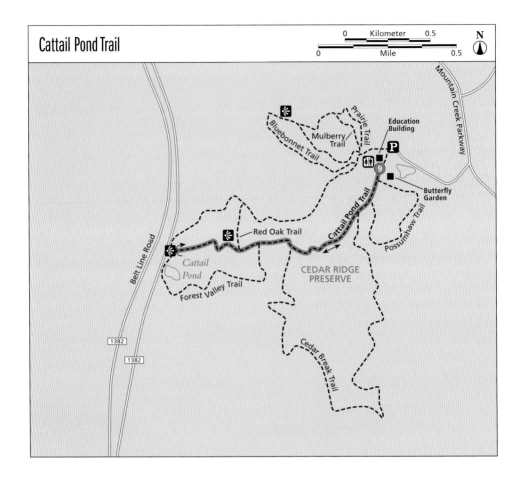

Miles and Directions

0.0 Enter the Cattail Pond Trail next to butterfly garden, then take a right at the junction with the Possumhaw Trail.

0.3 Stay to the right when the Cedar Break Trail splits off to the left. As the trail winds slightly downhill, it passes by rocky outcrops. It's fine to sit down and rest on the rocks, but resist placing your fingers in the crevices, where spiders and snakes may be hiding.

0.5 Stay to the right again when Cattail Pond Trail intersects with Cedar Break Trail. You'll wind through a forest of cedar trees where there's an overlook area that provides a nice view of Joe Pool Lake and surrounding neighborhoods, plus more than a few radio and cell phone towers. From here, the trail begins a sharper descent as it meanders down to the pond.

0.6 At the bottom of the hill, enjoy the view of the pond from a small bench before retracing your steps to return up the hill toward the trailhead.

1.2 Arrive back at trailhead.

WILD ORCHIDS

There are more than forty-five species of wild orchids in Texas, including a special, brownish maroon blooming type, the genus *Hexalectris*, or crested-coralroot, that gets its nutrients from fungus instead of traditional photosynthesis. There are seven *Hexalectris* species in the world, all in North America. Six of them are found in the United States, five of those in Texas and four in Dallas County. Cedar Ridge Preserve, with its sandy, limestone soils and oak and juniper forests, provides a particularly rich habitat for these unusual plants. Since 2004 University of Dallas biology professor Marcy Brown Marsden, her students, and volunteers have worked to document the plant locations, recording the GPS coordinates. Among the native species here are the Texas purple spike, known for its maroon flowers and yellow-orange crests, and the spring coralroot, which produces 0.5-inch-long flowers sporting white petals and reddish purple spots.

Hike Information

Local information: Cedar Hill Chamber of Commerce; (972) 291-7817; www.cedarhillchamber.org

Dallas Convention and Visitors Bureau, Dallas; (214) 571-1000; (800) 232-5527; www.visitdallas.com

Good eats: Veracruz Café offers some of the best fish tacos in town; 1427 N. US 67, Cedar Hill; (972) 293-8926; www.veracruzcafedallas.com

Organizations: Dallas Chapter of the National Audubon Society; (214) 398-8722; www.audubondallas.org

GREEN TIP
Use phosphate-free detergent—
it's less harmful to the environment.

10 Cedar Break Trail—Cedar Ridge Preserve

Located a dozen or so miles from downtown Dallas, this trail can feel totally remote even on sunny weekends. This rigorous up-and-down hike is a real workout and a challenge to those who say North Texas is totally flat. Unlike the Cattail Pond Trail, also in the Cedar Ridge Preserve, this trail does not offer mountaintop views, but it does provide a shaded canopy of trees and crosses over a small creek several times. It's a great hike for late fall, when leaves begin turning, even though many of the trees here, including the cedars, are evergreen.

Start: Butterfly garden
Distance: 1.9-mile loop
Approximate hiking time: 1 hour
Difficulty: Moderate
Trail surface: Packed dirt
Season: Oct through Dec
Other trail users: Birders
Canine compatibility: Dogs must be on leash
Land status: Operated and maintained by the Dallas Chapter of the National Audubon Society
Fees and permits: The Audubon Society accepts donations online at www.audubon dallas.org.

Schedule: Open 6:30 a.m. to dusk; closed Mon
Maps: National Geographic TOPO! Texas; Dallas Audubon Society
Trail contact: Dallas Audubon Society; (972) 709-7784; www.audubondallas.org
Other: On the third Sat of every month, the preserve has workdays with volunteers, including many Boy Scout troops, doing trail maintenance and plant restoration. No bicycles permitted on the trails.
Special considerations: Signs warn *not* to leave the marked trail due to poisonous snakes in the area.

Finding the trailhead: From I-20 take exit 458 to Mountain Creek Parkway. Drive 2.8 miles to Cedar Ridge Preserve on the right. The preserve's drive leads to a gravel parking lot. After parking, bear left by the building with restrooms, heading toward the butterfly garden. Follow the main trail about 500 yards to the woods where the Cattail Pond Trail begins by a large sign showing a map of the center's trails. GPS: N 32 38.276' / W 96 57.531'

The Hike

Start on the Cattail Pond Trail, which begins next to the preserve's restrooms, by the butterfly garden, bearing right as the Possumhaw Trail splits off to the left near the beginning. The same trail rejoins this trail just 0.3 mile later, making for an interesting detour if time permits. Signs on the left warn of the dangers of poisonous snakes, occasionally spotted in and along the trail, so keep an eye out. Stay to the right on the Cattail Pond Trail.

About 0.3 mile into the trail, the Cedar Break Trail intersects from the left; this is the return from the loop. Stay to the right on Cattail Pond Trail. Begin a light descent through rocky brush and cedar trees. At 0.5 mile the trail splits again. Bear

This wooded trail crosses a small creek several times.

left onto Cedar Break Trail, heading downhill to a small pond where Cedar Break Trail continues in a dense canopy of cedar trees. The trail loops around to rejoin the Cattail Pond Trail at 1.6 miles. The trails then wind back up to the butterfly garden and information center.

Miles and Directions

0.0 From restrooms/information center, go toward the butterfly garden, checking to see what species are enjoying the planted flowers and shrubs in the garden before continuing along the trail as it heads west toward Joe Pool Lake.

0.2 Bear right as Possumhaw Trail splits off, heading down the hill into woods of cedar, junipers, and cedar elms.

0.5 Bear left when Cattail Pond Trail continues toward the west. Cedar Break Trail takes you down the hill to the small pond. From here, the trail continues in the forest as it goes through a series of 50-foot-high hills, moving up and down. While the trail is well marked, it can be easily lost in certain times of the year, such as when fall leaves may obscure it.

1.6 The trail loops around and rejoins Cattail Pond Trail, heading uphill and into clearing where the butterfly garden and buildings by the main parking lot come into view.

1.9 Arrive back at trailhead.

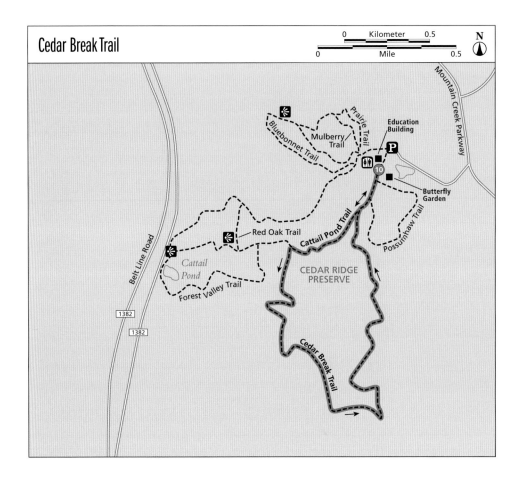

Hike Information

Local information: Cedar Hill Chamber of Commerce; (972) 291-7817; www .cedarhillchamber.org

Dallas Convention and Visitors Bureau, Dallas; (214) 571-1000; (800) 232-5527; www.visitdallas.com

Organizations: Dallas Chapter of the National Audubon Society; (214) 398-8722; www.audubondallas.org

11 Breckenridge Park Trail

This 417-acre park is a popular destination, particularly during soccer season, when the parking lots are jammed with local families toting tykes to weekend games. This hike makes the most of the park's 4.5 miles of trails, combining an out-and-back trail with a loop around the park's 10-acre lake.

Start: Across the road from the parking lot
Distance: 3-mile balloon
Approximate hiking time: 1 to 1.5 hours
Difficulty: Easy
Trail surface: Paved surface
Season: Mar through May when wildflowers are in bloom
Other trail users: Cyclists, anglers
Canine compatibility: Dogs must be on leash
Fees and permits: None
Schedule: Open daily sunrise to sunset

Maps: National Geographic TOPO! Texas; Richardson Parks and Recreation
Trail contact: Richardson Parks and Recreation Department; (972) 744-4300
Other: Bring a camera for great shots of spring wildflowers and binoculars for bird watching. On Saturday, parking lots may be crowded with soccer families.
Special considerations: Portions of the trail may be closed after heavy rains.

Finding the trailhead: From Plano take President George Bush Turnpike east to the Renner Road exit. Turn left onto Renner and travel east about 3 miles, turning right (south) onto Brand Road. The park is located at 3300 Brand Rd; turn right into the entrance onto Park Vista Road and follow around to parking lot A. The trailhead is located directly across the road from the restrooms by the parking lot. GPS: N 33 00.297' / W 96 38.067'

The Hike

It's hard to believe that this pastoral escape is partially built on an old city landfill. Luckily, the land was reclaimed, and now Breckenridge Park serves as a much-needed respite from the daily grind and gridlock of Telecom Corridor—the nickname derived from the high-tech firms that call Richardson and neighboring cities home.

The park includes more than 25 acres of wildflowers and was the former home of the city's annual Wildflower Arts and Music Festival before it moved to the more urban Galatyn Park. The park is still the best viewing spot for the city's annual July 4 fireworks display. On other days the loudest noises are cheers from the dozen-or-so soccer fields that draw area families for weekend games. Families use the park's wide trails to teach kids bike-riding and fish along the banks of the pond and adjacent Rowlett Creek.

To get to the trailhead, look for the restrooms located by Parking Lot A, then cross the one-way street to the beginning of the paved trail. From here, the trail heads down a gentle hill away from the soccer fields. When the trail splits, bear right, heading over a bridge over Rowlett Creek. The trail enters an open field, winding

The trail winds through a wooded area as it crosses Rowlett Creek.

along the creek. Apart from soccer moms and dads, the park's noisiest residents will likely be found along this part of the trail—ducks and swans who waddle around the creek's banks.

After passing under Renner Road, the trail dead-ends, so you have to turn around here, making your way back along the creek and re-crossing the bridge. At 1.6 miles, bear right at the trail split, and then right again onto the trail heading into the woods next to the rushing waters of Rowlett Creek. Listen for the rat-a-tat of woodpeckers as the trail passes through a dense forest of towering oaks and elms. The trail enters open space again, passing by the park's 10-acre pond on the left. The lake is stocked with bass, catfish, perch, and crappie, but anglers must adhere to the park's catch-and-release policy. The trail winds around the lake, passing picnic pavilions and a playground then heading up a small hill back to the soccer fields and Parking Lot A.

Miles and Directions

0.0 From trailhead, bear left and head down the hill. The paved sidewalk passes by restrooms as it moves away from the soccer fields toward a wooded area with a small creek.

0.1 Bear right, taking the trail over abridge into an open meadow by the creek and then crossing under Renner Road. Some anglers may be casting their lines here, while ducks and geese waddle across the path on their way to the water.

0.7 Turn around and circle back on the paved path, retracing the trail as it follows the creek.

Breckenridge Park Trail

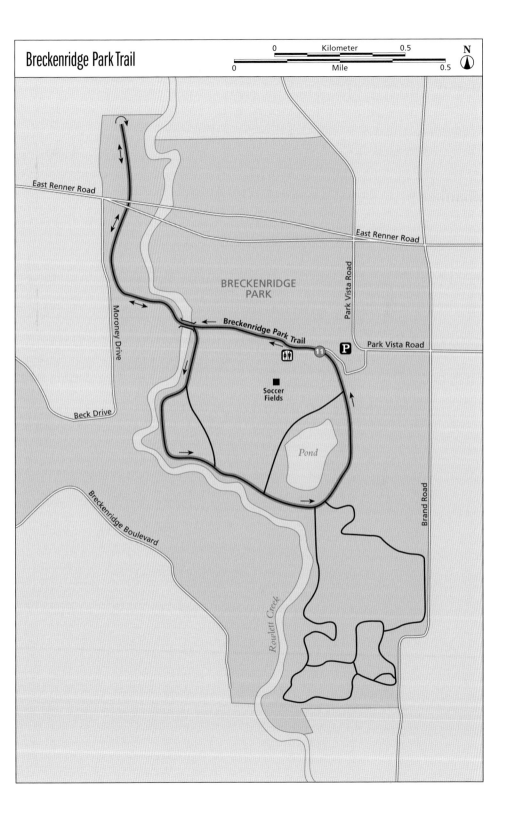

Kilometer
0   0.5

Mile
0   0.5

N

East Renner Road

East Renner Road

BRECKENRIDGE PARK

Park Vista Road

Breckenridge Park Trail

Park Vista Road

Moroney Drive

11   P

Beck Drive

Soccer Fields

Pond

Brand Road

Breckenridge Boulevard

Rowlett Creek

1.6 Bear right at the junction and keep right when trail splits, heading into woods surrounding Rowlett Creek. Here, listen for the sounds of woodland birds such as woodpeckers and cardinals.

1.9 Bear right at trail intersection, passing pond on left. The trail moves through a picnic area and a playground.

2.5 Pass picnic pavilion on right and cross over bridge, looping back toward parking lots.

3.0 Arrive back at trailhead.

Hike Information

Local information: Richardson Convention & Visitors Bureau; (972) 744-4034; www.richardsontexas.org

Attractions/events: The annual Wildflower Arts and Music Festival in May includes a 5K trail walk; www.wildflowerfestival.com

Good eats: LA Burger brings Korean and West Coast flavors to burgers, tacos and rice bowls; 2000 N. Plano Rd., Suite 115; Richardson; (469) 547-2727

GREEN TIP
Keep to established trails as much as possible.
If there aren't any, stay on surfaces that will be least
affected, like rock, gravel, or dry grasses.

12 Arbor Hills Loop

Popular with families, scout troops, hikers, and geocachers, this paved trail winds uphill through woods and Blackland Prairie, culminating in a hilltop view of surrounding Plano before looping back to the trailhead. Located in West Plano, the 200-acre park's 2.7 miles of trails and its late operating hours make it a popular destination for night hikers.

Start: Just left of the large building at the entrance
Distance: 2.3-mile loop
Approximate hiking time: 1 hour
Difficulty: Easy
Trail surface: Paved path
Season: Apr through May
Other users: Cyclists, in-line skaters
Canine compatibility: Dogs must be on leash

Land status: City park
Fees and permits: None
Schedule: Open daily 5 a.m. to 11 p.m.
Maps: National Geographic TOPO! Texas; maps available online at http://pdf.plano.gov/parks/ArborHills.pdf
Trail contact: Plano Parks and Recreation; (972) 941-7250

Finding the trailhead: Take Dallas North Tollway to the Parker Road exit. Turn left on West Parker Road and travel 1 mile; the preserve is on the right, just past Midway Road at 6701 W. Parker Rd. The trail begins to the left of the large building at the entrance that features restrooms and a large map of the park's paved and unpaved trails. GPS: N 33 02.898' / W 96 50.865'

The Hike

Just a few miles from the corporate headquarters of J. C. Penney and Frito Lay, this 200-acre park offers more than 2.2 miles of paved trails plus plenty of unpaved alternative routes to escape urban living with, of all things, a hill amid Plano's famously flat terrain. To take in the view at sunrise or sunset, a shorter 1-mile hike from the park entrance to the observation tower typically takes 15 to 20 minutes

From the parking lot, head to the large stone building at the entrance, where picnic tables and restrooms are available. There's also a large map of all the park's trails—both paved and unpaved—on the right wall across from the restrooms and more information about the diverse ecosystems in the park, including riparian wetlands, Blackland Prairie, and upland forest. On most weekends, the park is jammed with families taking to the paved trails with strollers, scooters, bikes, and in-line skates. Mountain bikers also flock to the park and its network of unpaved trails that sprout off the side of the main trail. While hikers are welcome to use the trails, maintained by the Dallas Off-Road Bicycle Association, they are typically closed for several days after rains. Hikers who want to hit those trails should check www .dorba.org before heading out.

The best views are available at sunrise and sunset from this stone tower.

From the entrance building, the paved trail heads down a slight incline, passing by a playground on the right. It then moves into a forest, crossing over a small stream before heading through a Blackland Prairie, so named for the gumbo-like soil. The soil is thick and dense but provides the perfect home for an abundant variety of wildflowers, including Mexican hat, a yellow-and-red wildflower common in late spring, and bluebonnets, the official state flower of Texas. Both typically are in bloom in late March through April.

From the main trail, you'll take a left and hit the Tower Trail at 0.3 mile. Head uphill toward the large stone observation tower; a shortcut to the tower is available on the right, but stay straight and enter the forest, slowly winding up the hill behind the tower, and bear left at the fork near the top of the hill toward the tower. Consider timing your hike to hit the tower at sunrise or sunset for a memorable view of the park and surrounding subdivisions and office high-rises. The park is also a favorite of those who enjoy night hikes, and the city website recommends wearing reflective clothing when hiking at night. The Dallas Sierra Club also organizes periodic night hikes at the Arbor Hills Nature Preserve. For more information go to www.dallas sierraclub.org (see "Night Hiking" sidebar).

From the tower the trail heads back downhill, bearing right at 1.3 miles when it reaches the park's main trail then reenters the prairie. At the next junction, the trail bears left and heads into the forest, crossing a bridge over India Creek. The trail continues straight as it winds back up to the parking lot and the trailhead.

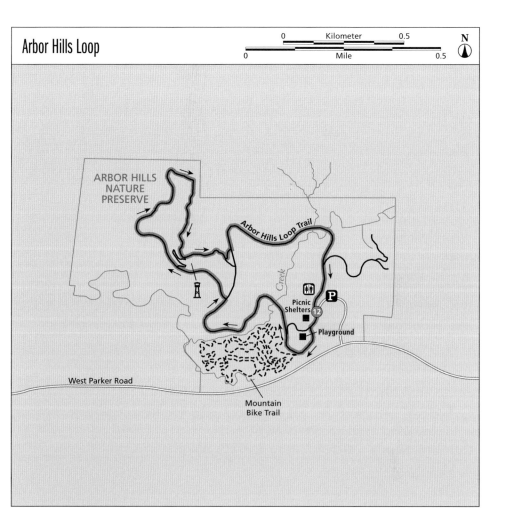

Miles and Directions

0.0 Start the trail by the large stone pavilion and picnic area adjacent to the parking lot.

0.2 Pass by a playground on the right. (**Option:** There are some unpaved trails on the left that are popular with mountain bikers and could provide an alternative hike, but be careful to give cyclists the right-of-way since these trails are maintained by the Dallas Off-Road Bicycle Association. They may also be closed after a rain.)

0.3 Stay to the right as the trail splits; head into forest and cross over a bridge. Bear to the left as the trail begins to head up the hill to the tower.

0.6 Stay to the left when the trail splits, heading uphill toward the tower as the path winds around through the woods.

1.3 As the trail reaches the top, bear to the right and enter the open-air tower to take in the view. (**Option:** You can omit the tower by going straight and heading back down the hill.)

1.4 Take in the view from the tower and turn around, retracing your steps to the main trail as it heads down the hill back to the main area of the park.

1.6 Go left when the trail meets up with another paved path, and head into a forested area.

1.7 Cross over a second bridge.

2.0 Continue straight when trail splits, heading into opening by the parking lot.

2.3 Arrive back at trailhead.

Hike Information

Local information: Plano Convention and Visitors Bureau; (800) 817-5266; www .visitplano.com

Good eats: Jorg's Café Vienna serves Austrian and German fare to the strains of polka music; 1037 E. 15th St., Plano; (972) 509-5966; www.jorgscafevienna.com

NIGHT HIKING

Night hikes can feel like a wonderful odyssey through a mysterious landscape with the outlines of plants and stones cloaked in darkness. In the summer, when daytime temperatures can top 100 degrees, night hiking is a great alternative to a day trek, but be sure the trail is open—many parks close at sunset—and be sure to bring a cell phone, which can come in handy if a flashlight runs out of power. Here are some other tips:

- Choose a well-marked trail. The paved path at Arbor Hills Nature Preserve, which is open until 11 p.m., is a great option.
- Wear reflective clothing. Some cyclists also enjoy nighttime jaunts, so it's a good idea to be easily spotted.
- Go when the moon is full. Once eyesight gets acclimated, it's often possible to hike by moonlight, but carry a flashlight just in case because it may be cloudy. It's not a bad idea to also have a spare.
- Bring a GPS unit or a compass or both. It is much easier to get lost in the dark. Landmarks are difficult to spot, and it is much easier to accidentally get off the trail.
- Bring water. It may be cooler at night, but you still need to drink.
- Consider a guided hike. The Dallas Sierra Club organizes periodic night hikes at the Arbor Hills Nature Preserve. For more information go to www.dallassierraclub.org.

13 Spring Creek Preserve Trail

This trail winds through a climax forest featuring some of the region's oldest trees, including some believed to be more than 300 years old. It is the only spot in the world where eight different types of oaks grow together in one ecosystem, making it a destination during late autumn weekends when the leaves are peaking. This level, paved trail leads to an overlook of a stream, where turtles rest atop logs and woodpeckers hammer overhead.

Start: Preserve parking lot
Distance: 0.75-mile out-and-back
Approximate hiking time: 20 minutes
Difficulty: Easy
Trail surface: Paved, stroller- and wheelchair-accessible
Season: Oct through Dec
Other trail uses: Birders
Canine compatibility: No dogs permitted
Land status: Preserve

Fees and permits: None
Schedule: Open daily 6 a.m. to 11 p.m.
Map: National Geographic TOPO! Texas
Trail contacts: Garland Parks and Recreation Department; (972) 205-3589
  Society for the Preservation of Spring Creek; www.springcreek forest.org
Other: No bikes are allowed on the trail, making it one of the area's rare paved and yet bike-free trails.

Finding the trailhead: From Plano, take President George Bush Turnpike to the Holford Road exit. Turn right (south) onto Holford Road. About 0.5 mile down the road, look for entrance to the preserve on the left at 1770 Holford Rd. The paved trail begins in the back of the preserve's parking lot. GPS: N 32 57.864'/W 96 39.183'

The Hike

This 83-acre preserve just south of the George Bush Turnpike in Garland gives a glimpse of what North Texas looked like before it was plowed under and paved over. The Preservation Society for Spring Creek Forest reports that more than 630 species of plants and animals have been observed here, making it a "relic forest." This bottomland forest has a unique, dominant overstory of chinquapin, bur, and Shumard oaks with green ash, hackberry, American elm, pecan, sycamore, and black walnut common. Many of these trees, estimated to be 100 to 200 years old, rise to heights of 100 feet, with trunks 4 feet thick.

The forest is home to a wide variety of wildflowers, including Solomon's seal and trout lilies; common vines are mustang grape and Alabama supplejack. Wildlife often spotted along the trail includes cricket frogs and box turtles that enjoy parking atop partially submerged logs in the creek. Snake species found here include Texas garter snakes as well as copperheads, cottonmouths, and rattlesnakes. This trail leads to a small viewing area of the creek, where you can relax under the dense canopy of trees

The serene wooded creek will calm jittery nerves.

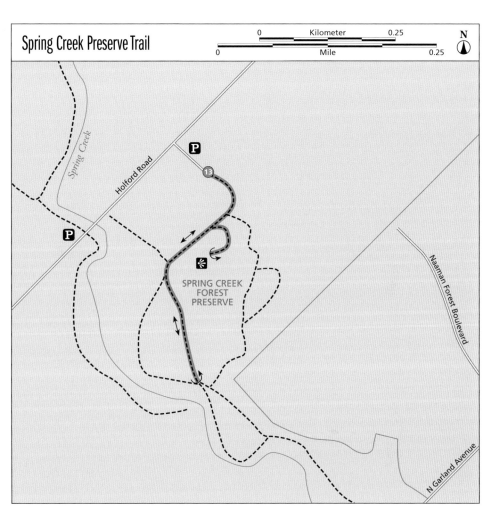

and take in the soothing sounds of the rushing water and birdcalls. Unfortunately, litter also piles up in the stream, blemishing the otherwise pastoral experience.

The forest's diverse ecosystem attracts birds year-round, making it great for bird lovers. Painted and indigo buntings, blue grosbeak, yellow-billed cuckoo, red-eyed vireo, scissor-tailed and great-crested flycatchers, western kingbird, and Swainson's hawk are commonly spotted here in the summer. During winter, sparrows can be abundant, with Harris's, swamp, Lincoln's, chipping, field, white-throated, song, LeConte's, and savannah sparrows as well as dark-eyed junco and spotted towhee. Fox sparrows can be found along the hedgerow that extends northwest of the parking lot. The Preservation Society for Spring Creek offers a comprehensive list of the bird species that have been spotted here at www.springcreekforest.org.

Well maintained by the Preservation Society, the trail is easily accessible for all ages and abilities and is perfect for a quick hike, but for those wanting more of a workout, and a bit more solitude, head across Holford Road to the Spring Creek Park Preserve, which features several longer and more primitive, unpaved trails and picnic tables. This side of the park has younger trees, including short-lived cottonwoods and hackberry trees with a less-dense canopy, allowing for better wildflower blooms. Birders love the preserve, where common species spotted include Carolina wrens, tufted titmice, and various hawks.

Miles and Directions

0.0 Trail begins in the back of the parking lot by an information sign listing rules and restrictions and heads to the adjacent paved trail.

0.1 As trail splits, bear right, following the trail farther into woods where it winds along a stream.

0.3 Trail dead-ends at the stream. Turn around and follow the path back to the split.

0.5 As the trail divides, veer right to immediately find a lookout point offering a nice stream view. Turn back to return to the parking lot.

0.75 Arrive back at trailhead.

Hike Information

Local information: Garland Chamber of Commerce; (972) 272-7551; www.garlandchamber.com

Attractions/events: The North Texas Chapter of the Texas Master Naturalists holds free weekend discovery walks that detail local flora and fauna. Upcoming walks are listed on the website www.public.ntmm.org.

Good eats: Super Chix serves up breaded and grilled chicken plus frozen custards and milkshakes. 1551 E. Renner Rd. Ste. 830, Richardson; (469) 466-1500

Organizations: Preservation Society for Spring Creek Forest; www.springcreekforest.org

GREEN TIP
Use a solar-powered charger to recharge electronics.

BUR OAK

Known to live for 200 to 400 years, bur oak is also called prairie oak, blue oak, scrub oak, or mossycup oak. It is found in the wild in deep, rich bottomlands, where it attains a large size, and on dry ridges and western slopes, where it is small and gnarled. It is called "bur" oak because its acorns have bristly husks or caps.

Bur oak is regarded as a prairie tree species because it was often associated with the prairie-forest border in the days before prairies were turned into farmland. The bur oak was one of the first trees to jump into that all-grass ecosystem and find a way to adapt. Because of its relatively thick, fire-resistant bark and natural resistance to drought, it historically competed successfully with prairie grasses, surviving the heat of the flash grassfires that swept over large areas during dry periods.

Bur oaks have the largest acorns of any North American oak tree, growing to a thickness of 1.5 inches. A bur oak tree bears heavy crops of nuts every few years. This strategy, called masting, overwhelms the ability of animals to eat all the acorns in that year, thus ensuring that some of the acorns will survive to form a new generation of trees. A large bur oak might produce 5,000 acorns in a single year. This heavy production occurs about every three to five years. But of those, only twenty-five to fifty might actually sprout, and fewer than half of those will make it to maturity.

14 Heard Sanctuary Wood Duck Trail

This comprehensive nature preserve offers a museum and small zoo along with a wide variety of trails through wetlands, prairies, and forests, where educational markers identify plants and encourage conservation. A great resource for learning more about Texas ecosystems, the Heard provides many guided hikes and interactive exhibits. This trail includes the Heard's Animals of the World Exhibit as it winds through a grassy prairie into a wooded wetland and, eventually, onto a boardwalk overlooking a pond where turtles sun themselves on rocks and ducks dive for fish.

Start: Behind the museum
Distance: 3.5-mile balloon
Approximate hiking time: 1 hour
Difficulty: Moderate; can be more challenging after rain when trails are slippery
Trail surface: Packed gravel with some portions on a wooden boardwalk with rails
Season: Mar through Nov
Other trail users: Nature education classes, school field trips
Canine compatibility: Dogs not permitted
Land status: Private preserve
Fees and permits: Small admission fee

Schedule: Mon to Sat 9 a.m. to 5 p.m.; Sun 1 p.m. to 5 p.m.
Maps: National Geographic TOPO! Texas; printed maps available at education center
Trail contact: Heard Natural Science Museum; (972) 562-5566; www.heardmuseum.org
Other: Indoor exhibits are accessible to wheelchairs and strollers, but nature trails are not. Trails are not paved and are only accessible to running strollers (not umbrella strollers). Plans are under way for more accessibility; call (972) 562-5566 for details.

Finding the trailhead: Take US 75 north from Dallas to McKinney and travel to exit 38A. Proceed east to TX 5; go 0.75 mile, then turn left on FM 1378 and drive approximately 1 mile to the museum entrance on the left. The trailhead is on the other side of the parking lot, behind the museum, on the deck overlooking a pond. GPS: N 33 09.554' / W 96 36.913'

The Hike

What is now the popular Heard Natural Science Museum and Wildlife Sanctuary goes back to the life and dreams of Bessie Heard, the eldest of five daughters, born in 1886 to one of Collin County's founding families. She never married, but instead poured her energy into civic pursuits including establishing this museum and sanctuary in 1964. She died in 1988 at the age of 101. Miss Bess, as she was affectionately known, was passionate about encouraging children's love of nature, and her legacy continues to grow with the facility's ever-expanding array of exhibits and events.

The Heard's facilities include the 25,000-square-foot museum with exhibits on dinosaurs, snakes, and an up-close look inside a beehive. The Animals of the World exhibit features non-native animals as well as a collection of native Texas reptiles. There is also a native plant garden that demonstrates how the native species can be incorporated into an urban landscape, and a butterfly garden that incorporates butterfly food plants such as Mexican butterfly weed, wild indigo, little bluestem, and passionflower vine.

The 289-acre center offers more than 3 miles of trails and is home to more than 240 species of animals. A special upland portion of the sanctuary is being managed to provide habitat for the endangered Texas horned lizard, or horned frog, a 6-inch reptile that shoots red liquid from its eyes to repel attack. Other animals found here include flying squirrels, alligator snapping turtles, and the occasional bobcat. As you enter the trail, a sign warns about the dangers of copperhead snakes, whose reddish brown color can blend in with the sandy dirt trail. Keep an eye out as you walk for snakes that may be sunning themselves on the trail. This route combines the 1-mile Bluestem Trail, named for a grass that grows to 4 feet tall, and the 1-mile Wood Duck Trail, to sample a variety of ecosystems.

From the education center, exit to the back patio and look for the trail marker, bearing left and heading toward the center's outdoor animal exhibits. True to its sanctuary name, Heard provides a home for wayward and injured animals including several exotic species as well as Texas natives. Detour from the trail through the exhibits then pick it up again, bearing right into the Blackland Prairie. Here you'll see an educational marker explaining that only a tiny fraction, less than 0.04 percent, remains of the 12 million acres of Blackland Prairie that once covered Texas. The trail winds through a forested wetland and becomes a boardwalk over the mud. The Bluestem

The Wood Duck Trail reaches a wetlands area that is home to many types of birds and amphibians.
HEARD WILDLIFE SANCTUARY

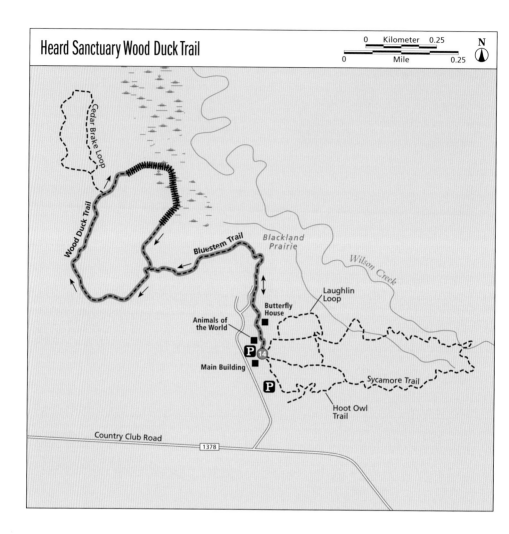

Heard Sanctuary Wood Duck Trail

0   Kilometer   0.25

0   Mile   0.25

N

Cedar Brake Loop

Wood Duck Trail

Bluestem Trail

Blackland
Prairie

Wilson Creek

Laughlin
Loop

Butterfly
House

Animals of
the World

Main Building

Hoot Owl
Trail

Sycamore Trail

Country Club Road

1378

Trail ends near a large picnic pavilion; bear right and pick up the Wood Duck Trail, a boardwalk over a pond, where several benches provide ideal wildlife watching. The trail curves back around to meet up with the Bluestem Trail, where you can retrace your steps back to the education center.

Miles and Directions

0.0   Enter the education center and walk through to the back, exiting to a terrace. Look for signs for Bluestem Trail to the left and begin walking into woods toward the zoo.

0.1   The small zoo area is on the left; detour through exhibits or continue along the main trail through the Animals of the World Exhibit, which includes exotic birds, such as the blue-and-gold macaw and Muluccan cockatoo, as well as native Texas species, such as the nine-banded armadillo and an albino raccoon.

0.4 The trail heads through a Blackland Prairie area with informative signs explaining its unique ecosystem.

0.6 Cross over a gravel service road and continue straight into woods. (**FYI:** Certain parts of the trail travel over a wooden boardwalk to help hikers avoid the mucky soils. For those with strollers, the trail is doable, but requires some lifting and navigating the sometimes rocky paths.)

0.7 Bear left, following the sign for the Wood Duck Trail, and head toward the pond.

1.0 Cross the service road and continue on boardwalk over the pond. Here a few benches enable you to enjoy watching the pond's wildlife, including turtles that like to sun themselves on the rocks.

1.4 Cross the road and take the trail back into forest.

1.6 Cross the service road and head into an open prairie area; pick up the Bluestem Trail and head back to the education center.

3.5 Arrive back at trailhead.

Hike Information

Local information: McKinney Convention and Visitors Bureau; (888) 649-8499; www.visitmckinney.org

Good eats: Baker's Drive-In is an old-school burger joint that's been enjoyed by generations of McKinney residents; 1001 S. McDonald St., McKinney; (972) 542-4050

Hike tours: Special night hikes are often scheduled by the museum; call for more information.

Organizations: Heard Natural Science Museum and Wildlife Sanctuary; (972) 562-5566; www.heardmuseum.org

NATURE ADVENTURES

The Heard offers a variety of adventurous options for nature lovers looking to push their limits. For example, a leadership and team-enrichment program includes such classes as a new High and Low Elements Rope Course. There are also many guided hikes, including popular night hikes.

An EcoAdventures Paddling Program includes three-hour, guided wetlands canoe tours, moonlight canoe trails, and a special two-day Girls Getaway Camping and Paddling Trip for ages 7 and up. For the latest information go to www.heardmuseum.org.

15 Parkhill Prairie Trail

Located in extreme northeast Collin County, this out-and-back hike runs through a 436-acre grassland that includes a 52-acre remnant of Blackland Prairie. It's best enjoyed in the spring and early summer when it is carpeted with wildflowers, such as wild petunia, Indian paintbrush, winecup, purple coneflower, and goldenrod.

Start: Main parking lot
Distance: 1.8-mile out-and-back
Approximate hiking time: 40 minutes
Difficulty: Moderate
Trail surface: Grass
Season: Mar through June
Other trail users: Birders, kite flyers

Canine compatibility: Dogs must be on leash
Land status: City park
Fees and permits: None
Schedule: Open daily sunrise to sunset
Map: National Geographic TOPO! Texas
Trail contact: Collin County; (972) 424-1460, ext. 3744

Finding the trailhead: From McKinney go east on US 380 toward Farmersville. Take TX 78 north to Blue Ridge. Near Blue Ridge, turn right onto CR 825, heading east. Turn right onto CR 668 and travel 2 miles to the park on the left. The trailhead is just inside the park by the main parking lot. GPS: N 33 16.262' / W 96 17.864'

The Hike

This hike through the vast open prairie provides a glimpse of what early settlers in the area encountered when they first arrived. The park was funded through an initiative to preserve open spaces in rapidly developing Collin County and feels worlds away from the Metroplex. The bucolic drive to the park winds by ranches and farms, crossing over Pot Rack Creek.

The 436-acre preserve includes a 52-acre piece of native Blackland Prairie. Before European settlers came to the Central Plains and began tilling its soils for crops and using it for grazing lands, it was covered by the Blackland Prairie, which has a special mix of soils and mineral deposits that support a diverse array of plant and animal species. Dubbed "Black Velvet," the dark soil enjoyed deep calcareous deposits and became famous for high productivity. They were formed by the frequent fires that swept the plains and also by vast herds of buffalo that grazed here. Today the Blackland Prairie is considered the most endangered large ecosystem in North America. In Texas, only a tiny fraction remains, less than 1 percent of the original 20 million acres that once covered three-fourths of the state from the Red River south to San Antonio.

The prairie's diverse ecosystem includes more than 200 plant species including native grasses such as bluestem, big bluestem, and yellow Indian grass, as well as wildflowers such as prairie parsley, milkweed, coneflower, Mexican hat, gay feather, azure sage, goldenrod, Texas giant sage, and, of course, bluebonnet and Indian paintbrush.

This Blackland Prairie is just as the early settlers would have seen.

Parkhill Prairie is home to the Parkhill Prairie crayfish, *Procambarus steigmani*. Only 2 to 3 inches long, these crayfish burrow into the ground and live in gray mounds, dubbed crayfish chimneys. They are most active at night, when they leave the mound to feed. They are frightened by white light, so use a red-filtered flashlight to observe these unique creatures.

NATIVE PRAIRIES OF TEXAS

With less than 1 percent of the tallgrass prairies of Texas remaining today, the flora and fauna that call the region home face a greatly reduced habitat.

But the Native Prairie Association of North Texas is working to preserve what remains of the fast-disappearing ecosystem, buying up parcels of land as they become available. The nonprofit organization and land trust protects more than 1,200 acres of native Texas prairie, including 100 acres of endangered tallgrass prairie, and promotes prairie restoration.

The organization also holds frequent workshops and field trips exploring the plant and animal life of the prairies. For more information go to www.texas prairie.org, or call (512) 772-4741.

Parkhill Prairie is one small fragment that remains of the Blackland Prairie, named for its rich black soils.

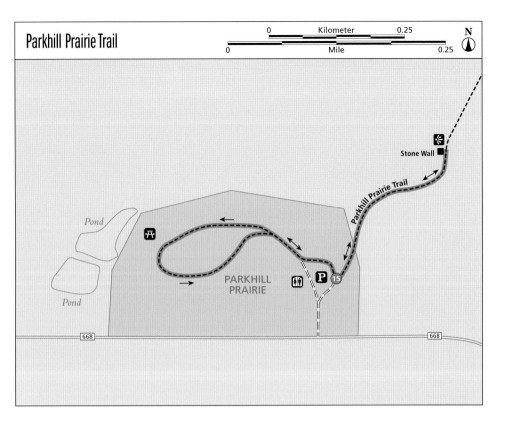

Parkhill Prairie Trail

Because most of the trail is open, it's best hiked on a cool, sunny day, ideally during the peak wildflower blooming time of April through June. The park has several covered pavilions with cooking pits, making it a great spot for picnicking.

The trail can also be hard to follow if it hasn't been mowed recently, and be aware that during much of the year, insects such as grasshoppers will pop out of the grasses with your every step so long pants are advisable. Fire-ant mounds are evident as well; avoid wearing open-toed shoes.

To help preserve the land as prairie, the county, working with The Nature Conservancy, schedules periodic burns to control invasive plant species. You may find charred tree trunks along the trail.

From the parking lot, the trail begins by the restrooms. Follow the mowed lane up and down the rolling hills until the trail arrives at an overlook with a half-stone wall. This marks the turnaround spot; head back along the trail to the parking lot.

Miles and Directions

0.0 Trail begins by the first parking lot to the right of the entrance. Look for a kiosk with information about native prairie flora and fauna. From here, follow the mowed path through the grasslands up a small hill.

0.8 Reach a viewing spot with a small stone wall and turn around to retrace the path back to the parking lot. The hike could end here, but for a longer hike, take the paved drive out of the parking lot as it passes by the restroom building.

1.2 Pass a covered picnic pavilion on the right, and continue following the road as it curves around. There's a side trail down to a small pond to the right, which makes a nice spot for fishing or picnicking.

1.5 Pass back by the restrooms and continue to the parking lot and trailhead.

1.8 Arrive back at trailhead.

Hike Information

Local information: Farmersville Chamber of Commerce; 2051 CR 655, Farmersville; (972) 782-6533

Attractions/events: Famous as the home of the Ewing clan in the television series *Dallas,* Southfork Ranch is a real tourist attraction that has managed to keep tourists coming years after the original series signed off in 1991 and through the reboot that aired 2012–2015. The ranch is open daily, and tours include a museum of memorabilia including the gun that shot J.R., Lucy's wedding dress, and Jock's Lincoln Continental; 3700 Hogge Rd., Parker; (972) 442-7800; www.southforkranch.com

Good eats: The Brownie Cottage serves more than forty variations of the popular baked treats plus traditional breakfast and lunch fare; 205 Hwy. 78, Farmersville; (972) 837-6904

Organization: Collin County Recreation & Sports; (972) 424-1460

Nearby resources: The nearby Sister Grove Park, located off CR 562 east of Princeton, is a 75-acre park with a hike/bike trail open for day use. The park has picnic tables and restrooms, and the trail leads through a grassy field into the woods on the edge of Lake Lavon. The trail here is maintained by the Dallas Off-Road Bicycle Association (www.dorba.org) and may be closed after heavy rains.

16 Trinity Trail at Lake Lavon

A favorite with horseback riders as well as hikers, this scenic 3-mile hike winds by the shores of Lake Lavon through grassy areas and hardwood forests. It is also home to one of the state's largest sycamore trees. The trails here are for horses first, so be sensitive to the needs of horseback riders, and be sure to watch your step while enjoying the great view of the lake and its adjacent grasslands and glens.

Start: Gravel parking lot
Distance: 3-mile out-and-back
Approximate hiking time: 1 to 2 hours
Difficulty: Moderate to difficult given the mucky soils in this area
Trail surface: Dirt that can be muddy for days after a heavy rain
Season: Mar through June
Other trail users: Birders, horseback riders
Canine compatibility: Dogs must be on leash, but given the number of horses on this trail, it's easier not to bring pets or at least be sure they are comfortable around horses.
Land status: US Army Corps of Engineers watershed
Fees and permits: None
Schedule: Open daily sunrise to sunset
Map: National Geographic TOPO! Texas
Trail contacts: US Army Corps of Engineers; (972) 442-3141; www.swf-wc.usace.army .mil/lavon/Trinity Trail Preservation Association; (972) 824-3369; www.trinitytrailriders.org

Finding the trailhead: From Dallas take I-75 north to Allen; exit at Bethany Drive and turn right. Head east about 5 miles on Bethany, which becomes Lucas Road. In about 0.5 mile, turn left at the stoplight onto FM 3286. Drive about 0.8 mile, turning right on Brockdale Park Road. Go about a mile—if you get to the bridge over Lake Lavon, you have gone too far. Look for horse trailers parked on the right side of the road; pull into the parking lot here and walk through the parking area to the southwest side, where the trail begins on the other side of the pipe fence. GPS: N 33 04.802' / W 96 32.969'

The Hike

Traveling along the western shore of Lake Lavon, this hike passes through several ecosystems including open prairie, marsh, and woodlands. Animal species that have been spotted here include the black-tailed prairie dog, porcupine, fox, bobcat, and river otter. The lake, created in 1953 for flood control and water storage, draws a variety of bird species including the common loon, pelican, egret, heron, and wood duck.

The all-volunteer Trinity Trail Preservation Association maintains this trail on US Army Corps of Engineers land. The entire length of the trail runs 25.5 miles, but this hike covers only a small portion of the trail, which is closed to bicycles and motorized vehicles. Hikers do share the trail with horseback riders, so watch your step. Hikers who see horses approaching should give a standard hello so that the horses are not spooked by a mysterious figure moving on the trail—the sound of a human voice lets them know the figure is human and therefore not likely to be a threat.

Walk along the lakeshore and through meadows of grass.

The trail, more than any other in the guide, is very much in the Blackland Prairie's gumbo soils. Even on perfectly dry days, the trail can be more challenging than others in the area because hikers tend to sink down a bit with every step, even more than on trails that move through sand. It's wise to give yourself some extra time or not attempt as far a distance given the workout these soils provide.

CHAMPION SYCAMORE

In 2009 a volunteer with the Trinity Trail Riders was helping map out a proposed northern extension of the trail near the town of Lucas when he happened to spot a giant sycamore tree near Lake Lavon. The tree turned out to be 101 feet tall, with a circumference of 25.5 feet. The tree has three massive trunks that wind together. Counting the third trunk, it is possibly the largest tree in the Dallas/Fort Worth area. Experts estimate that it could be 200 years old.

To find the tree, take I-75 to the exit at Bethany Road and head east for 6 miles to FM 1378. Turn right onto FM 1378 and go to the stoplight and Lucas Food Store where you turn left onto TX 3286. Drive 2.4 miles, go over the first Lavon Lake bridge, then turn left onto Snider Lane, which is before the second bridge. Drive 0.6 mile and look for the white-pipe fence on the right. Hike north for 4.5 miles and look for the champion tree by a picnic table on the banks of Wilson Creek.

CEDAR—CAN GOOD TREES GO BAD?

Throughout Central Texas and on up into North and West Texas, the rocky limestone soils are a perfect habitat for many types of junipers—which are sometimes mistakenly called cedars or red cedars. These trees are home to many species of birds that appreciate the junipers' blue-purple berries—actually female seed cones—including the  golden-cheeked warbler, which nests in older stands of ash cedar in the spring, building its nest from the bark, which comes off in long strips.

Hikers can easily recognize junipers or cedars from their small green leaves and familiar scent, particularly evident after a rain. The Apache used juniper berries as a sweetener, and some tribes reportedly used it as an appetite suppressant during times of famine. Europeans use juniper berries to flavor dishes and drinks, such as gin and even beer (be warned that picking and eating raw juniper berries can lead to nausea and stomachaches).

During the Dust Bowl drought of the Great Depression, farmers were encouraged to plant junipers as windbreaks because they thrive in adverse conditions, being both drought and cold tolerant. But over the last century, parts of Central and North Texas up through the Central Plains have seen such a rise in the number of cedars that they threaten native hardwoods, grasslands, and even the water table because they are thirstier than the plants they crowd out. Their unique root structure enables them to thrive in dry soils, but their roots tap into precious aquifers, lowering the water table and decreasing watershed levels. A mature cedar tree can use more than thirty gallons of water per day, and its leaves can intercept up to 25 percent of rainfall, grabbing the water before it can even hit the ground.

Many Texas ranchers including President George W. Bush have waged war on cedar: He was famously shown at his Crawford ranch on a tractor regularly clearing brush that included cedar shrubs. In addition to removing the trees mechanically, ranchers and other landowners have turned to chemical herbicides, controlled fires, and even goats—which will eat cedar if little else is available. Perhaps the biggest victims of juniper or cedar are allergy sufferers who start sneezing and wheezing around Thanksgiving and Christmas, when juniper pollen hits the air. The pollen typically peaks in January and can remain elevated through April.

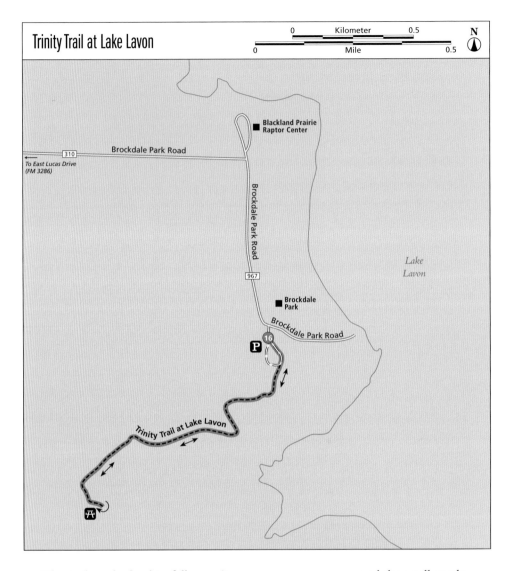

Trinity Trail at Lake Lavon

Blackland Prairie
Raptor Center

Brockdale Park Road

310

To East Lucas Drive
(FM 3286)

Brockdale Park Road

967

Lake
Lavon

Brockdale
Park

Brockdale Park Road

P 16

Trinity Trail at Lake Lavon

The trail can be hard to follow as it moves over grassy areas, and the small creeks can become muddy marshes after a rain, so avoid hiking this trail in wet weather. After extremely heavy rains, the trail is closed to prevent erosion. Some hikers try to make the 9-mile trek from Brockdale Park to East Fork Park, either doing it as an overnight out-and-back or setting up a car shuttle. It's common to find at least one horse trailer in the parking lot by the trailhead, easily identified with white-pipe fencing.

The hike begins in an open grassy area atop a small hill overlooking the lake. At the trailhead, take the larger trail to the right and follow the wider trail that heads south into the woods. At 0.3 mile, the trail moves down a small hill to a boggy area where water gathers. While the trail has a culvert beneath it to funnel water to the lake, the soils here can be muddy even a week after a rain.

Here, the trail moves into a partially open area with scattered trees such as junipers and hollies as well as deciduous cedar elms and sycamores. One of North Texas's largest champion sycamores is located on the Trinity Trail around the northwest shore of the lake. Hikers who would like to take in the massive tree should enter the Trinity Trail from the Highland Park Trailhead and bear left, following the trail for 4.5 miles, where the tree is located by a creek and picnic table.

The trail moves into and out of forested areas at 0.7 mile, providing a great variety of plants and wildlife including various woodland bird species such as robins and cardinals as well as grassland birds such as dickcissels and meadowlarks. At 1.5 miles the trail reaches a shaded picnic spot, providing a nice place to rest before retracing your steps back to the trailhead. (**Option:** More ambitious hikers may opt to continue along this trail for 5 miles to reach Colin Park and its lakeside picnic tables. For this longer hike, turn around at the picnic tables and retrace your steps to the trailhead.)

Miles and Directions

0.0 Trail begins in Brockdale Park; look for horse trailers lining the parking lot on busy weekends. Find a parking spot and make your way to the south side of the lot, where the trailhead is on the other side of a white-pipe fence and horse mounting station.

0.1 Bear right on the trail as it winds down a small hill through a grassy prairie. (**FYI:** Enjoy the view of the lake since it's the only time the lake will be in view.)

BLACKLAND PRAIRIE RAPTOR CENTER

Located in Brockdale Park, the Blackland Prairie Raptor Center, a nonprofit agency dedicated to preserving birds of prey and other wildlife whose habitat in the tallgrass prairie has been destroyed by development. By educating the public about the important role raptors play in the ecosystem, the program's instructors hope to increase awareness about their plight. Their "Raptor Ambassadors" include kestrels, hawks, falcons, and owls that have suffered injuries that make them non-releasable, or that grew up in the care of humans and never developed the skills to survive in the wild. The raptor center continues to grow in its new home by Lake Lavon, which was made possible by many private donors, including the Collin County Open Space initiative, the US Army Corps of Engineers, and Pinnacle Excavation. The center also includes a Native Plant Demonstration Trail that shows plants able to survive the tough Texas climate.

The center houses and rehabilitates injured birds, such as red-tailed hawks, and gives educational programs on hawks, owls, and falcons at its Brockdale Park facility on the first Saturday of many months—call or check for upcoming events, schedule, and educational workshop; (469) 964-9696; www.bpraptorcenter.org.

0.3 The trail passes over a boggy area where water collects, then begins alternating between grassy areas and wooded glens.

0.7 The trail moves through an area populated with spruce pines, junipers, and hollies including possumhaw holly, named in part because possums have been known to prefer the tree as a hiding spot.

1.5 The trail reaches a shaded picnic area, which makes a nice turnaround spot. Retrace your steps back to the north and the trailhead by the parking lot.

3.0 Arrive back at trailhead.

Hike Information

Good eats: An outpost of the DFW–based Palio's Pizza Café serves pastas, pizzas, and calzones; 407 W. Princeton Dr., Princeton; (469) 378-3637.

Organizations: Trinity Trail Preservation Association; (972) 824-3369; www.trinity trailriders.org

GREEN TIP
Consider the packaging of any products you bring with you.
It's best to properly dispose of packaging at home before
you hike. If you're on the trail, pack it out with you.

Honorable Mentions

Here are some other great trails in this region:

A Great Trinity Forest Trail Joppa Preserve

Part of the Dallas County Open Space Project, the 307-acre Joppa Preserve was named after one of the area's first post-Civil War "Freedmen" communities, which was located near the preserve's Lemmon Lake. Today the preserve is a popular spot for picnics including Juneteenth celebrations. The paved trail travels through the Great Trinity Forest, along the Trinity River, and connects to trails at the nearby Trinity River Audubon Center. Following the shores of Little Lemmon Lake and Lemmon Lake, the trail includes a footbridge between the two lakes was the location for the Texas Ranger scene in the 1967 film *Bonnie and Clyde*. There are warning signs alerting hikers that alligators inhabit the lakes, noting, "They can run 40 mph in a straight line-dash." There is no fee to enter the preserve, operated by the City of Dallas; www.dallasparks.org/Facilities/Facility/Details/Joppa-Preserve-543. From downtown Dallas, take I-45 south to South Central Expressway to River Oaks Drive. The preserve is located at 4911 River Oaks Rd., Dallas.

B Dogwood Canyon Audubon Center

Opened in 2011, the 200-acre Dogwood Canyon Audubon Center located just south of Cedar Hill State Park has two trails—the stroller-friendly 0.5-mile Canyon Floor Trail and the more challenging 1.65-mile West Loop Trail, which has a 150-foot elevation change in the first 0.5 mile and offers a view of nearby Joe Pool Lake. The center and its trails are closed Sunday, Monday, and major holidays. Leashed dogs are only welcome on Saturday. Trails are open during the center's operating hours—9 a.m. to 5 p.m. Tuesday through Saturday—and hikers are asked to sign in and out at the gift shop. The center shares a parking lot with Cedar Mountain Nature Preserve, operated by the City of Cedar Hill, which is a different entity from Cedar Ridge Preserve, operated by Audubon Dallas. Hiking trails at the Cedar Mountain Nature Preserve do not connect to those at Dogwood Canyon. From Dallas, take I-35 south to US 67 south; proceed on US 67 a few miles south of the I-20 intersection and take the FM 1382 exit. Turn right on FM 1382. After passing through the traffic light at New Clark Road, look for Newman International Academy on the left. The next left turn will be for Dogwood Canyon Audubon Center; www.dogwood.audubon.org; (469) 526-1980.

C Lake Texoma Cross Timbers Trail

Dubbed the "toughest little trail in Texas," this challenging trail offers plenty of ups and downs as it traces the shoreline of Lake Texoma. The downside of the trail (literally) is the steep drop-offs in places due to erosion from the lake. Also, the trail can be very slippery (and in parts covered with water) after a heavy rain. Be aware of large patches of poison ivy in places. The payoff for this little-used trail is plenty of wildlife, including deer, scores of birds—including the occasional bald eagle—and, if you move softly and slowly, even a bobcat or two. The full trail runs about 14 miles, making it popular with hikers looking for a weekend overnight hike, but it can easily be modified by trekking to about the 5-mile mark, where a rocky ledge provides a prime spot for picnicking, then heading back to the trailhead, or by turning around at the marina, located about 2 miles into the trail. From Dallas, take US 75 north until you get to Sherman, then take US 82 west to Whitesboro. From Whitesboro, take US 377 north for about 12 miles. The entrance to Juniper Point East will be on the right side just before the bridge on Lake Texoma. From that park's entrance, bear left into the western side of the park, then when the road splits, bear to the left again and look for the dirt parking lot on the left. The trailhead is located by the parking lot; US Army Corps of Engineers; (903) 465-4990.

D North Trail Lake Tawakoni State Park

In 2007 park rangers at Lake Tawakoni discovered a vast spider web crawling with millions of spiders spreading over several acres on a peninsula located at Lake Tawakoni State Park. It was, it turns out, the result of at least thirteen different species of spiders involved in spinning the massive webs that brought worldwide media attention to the small state park an hour east of Dallas. The most common spider found in the collected samples was the Guatemalan long-jawed spider, according to tests done by Texas A&M University. Scientists believe the massive webs were the result of an unusually wet summer that exploded that park's insect population, providing the multitudes of spiders ample feeding. The webs have since dissipated, but the state park still makes a fun and interesting outing. The 1.1-mile North Trail loops around the peninsula where the webs were discovered, providing nice venues for watching ducks and cranes along the shore. Scientists haven't fully explained why the spider webs emerged—or if they will return—so those with arachnophobia may want to hike elsewhere just in case. There is a small entrance fee per person or use the Texas State Parks Pass. Take US 20 east out of Dallas for about 35 miles. Exit at TX 47 to Wills Point (exit 516) and go left. Stay on TX 47 for about 11 miles and turn left onto FM 2475. The park is about 3 miles down FM 2475; (903) 560-7123.

The Mid-Cities
and Denton County

Dallas/Fort Worth's middle cities are home to the Eastern Cross Timbers, where you'll find leafy trails that can provide escape from summer heat. The region's many creeks, rivers, and lakes also offer trails where hikers can view wildlife, including many species of birds and butterflies that migrate through each spring and fall.

While Mid-Cities residents appreciate the area's proximity to Dallas and Fort Worth, the area is also filled with parks and nature preserves where families can enjoy a quick hike together. Places such as Lake Grapevine's Horseshoe Trails, L. B. Houston Nature Trail, Little Bear Creek Park, and River Legacy Park can seem worlds away from busy freeways and bustling Dallas/Fort Worth International Airport.

Denton County is home to popular lakes, such as Lake Lewisville and Lake Ray Roberts, that also offer scenic trails for hikers who enjoy water views. History lovers can enjoy hikes that combine local lore including the supposedly haunted Old Alton Bridge.

Many hikes in the Mid-Cities and Denton County have water views (North Shore Trail).

17 Cottonwood Nature Trail

This 1.3-mile loop on the shores of Lake Lewisville passes by a restored 1870s pioneer cabin and winds by the lake where wood ducks, wading birds, and other waterfowl can be spotted from a camouflaged blind. A side trail called the Cicada Loop identifies various types of trees and plants in an informative tree walk.

Start: Lake Lewisville Environmental Learning Area picnic pavilion
Distance: 1.3-mile loop
Approximate hiking time: 1 hour
Difficulty: Easy
Trail surface: Packed dirt, some gravel
Season: Oct through May
Other trail users: Birders, school field trips
Canine compatibility: Service dogs only

Land status: Nature preserve/educational center
Fees and permits: Small fee
Schedule: Fri, Sat, Sun only; Nov 1 through Mar 1, 7 a.m. to 5 p.m.; Mar 2 to Oct 31, 7 a.m. to 7 p.m.
Map: City of Lewisville: https://www.cityoflewisville.com/home/showdocument?id=9413
Trail contact: Lake Lewisville Environmental Learning Area; (972) 219-7980; www.llela.org

Finding the trailhead: From Dallas take I-35E north to Lewisville; exit at Valley Ridge Road. Go east to the stoplight at Mill Street. Turn left onto Mill Street and travel to Jones Street, which dead-ends at the education center's front gate at the intersection with North Kealy Avenue. The trailhead is about 0.5 mile from the entrance on the right by a large picnic pavilion. GPS: N 34 41.12' / W 96 59.121'

The Hike

Located in the Lake Lewisville Environmental Learning Area, this hike is a popular field trip for area school kids during the week, who use the large pavilion at the trailhead for picnic lunches. The center also serves older students, college undergraduates, and graduate-level researchers, who use it for fieldwork. Since 1997 the center has been involved with research and training in the use of prescribed fire to preserve and restore prairie lands.

A variety of special events are held each month including a bison tour on the last Sunday of each month, at which visitors can get up-close and personal with the amazing creatures that once roamed the entire Central Plains. There are also monthly bird walks and opportunities to travel the Elm Fork of the Trinity River by kayak on a 6-mile water adventure. Check the website for the most up-to-date calendar of events.

While the protected area is located in the middle of the sprawling suburbs of north Dallas, it feels isolated apart from the occasional roar of an airplane overhead. Animal species that have been spotted here include bobcats, white-tailed deer, coyotes, and mink, and, after a rain when the dirt trail is muddy, it's possible to spot a variety of tracks.

The trail begins by the parking lot to the far right of the large picnic pavilion. Three trails begin here: the 1.3-mile Cottonwood Trail, 0.3-mile Cicada Trail, and 1.4-mile Redbud Trail. It's easy to combine this trail with the Cicada, which winds through the woods, or add on the Redbud, which travels by the Elm Fork of the Trinity River.

The Cottonwood Nature Trail begins in an open grassy area on a gravel road that winds into a forest by a preserved log cabin and outbuildings. Bear to the left to take the trail to the cabin, where on the third Saturday of each month, volunteers are on hand to guide visitors through the Minor-Porter cabin and talk about the history and daily lives of the families who lived there. William Tipton Minor came to Texas from Alabama and bought property in 1869 in the area that's now Highland Village. He married Mary Nowlin and built the log home for his new bride. Mary died in 1879, and the couple had no children. Today the cabin gives modern-day families an idea of what life must have been like for those early settlers.

After passing by the cabin, the trail curves around to a large beaver pond where a covered observation area provides an ideal spot to watch waterfowl and perhaps stop for a brief picnic. At the 0.8-mile mark, the trail splits. Go straight, continuing through the open grassy area, to reach the trailhead. **(Option:** For a longer hike,

This charming bird blind offers great views of local wildlife.

SUNNY BLOOMS

Sunflowers have been cultivated in Texas and the American Plains since pre-Columbian times. Native Americans used dyes made from the yellow flowers and black seedheads in basketry and weaving, and they ground the seeds for flour and used their oils for cooking and hairstyling. Nineteenth-century settlers believed growing the plants near their home would protect them from malaria.

bear right at the split and take the Cicada Trail, which winds through the forest. Informative markers name various tree species before the path connects back to the trailhead.)

Miles and Directions

0.0   Trail begins on the far west side of the picnic pavilion. From the trailhead, follow the wide, dirt road as it winds around a corner toward the forest.

0.35 The trail splits here; bear left to go to the pioneer homestead and cabin. Take a look at life for Texas's early settlers and learn more about the cabin's residents—the Minor-Porter clan.

0.5   From the cabin, retrace your steps back to the main trail, this time bearing left as the trail winds around a corner to provide a view of the water in a covered blind. The blind makes a great spot for bird watching.

0.8   From the blind, the trail winds through the woods and intersects with the Cicada Trail; continue straight as the trail moves through an open grassy area back to the trailhead. (**Option:** For a longer walk, bear right onto the Cicada Trail to stroll through a wooded area with information signs identifying major tree species in the region.)

1.3   Arrive back at trailhead.

Cottonwood Nature Trail

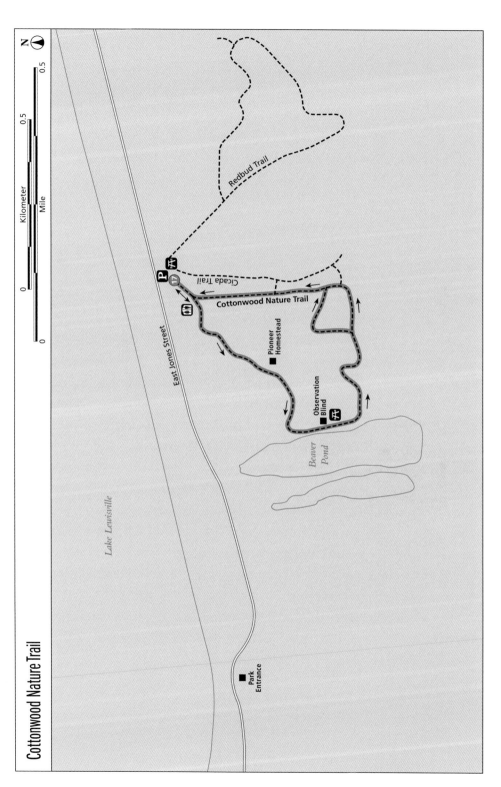

Lake Lewisville

East Jones Street

Park Entrance

Redbud Trail

Cicada Trail

Cottonwood Nature Trail

Pioneer Homestead

Observation Blind

Beaver Pond

Kilometer

Mile

N

0   0.5   0.5

0

Hike Information

Local information: Lewisville Convention and Visitors Bureau; (800) 657-9571; www.visitlewisville.com

Attractions/events: The City of Lewisville celebrates its annual Western Days Festival in September with entertainment, kids' activities, and the world tamale eating championship; Lewisville, (972) 219-3400; www.cityoflewisville.com

The Lion's Club International holds the Highland Village Balloon Festival in late summer; www.hvballoonfest.com

Good eats: The Lewisville outpost of the popular Fuzzy's Taco Shop offers breakfast burritos, amazing tempura shrimp tacos, and grilled veggie salads; 1288 W. Main St., Ste. 117, Lewisville; (972) 539-8226; wwwfuzzystacoshop.com

WILD TURKEYS

When new species are introduced into an ecosystem, they may have found a new home, but they can also crowd out native populations of plants and animals.

The Lake Lewisville Environmental Learning Area has an active wildlife repopulation effort designed to reintroduce species that once thrived in North Texas, but, for whatever reason, have seen their numbers decline. One example is Rio Grande wild turkeys. They were once very common in the Cross Timbers and Blackland Prairie, but their numbers declined dramatically. By 2005 there were no local breeding populations in the area. As part of an ecological restoration project, the center teamed with the US Army Corps of Engineers, the University of North Texas, Texas Parks and Wildlife Department, and the National Turkey Federation to trap, band, and release forty-nine Rio Grande turkeys in 2005. The turkeys were trapped in Jack County from a population near Jacksboro and moved to the learning area, where they were banded and released. Twenty-five of these birds were also fitted with radio transmitters, enabling graduate students to track their locations. The transmitters provided data on the mortality of the flock through the first year and information on the locations of good foraging habitat and roosting sites.

Now more wildlife species reintroductions are planned, including possibly reintroducing the black-tailed jackrabbit, plains pocket gopher, thirteen-lined ground squirrel, muskrat, black-tailed prairie dog, collared lizard, and Texas horned lizard.

18 North Shore Trail

This 3-mile out-and-back trail gets its name from its location—the north shore of Lake Grapevine—and is a favorite among North Texas hikers, joggers, and cyclists. The trail has lots of rocks and roots, plenty of winding curves, and lots of ups and downs. It may be too steep in places for small children or anyone with mobility issues. The payoff for those who tackle the arduous trek is glorious vistas of the lake. The trail splits in some places, with those heading north taking one track and those heading south taking the other. Hikers should yield to cyclists, a difficult challenge in places where the narrow trail is lined by thorny briars much of the year.

Start: Sheltered picnic table overlooking Lake Grapevine
Distance: 3-mile out-and-back
Approximate hiking time: 1.5 hours
Difficulty: Difficult in places where climbing over rocks is required
Trail surface: Packed dirt, rocks, and sand
Season: Oct through Mar
Other trail users: Mountain bikers, joggers
Canine compatibility: Dogs must be on leash
Land status: City park; watershed managed by US Army Corps of Engineers

Fees and permits: Small entrance fee
Schedule: Daily; hours vary, but generally 9 a.m. to 7 p.m.; gate is locked at 7 p.m.
Map: National Geographic TOPO! Texas
Trail contacts: US Army Corps of Engineers; (817) 865-2600; Dallas Off-Road Bicycle Association; (817) 481-3576; www.dorba.com
Special considerations: Some portions of the trail may be underwater if lake levels are high, and the trail can be washed away in places after very heavy rains. Call (817) 481-3576 for latest trail conditions.

Finding the trailhead: From DFW International Airport take US 121 north and exit at Grapevine Mills Parkway; head north past the massive mall. The road changes names, becoming International Parkway. Turn left onto Lakeside Village Boulevard and go through the travel circle to head south on Lakeside Parkway. Look for the Rockledge Park entrance on the left. GPS: N 32 58.975' / W 97 04.058'

The Hike

One of the, if not the, most popular hikes in the region, the trail can sometimes feel loved to death—with crowded conditions on many weekends. The Dallas Off-Road Bicycle Association (DORBA) estimates that an average of 800 bikes ride the trail each week, so hikers should be on the lookout and yield to passing cyclists. Only the most experienced mountain bikers can handle some of the steep "rock garden" passes of this trail, so they may be walking (or carrying) their bikes in these touchy technical spots.

Beautiful lakeside scenery makes this hike a winner.

The hike starts off at Rockledge Park by a covered picnic area and winds over narrow cliffside trails overlooking Lake Grapevine. Avoid this trail after a heavy rain, when it may be closed and even washed out or underwater in places. Even in perfect weather, the trail can be treacherous, with one misstep leading down a steep ravine into the water. In rainy conditions, the nearby paved Mustang Trails hike is a better option. Small children will need some supervision to safely maneuver the narrow trail in the beginning. Another option is to get on the trail at Murrell Park in Flower Mound (take International Parkway north then take a left at FM 3040 and another left on McKamy Creek Road then another left on Simmons Road).

The trail is just a few miles north of DFW International Airport, so the shadows of large-body planes hover overhead through portions of this hike. The area is also home to fossils. Some surfaced a few years ago when lake levels were very low. Due to damage from vandals, the fossils were covered up by the US Army Corps of Engineers, who oversee this lake and its watershed, and their location kept secret.

The trail follows the shoreline in the beginning before heading for a stretch in the Cross Timbers forest of oaks and elms. In places the trail splits, with hikers heading north bearing right and those heading south (back to the trailhead) bearing left. Even in the dense woods, the trail still offers the occasional glimpse of the lake as it weaves into and out of the forest.

At 1 mile, bear right at the first two forks. Cross over a small bridge and bear right when the trail widens out a bit then winds over a steep, rocky drop. At 1.2 miles, a

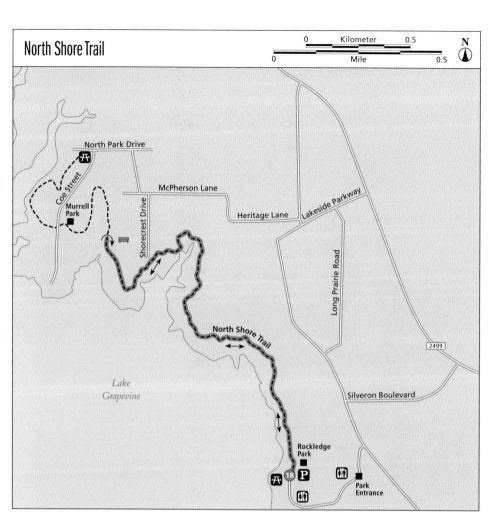

North Shore Trail

scenic overlook offers a view of the massive Gaylord Texan Resort before heading into a grassy meadow where thorny plants can threaten to overtake the path in places. At 1.5 miles, the trail comes to a long wooden bench, a good place to take in the view and rest a bit before heading back. (**Option:** For those seeking a longer hike, continue on the trail until it reaches the MADD Picnic Shelter at Murrell Park. This out-and-back adds an additional 3 miles, for a total of 6.)

Miles and Directions

0.0 The trail begins on the far north side of the parking lot by the restroom and a covered picnic table.

0.5 The trail splits, bear right to take the high road (northbound route). (**Caution:** The trail gets narrow here and is densely wooded, so be sure to listen for cyclists coming from behind and be ready to give them the right-of-way.)

The trail hugs the shores of Lake Grapevine, offering spectacular vistas.

0.6 The trail reaches a series of rocky, steep inclines designed to challenge mountain bikers.

0.8 The trail crosses over a bridge then winds to the left, providing a shaded resting spot with a nice vista of the lake for those who want to enjoy a snack or picnic with a view.

1.0 The trail moves down from the cliffs into a more grassy area where weeds, including thorny vines, can be a hazard.

1.2 Enjoy the scenic overlook view of the massive Gaylord Texan Resort.

1.5 Here the trail reaches a small bench and this hike's turnaround spot. (**Option:** For those seeking a 6-mile hike, simply continue along the trail another 1.5 miles until it reaches the MADD Picnic Shelter at Murrell Park. Turn around and retrace your steps to the trailhead.)

2.5 When the trail splits, this time bear right to take the southbound lane.

3.0 Arrive back at trailhead.

Hike Information

Local information: Grapevine Convention and Visitors Bureau; (800) 457-6338; www.grapevinetexasusa.com

Flower Mound Chamber of Commerce; (972) 539-4307; www.flowermound chamber.com

Attractions/events: The trail is popular with the North Texas Trail Runners, a group dedicated to ultra-running that sponsors many weekend race events including the Rockledge Rumble, held in November to honor American veterans; members also meet there on Saturday morning and Wednesday evening for a run; www.nttr.org

The Dallas Off-Road Bicycle Association (DORBA) has periodic races on the trail including the annual Northshore Fest in December; www.dorba.org

GREEN TIP

When hiking in a group, walk single file on established trails to avoid widening them. If you come upon a sensitive area, spread out so you don't cut one path through the landscape. Don't create new trails where there were none before.

19 Rocky Point Trail

This 3-mile out-and-back hike starts out in a suburban subdivision before heading into forests where it follows a shaded creek to the shores of Lake Grapevine. A couple of creek crossings are relatively steep, and low-water crossings will be wet after rains. Great year-round, this trail is much less heavily traveled than the nearby North Shore Trail, offering a more solitary experience as long as you don't mind the thorny vines encountered in the forested parts at the beginning of the trail.

Start: Just off High Road at a black-pipe fence
Distance: 3-mile out-and-back
Approximate hiking time: 2 hours
Difficulty: Moderately challenging with some steep climbs
Trail surface: Packed dirt, rocks, and sand
Season: Oct through May
Other trail users: Birders, horseback riders
Canine compatibility: Dogs must be on leash

Land status: Watershed managed by US Army Corps of Engineers
Fees and permits: None
Schedule: Open daily sunrise to sunset
Maps: National Geographic TOPO! Texas; www .swf-wc.usace.army.mil/grapevine/Recreation/ Trails/Rocky-Point-trail-2011.pdf
Trail contact: US Army Corps of Engineers; (817) 865-2600

Finding the Trailhead: From Dallas take FM 1171 (Cross Timbers Road) west from I-35E in Lewisville. Turn south onto High Road and look for a small parking lot 0.5 mile down the road on the left, just after Stallion Circle. There isn't a lot in the way of signage to indicate the trailhead. A low step at the end of a black-pipe fence leads to the start of the trail, where there is also a small marker by the trailhead. GPS: N 33 02.000' / W 97 09.000'

The Hike

It's easy to drive past the small parking lot, which holds only six or so cars or a couple of horse trailers, but this trail is growing in popularity as hikers look for a more secluded option to the busy North Shore Trail where mountain bikers crowd the trail on sunny weekends. Local horseback riders maintain the trail, and horses get the right-of-way. As on other trails where hikers meet up with horses, it's important to say hello in a normal conversational voice as horses and their riders approach so as to not spook the horses. Also, while dogs are allowed on the trail, be careful and considerate with the horses.

The trailhead is adjacent to the parking lot and starts out down a thin strip of lane between houses and along the fence of a private drive. (**Note:** Please stay on the public easement; don't enter private yards.) The trail passes by a home and its back-yard pool before moving into the woods along a fence line. At this point of the trail, thorny vines can be a problem, so wearing long pants is recommended even during summer. The trail then starts a gradual descent down a hill before getting a bit steeper as it approaches a rocky creek bed at about 0.4 mile.

This tree by the shores of Lake Grapevine shows damage likely due to lightning.

HOLLY WOODS

While holly berries are somewhat toxic to humans, they provide an important food source for many species of birds and other animals. The berries appear in fall when they are hard, but after several freezes, the berries soften up a bit and become less bitter, increasing their appeal to wildlife. North Texas's many native species of holly trees include yaupon holly and possumhaw, the widest-ranging native holly in the state. Hollies also provide an important refuge for birds, particularly cardinals whose red colors blend in with the bright red berries; the tree's sharp leaves deter predators.

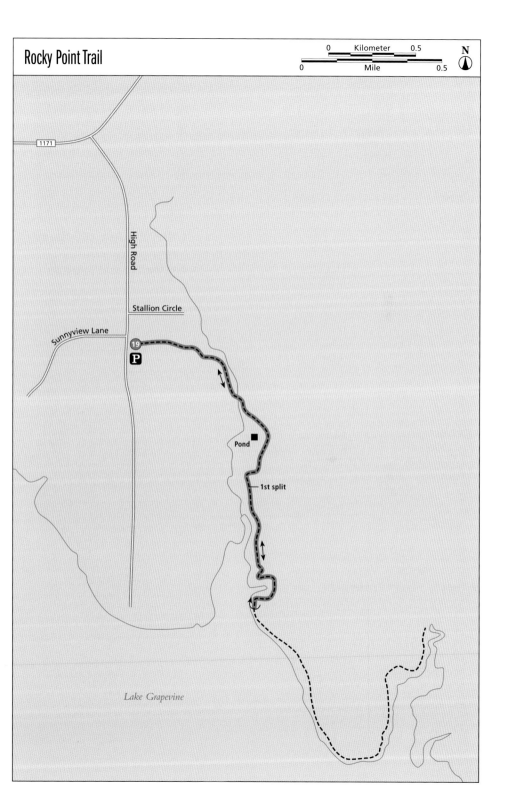

Rocky Point Trail

0   Kilometer   0.5

0   Mile   0.5

N

1171

High Road

Stallion Circle

Sunnyview Lane

19

P

Pond

1st split

Lake Grapevine

GOLDEN DAYS

Tall goldenrod is part of the sunflower family and blooms in Texas in September and October. Practitioners of herbal medicine use the plant to counter ills of the bladder and kidney. Native Americans chewed the leaves to help relieve sore throats and toothaches.

Goldenrods can also be used to make rubber, and inventor Thomas Edison cultivated a type of goldenrod that could be used to make tires. Automaker Henry Ford gave Edison a Model T that had rubber tires made from the plants, but its use never went beyond the experimental phase.

From here, the trail winds along the side of the creek, where green mosses cover the rocks and small waterfalls create a peaceful mood. The trail moves away from the creek briefly, then rejoins it and crosses over it—easily accomplished by either jumping over rocks or walking a dozen feet down the creek bed to where it narrows. The trail then moves by a small pond and back by some homes as it moves closer to the lake.

At about 1 mile, there is a split in the trail; bear right to continue toward the lake—the trail to the left goes up to a neighborhood where horseback riders can access the trail. The trail then winds back to the creek, which is larger here, becoming more like a small river as it meets up with the lake. Here the rooflines of some nearby residences can be spotted, but the overall feel of the trail is quiet and remote as it creeps closer to the lake's edge. The trail reaches the lake, passing by a group of hollies and cedar trees as it finally gains the shore. The dirt trail gives way to sand, making more of a challenge for hikers This sandy portion of the trail can also have sand spurs, so be careful to check for this prickly annoyance on socks and clothes.

During periods of little rain, the lake may be dried out, becoming a large brown beach, but most of the time, the lake here draws a variety of birds including herons and cranes, as well as ducks. At about 1.5 miles, the trail splits again; bear left then hike into the treed grove up the hill to reach Rocky Point and take in the panoramic view of Lake Grapevine before retracing your steps and returning to the trailhead.

Miles and Directions

0.0 Trailhead is located by a small parking lot. Trail heads down a grassy lane between property line fences and a private drive.

0.4 Trail heads downhill gradually at first, then on a steeper decline as it meets up with a small creek lined with moss-covered stones in a riparian forest.

1.0 Bear right at split, following the trail to a small pond.

1.2 The trail reaches the shore of Lake Grapevine—from here the rooftops of several homes and their boat docks are visible. This is a great bird-watching spot because cranes and other water birds perch on iron rails that rise out of the lake.

1.5 Bear left and head up a rocky hill toward Rocky Point. Leave the trail to walk into the grove of trees at the high point that overlooks the lake. Retrace your steps back to the trailhead.

3.0 Arrive back at trailhead.

Hike Information

Local information: Flower Mound Chamber of Commerce, (972) 539-0500, www .flowermoundchamber.com

Attractions/events: Keep Flower Mound Beautiful holds an annual Trash Bash and Fall Festival as well as monthly cleanups and composting classes; www.kfmb.org

20 Knob Hills Trail

The hike heads up and down rocky hills through a shrubby forest and over a couple of knobby bridges before coming to an overlook of a small creek, which is dry if there hasn't been any recent rain. The narrow trail is shared with mountain bikers, who are challenged by the sharp turns and some of the steep slopes here. Prickly pear cacti line the trail in many sections, adding to the degree of difficulty.

Start: Parking lot just east of US 377
Distance: 2.2-mile out-and-back
Approximate hiking time: 1 to 2 hours
Difficulty: Moderate
Trail surface: Packed dirt and rocks, some wooden bridges
Season: Oct through May
Other trail users: Mountain bikers, joggers

Canine compatibility: Dogs must be on leash
Land status: US Army Corps of Engineers watershed
Fees and permits: None
Schedule: Open daily sunrise to sunset
Map: National Geographic TOPO! Texas
Trail contact: Dallas Off-Road Bicycle Association maintains the trail; www.dorba.org

Finding the trailhead: From Dallas take TX 114 west to Roanoke, then turn right onto US 377. Go approximately 2.2 miles, crossing over Denton Creek, and look for a small dirt-and-gravel parking lot immediately to the right after the bridge. The incline to the parking lot is steep, so take the turn slowly. The trailhead is in the right back corner of the parking lot by a gate. GPS: N 33 02.831' / W 97 12.322'

The Hike

From the trailhead, which is a simple iron gate, the trail doesn't look like much—it's a rocky, dirt trail leading through scrubby grassland and bordered by prickly pear cacti. But the parking lot fills up on sunny weekends when mountain bikers hit the challenging up-and-down rocky inclines. Maintained by the Dallas Off-Road Bicycle Association (DORBA), this trail is closed after heavy rain.

The hike starts out in a grassy meadow of drought-tolerant wildflowers and native grasses before heading into a dense forest and reaching a creek. Most mountain bikers will do the full 9-plus miles of this out-and-back trail, but this hike travels only 1.1 miles down the trail to where it reaches a small creek, which can be dry during particularly arid summer months. The trail is narrow in places, and given the cacti on either side in some sections, it can be a bit of a challenge to make way for cyclists as they pass through. After this initial section in a dusty, rocky meadow, the trail moves over some decrepit and uneven wooden bridges and down a few steep slopes including a steep drop dubbed "Goatman's Hill," where some cyclists have gone flying over their handlebars, but it shouldn't be any problem for hikers.

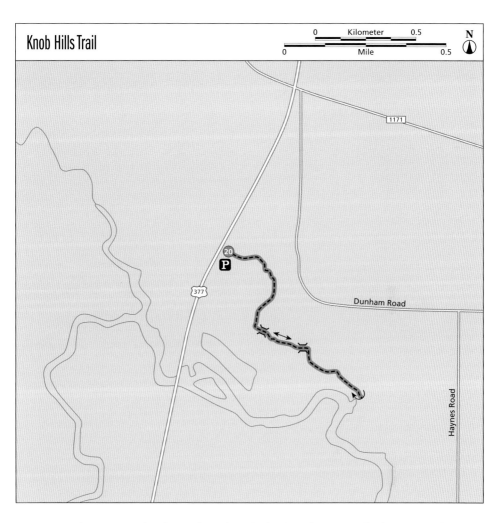

At about 1.1 miles, the trail reaches the banks of a seasonally dry creek. The overlook provides a nice resting spot before heading back to the trailhead.

Miles and Directions

0.0 Start at trailhead located at east side of gravel parking lot by an iron fence.

0.2 Trail splits—bear right as the trail winds through scattered trees.

0.5 Trail crosses over wooden bridges and passes through a small clearing.

1.1 The trail reaches an overlook by a small creek. Retrace your steps back to the trailhead.

2.2 Arrive back at trailhead.

Hike Information

Local information: Northwest Metroport Chamber of Commerce; (817) 837-1000; www.nwmetroportchamber.org

While the trail is dusty, some parts provide relief in the form of shade.

Attractions/events: Located at the intersection of I-35W and TX 114 is the Texas Motor Speedway, which has multiple major NASCAR events each year when thousands of race fans throng the highways into and out of the track; www.texasmotor speedway.com

Good eats: The original Babe's Chicken serves up comfort food, including plenty of the fried stuff at 104 North Oak St., Roanoke; (817) 491-2900; www.babeschicken .com

YEP, THEY'RE SHARP!

The prickly pear cactus was named the official state plant of Texas in 1995 by then-governor George W. Bush.

21 L. B. Houston Trail

This trail is largely for off-road cyclists, but hikers are welcome as long as they give cyclists right-of-way. Located just off TX 114 in Irving, the trail winds through a leafy glade then offers a prime picnic spot by the Elm Fork of the Trinity River. The hike begins in a grove of tightly packed laurels before joining the riparian forest along the river, home to wood ducks and northern cardinals. From there, the hike returns back through a meadow, returning to the trailhead located near a popular fishing spot on the river.

Start: Parking lot near information sign
Distance: 1.6-mile loop
Approximate hiking time: 1 hour
Difficulty: Easy, if you don't mind making way for mountain bikers
Trail surface: Dirt
Season: May through July
Water availability: No water available on the trail, so bring what you need
Other trail users: Off-road cyclists
Canine compatibility: Not recommended for dogs as hikers must frequently move aside for cyclists and the trail is often narrow
Land status: City park

Fees and permits: None
Schedule: Open daily sunrise to sunset
Map: National Geographic TOPO! Texas
Trail contact: Trail maintained by Dallas Off-Road Bicycle Association (DORBA); www.dorba .org
Special considerations: Trail is closed for several days after heavy rain. Check DORBA website for latest conditions before heading out. Trails are closed to all users on special workdays for trail maintenance, usually the last Sunday of the month. Check website for upcoming workdays.

Finding the trailhead: From Dallas take TX 114 west toward DFW International Airport. Exit at O'Connor Boulevard, heading right, and then turn right on Riverside Drive. Turn left onto California Crossing and look for a gravel parking lot on the right, across from the National Guard Armory. The trailhead is by the information sign. GPS: N32 51.59' / W96 55.22'

The Hike

The trail takes you on a winding path through a dense forest by the Trinity River, including a great riverside resting spot to check out turtles, snakes, and herons. Maintained by the Dallas Off-Road Bicycle Association (DORBA), the park is overcoming its shady reputation as a drinking spot. (It is located not far from liquor stores at the Dallas city limits on Northwest Highway.)

With more than 7 miles of singletrack trails, the park is a major draw for cyclists testing their skill and nerves on the winding paths. The trail is maintained by and for off-road bicyclists. There's a pond by the parking lot, where local anglers like to try their luck. Look for the park regulations posted on a small billboard; the trailhead is to the right. The loop is designed to be done counterclockwise, so start the trail by

The tree-canopied trail approaches the Trinity River.

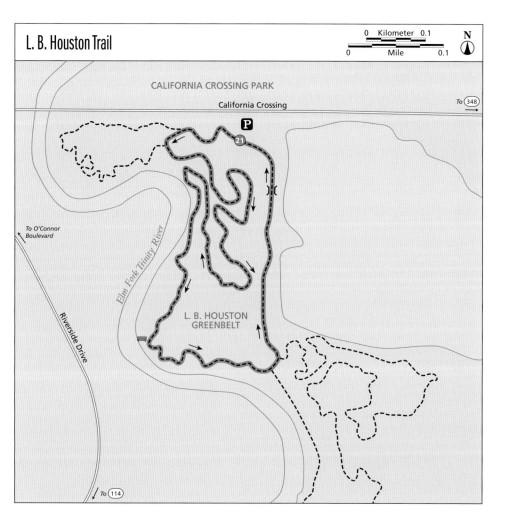

CALIFORNIA CROSSING PARK

California Crossing

To 348

To O'Connor Boulevard

Elm Fork Trinity River

Riverside Drive

L. B. HOUSTON GREENBELT

To 114

turning right and moving into the forest. Here the very dense growth of low trees feels almost jungle like, which no doubt adds to the challenge of biking it. But for hikers it's just a matter of watching for low-lying branches and listening for cyclists coming up from behind—they get the right-of-way here.

The narrow trail often has room for only single-file hiking as it meanders toward the river. At the 1-mile mark, there's a small bench for taking in the view at the Trinity River Overlook, but unfortunately there's not a lot of other room along the trail here.

Despite being surrounded by major freeways and bustling high-rises of Las Colinas, the park has abundant wildlife, with butterflies and birds flitting in and out of the tree canopy down to the river. The trail crosses a small bridge and enters an open meadow at about 1.4 miles. From here you can see the trailhead; turn left and follow the dirt road back to the parking lot. For those seeking a longer hike, simply stay straight as the trail meanders through the dense forest and eventually leads to the parking lot and trailhead.

Miles and Directions

0.0 Start at the trailhead to the right of the billboard and turn right onto the trail.

0.1 The trail heads into woods, tightly winding in hairpin curves through a dense canopy of low trees and shrubs.

1.0 Come to the Trinity River Overlook.

1.4 Bear left, heading toward an open meadow. Picking up a two-lane dirt road, turn left to return to the trailhead.

1.6 Arrive back at trailhead.

Hike Information

Local information: Irving Convention and Visitors Bureau; (800) 247-8464; (972) 252-7476; www.visitirving.com

Dallas Off-Road Bicycle Association (DORBA); www.dorba.org

Good eats: The buffet at Terra Mediterranean is a great place for a post-hike repast; 5910 N. Macarthur Blvd., Irving; (972) 401-3900; www.terramediterranean.com

Attractions/events: *The Mustangs of Las Colinas*, the largest equestrian statue in the world, is located just a few miles away in Williams Square Plaza; 5205 N. O'Connor Dr., Irving; (972) 869-9047; www.mustangsoflascolinas.com.

GREEN TIP
If you're driving to or from the trailhead, don't let any passenger throw garbage out the window. Keep a small bag in the car that you can empty properly at home.

22 Loyd Park Trail

This 1-mile loop trail through hardwood bottomland skirts the edge of Walnut Creek by Joe Pool Lake, where some try their luck at catching crappie, catfish, and bass. It's pricey to enter the park, but the payoff is clean facilities and a well-marked trail that's relatively empty even on sunny weekends.

Start: Back of parking lot, left of restrooms, at Campsite 1
Distance: 1-mile double loop
Approximate hiking time: 30 minutes
Difficulty: Easy
Trail surface: Packed dirt
Season: Apr through Nov
Other trail users: Anglers, birders, and horseback riders

Canine compatibility: Dogs must be on leash
Land status: Operated by the City of Grand Prairie
Fees and permits: Per vehicle entry fee
Schedule: Open daily 24 hours
Map: National Geographic TOPO! Texas
Trail contact: Grand Prairie Parks and Recreation; (817) 467-2104; www.grandfungp.org

Finding the trailhead: From DFW International Airport take TX 360 south to Ragland Road; turn left onto Ragland at the light. The park is about 0.5 mile down the road at 3401 Ragland Rd. After entering through the gate, turn right and follow the park's main road until it dead-ends. The trailhead is at the back of the parking lot by the restrooms. GPS: N 32 35.895' / W 97 04.112'

The Hike

The City of Grand Prairie's 791-acre Loyd Park on Joe Pool Lake offers equestrian, mountain biking, and hiking trails along with cabins and campsites, picnic areas, and a swimming beach. For hikers looking for an overnight trip with rustic cabins and plenty of other diversions, from fishing to beach volleyball to boating, the park is a great option. The city charges an entrance fee per vehicle (higher on popular holiday weekends, such as Labor Day and Memorial Day). While the park is extremely busy on sunny summer weekends, when the wait to get inside the gates can top thirty minutes, the hiking trail, situated at the far west side of the park, feels remote. Perhaps that's because so many park-goers make a beeline right to the park's picnic pavilions, playground, and sandy beach swimming area.

The hiking trail is located at the west end of the park, just past the camping sites and near a building housing large, clean restrooms. The trail heads into the dense woods and early on, at about the 0.3-mile mark, there's a split. Bear right and head toward the banks of Walnut Creek where it's common to see one or two folks trying their luck at bank fishing. This trail is gorgeous in the fall when its canopy of deciduous trees turns vibrant red and orange, and in summer when the green leaves provide welcome shade from the sun.

Fish or swim in Joe Pool Lake.

In late summer the trail is littered with the bright green fruit of the Osage orange tree, sometimes called horse apples. The trail winds away from the creek through the woods, coming to a split. Bear right to continue on the loop back to the trailhead. (For a longer hike, bear right and continue along the creek's banks. See Options below.)

Miles and Directions

0.0 The trailhead is located past the camping sites in the far side of the parking lot by restrooms. From the parking lot, the trail heads into the dense woods along a wide, dirt path.

0.3 As the trail splits, bear right and head toward the creek's banks and follow it for about 5 yards. This spot makes an excellent fishing site or a shaded campground hideaway.

0.4 The trail moves into the woods, where it narrows as it passes by an Osage orange tree.

0.6 The trail comes to a split; bear right to continue on the loop.

1.0 Arrive back at trailhead.

Options

For a longer hike, bear right at 0.4 mile and continue along the creek's banks, following the trail for about 0.5 mile out and back until it returns to this junction. The trail then joins the Princess Trail at 0.6 mile; bear left at the juncture and return to the trailhead and the parking lot.

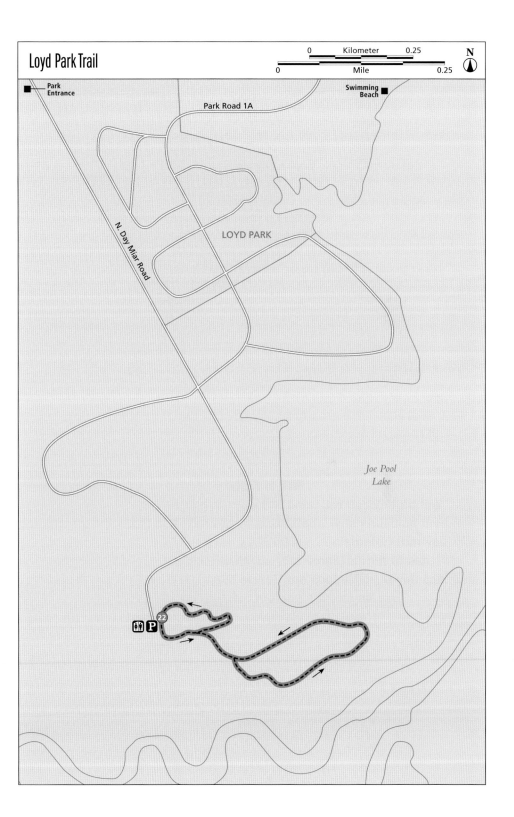

Loyd Park Trail

0   Kilometer   0.25

0   Mile   0.25

N

Park
Entrance

Park Road 1A

Swimming
Beach

N. Day Miar Road

LOYD PARK

Joe Pool
Lake

22

THE GRAND PRAIRIE

The 7-million-acre Grand Prairie includes the flatlands just west of the Blackland Prairie in north-central Texas. This unique area of approximately 15 million acres of alternating woodlands and broad grassy prairies offered a bountiful harvest of essential survival ingredients to the Native American cultures from the pre-history era through the settlement of Texas. A mild enough climate, good soil, and frequent rains fostered prairie grasses in quantities to support large herds of horses and buffalo. Several salt deposits were featured along with large, freshwater springs as special attractions among the many migratory Native American trails.

The only buffalo wallow known to exist in Grand Prairie—and possibly the entire Dallas/Fort Worth area—is located by the Mountain Creek Retirement community (2305 Corn Valley Rd.). The southwest corner of Freetown and Corn Valley Roads is now part of a protected preserve.

A buffalo wallow begins when buffalo paw dry dirt to break up the grass surface. The animals then roll in the dirt to dust themselves for fly and mosquito control. Over time, the wallows become muddy, with the mud acting as even more effective insect control. Today wallows are seldom found due to farm cultivation and urban development. This site's large, rounded indentations provide proof that buffalo once roamed this area freely.

When the railroad came to Grand Prairie around 1875, the area was still populated with buffalo herds. The Trinity River plains made an excellent home for buffalo, but increased hunting, farming, and development caused the animals to disappear from the area.

These wallows were discovered by Muriel Adair, whose grandfather, James Alfred Adair, came to Texas in the 1880s on a Missouri wagon train, settling the land just north of the existing wallows.

The land on which the wallows reside was originally 125 acres settled by generations of the Galloway family beginning in 1911. Most farmers would have tried to plow the wallows and plant crops. However, the mucky soils located in the wallows were bad for most crops. The Galloways never tilled the wallows on their property, and a thicket grew up around them. After the Galloways left the farm, the land remained vacant. The Grand Prairie Housing Finance Corporation bought the land in 2002, building the Mountain Creek Retirement Living Center and left the wallows as open space in the design of the complex, preserving this unique relic of the past for all time.

If you don't want to pay the fee to enter and hike in Loyd Park, opt for the Northside Impoundment Trail, a wide, gravel road located on a berm built to form the lake. The trail can be accessed near the Lynn Creek Marina off Mansfield Park and Lake Ridge Parkway. Park in Lynn Creek Marina by Gate 2. The trail is about 3 miles long, making it a 6-mile out-and-back hike. Dogs are allowed as long as they are on a leash. The hike rises as it gets to the top of the dam then is a flat cement road as it crosses the dam.

Hike Information

Local information: City of Grand Prairie; (817) 467-2104; www.grandfungp.org
Good eats: The Oasis at Joe Pool Lake offers a great view and a casual vibe that comes with lakeside dining and drinks. Located by Lynn Creek Marina; 5700 Lake Ridge Pkwy., Grand Prairie; (817) 640-7676; www.theoasisrestaurant.com

HORSE APPLES

The fruit of the Osage orange tree, called horse apples or hedge apples, is a popular late-summer fare for the squirrels that typically sit at the base of the tree and pick apart the tough, stringy fruit to get to the coveted seeds inside. The trees were once used as hedgerows before the invention of barbed wire. Their strong, dense wood was prized by Native Americans, who used it to make bows. Only female trees produce the fruit, which can reach 6 inches in diameter.

23 River Legacy Park Trail

This flat, paved trail is popular with joggers, cyclists, and hikers alike. The park's 1,300 acres include 8 miles of trails along the West Fork of the Trinity River, where the river's steep banks are lined with mature bottomland hardwoods drawing abundant wildlife. This hike covers the west side of the park, where the trail is shaded by massive gnarled oaks and is a bit less traveled perhaps due to the adjacent sewage treatment facility. A bench perched by the riverbank provides a nice mid-hike picnicking spot.

Start: Parking lot
Distance: 3.2-mile out-and-back
Approximate hiking time: 1 to 2 hours
Difficulty: Easy
Trail surface: Paved concrete
Seasons: Feb through May; Oct through Dec
Water availability: Water fountains and restrooms at trailhead
Other trail users: Cyclists, in-line skaters, joggers

Canine compatibility: Dogs must be on leash.
Land status: City of Arlington Parks and Recreation
Fees and permits: None
Schedule: Open daily 5 a.m. to 10 p.m.
Maps: Trail maps available at park entrance or online at www.riverlegacy.org
Trail contact: Arlington Parks and Recreation; (817) 459-5474; www.naturallyfun.org

Finding the trailhead: Take Cooper Street North to Green Oaks Boulevard, then turn left and go 0.25 mile to the entrance of River Legacy Park. Take the park drive to the end. Trail begins by the parking lot. GPS: N32 47.508' / W097 06.764'

The Hike

River Legacy Park is a major destination for Arlington-area residents year-round, including special events such as the Cardboard Boat Regatta held in the spring. Its Living Science Center includes informative exhibits on natural history and native plants and animals, as well as tips on living green. In fact, much of the center itself was

WOLF SPIDERS

River Legacy Park is home to a colony of wolf spiders, named for their hunting prowess. Brown and black with some striping, these spiders hunt at night and can be seen when their two large eyes reflect the light from a flashlight or headlight. (They actually have eight eyes arranged in three rows with two large eyes in the middle row.) Unlike other spiders, they form webs for protection during the day, not to hunt and capture prey. Many wolf spider females carry their eggs everywhere they go until they hatch. The baby spiders then cling to their mother's abdomen. Wolf spiders can bite, but their venom is not considered toxic to humans.

constructed using sustainable design and recycled materials.

The trailhead is located at the back of the park's drive just north of the science center, making it an easy addition to the hike. Several small trails jut out from the park's main trail along the Trinity River here, but the best place to meet up is the small trail to the far right, heading into the woods and over a bridge. If time permits, take a brief detour bearing to the right on the main trail and crossing a bridge over Snider Creek to quickly check out a dense thicket of trees that's home to a colony of wolf spiders, which form webbing as a daytime shelter, not to catch prey. Turn around, heading west on the main trail. The wide trail winds along the river, which is to the right, and the park's picnic tables and fields are on the left.

Stop at the park's Living Science Center before hitting the trail to grab brochures identifying the different plants and animals in the park, including an informative handout on animal tracks. The center is open 9 a.m. to 5 p.m. Tuesday through Saturday.

Cross over Snider Creek.

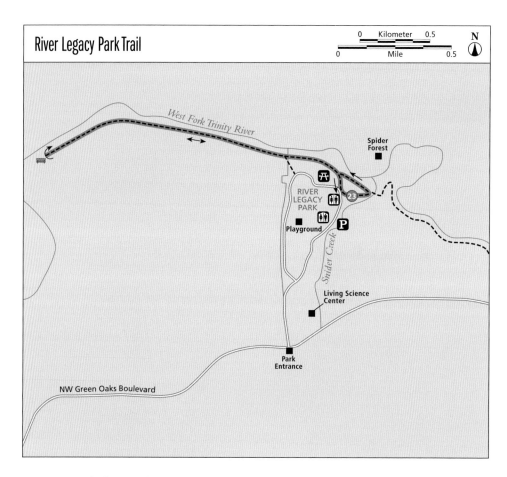

River Legacy Park Trail

0   Kilometer   0.5
0   Mile   0.5

N

West Fork Trinity River

Spider Forest

RIVER LEGACY PARK

Playground

Living Science Center

Snider Creek

Park Entrance

NW Green Oaks Boulevard

At 0.5 mile, bear right at a fork, staying on the main trail as it continues along the river. The city's sewage treatment center is located on the other side of the river here, so smells related to processing the sewage of more than 300,000 people waft over the trail. The churning sounds of a natural gas well may also be heard—an indication the trail passes the Barnett Shale, a rich underground reservoir of natural gas and some oil that lies under much of the region. The paved trail ends at 1.6 miles, where a picnic spot by the river provides a pleasant place to relax and take in wildlife before heading back to the trailhead.

Miles and Directions

0.0   Trail begins behind the parking lot. Bear right at the first trail split just a few yards beyond the trailhead and head toward the wider, main trail as it heads into the woods.

0.1   Bear left when you meet up with the main trail.

0.5   Bear right at a fork to stay on the main trail, following the river.

1.6   The trail ends; turn around to head back, retracing your steps back to the parking lot.

3.2   Arrive back at trailhead.

Hike Information

Local information: Arlington Convention and Visitors Bureau; (800) 342-4305; www.arlington.org

Organizations: River Legacy Foundation; (817) 860-6752; www.riverlegacy.org.

BOBCATS

Bobcats are generally solitary animals, but a few have been spotted at River Legacy Park, which offers a Bobcat Blog on its website, www.riverlegacy.org. These cats are often seen during feeding times in the early morning and late afternoon around the park's creeks and riverbeds. They are usually well camouflaged and will typically avoid humans. Hikers who encounter a bobcat should take the following precautions:

· Quietly watch the animal from a distance.

· Make sure the bobcat has an escape route and do not try to corner it.

· Never approach a mother bobcat with cubs. She will try to protect them if she feels you might be a threat.

The Living Science Center at River Legacy Park offers informative exhibits on bobcats and other mammals found in the park. The center, located at 703 NW Green Oaks Blvd., is open 9 a.m. to 5 p.m. Tuesday to Saturday; (817) 860-6752.

24 Little Bear Creek Trail

A popular dog park adjacent to this trail makes it ideal for canines. Educational markers identifying various tree species, a scenic dock overlooking a large pond, and well-maintained fields and a playground make for an enjoyable outing for kids and adults.

Start: Parking lot next to Bear Creek Dog Park
Distance: 2-mile out-and-back
Approximate hiking time: 1 hour
Difficulty: Easy
Trail surface: Mostly paved with some gravel and dirt
Season: Feb through May
Other trail users: Cyclists, joggers, dog walkers
Canine compatibility: Dogs must be on leash
Land status: City park
Fees and permits: None

Schedule: Open daily 7 a.m. to 11 p.m.
Maps: National Geographic TOPO! Texas; City of Euless Parks and Recreation; www.euless.org/pacs/trails.htm
Trail contact: City of Euless Parks and Recreation Department; (817) 685-1429
Special considerations: The park's fields are very popular on weekends for soccer and flag-football games, and the dog park also draws crowds, so parking can be a pain.

Finding the trailhead: From TX 183, take TX 360 north and exit at Mid-Cities Boulevard. Head west on Mid-Cities Boulevard and turn left at Bear Creek Parkway; the park is 0.25 mile on the right. The trailhead is by the parking lot next to the dog park. GPS: N32 51.901'/W97 04.156'

The Hike

Just a couple miles west of Dallas/Fort Worth International Airport, this trail follows Little Bear Creek just before it meets up with Big Bear Creek and meanders along a tree-lined greenbelt through two city parks. The 4-acre dog park means lots of canines are typically walking along the paths. Waste bags and periodic dumping stations are provided along the trail.

Start the trail by the main parking lot next to the dog park and head toward three tree-lined creek areas. Veer left off the paved path onto the gravel trail for a walk along the creek banks on the Texas Outdoor Education Trail, which has detailed descriptions of various tree species. Signs that read Bear Crossing don't refer to actual bears, but are spots where paths cross over Little Bear Creek. Several dirt trails spring off the main trail, leading down to the creek for a closer look at the wildlife there.

At about 0.25 mile, bear right as the trail enters a more open area alongside playing fields. At about 0.5 mile, bear left to take in the scenic view of a pond with an observation deck, a nice birding spot, then rejoin the main trail. Follow the wide paved path along the creek until you reach the spot where Main Street crosses over the trail. This is the turnaround, but if you would like to hike a bit farther, the trail continues through Bob Eden Park, where you can add another mile to the hike, turning around at the playground there.

Top: The trail passes playing fields and a playground as well as crossing the creek several times.
Bottom: The dock overlooks a large pond teeming with wildlife.

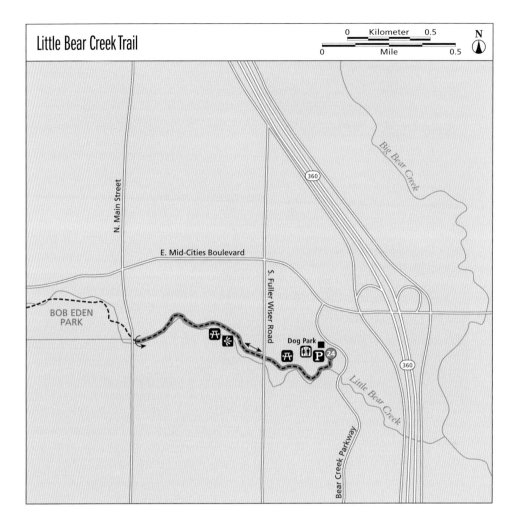

Little Bear Creek Trail

Miles and directions

0.0 From the parking lot by the dog park, locate the trailhead where the paved path heads toward the tree-lined creek.

0.25 Bear right as the trail enters an open area by playing fields.

0.5 Take a left walking down to an observation deck over a pond.

1.0 The trail heads under Main Street. Turn around here and retrace your steps back to the trailhead.

2.0 Arrive back at trailhead.

Hike Information

Local information: HEB Chamber of Commerce; (817) 283-1521; www.heb.org

HIKING WITH DOGS

Many hikers enjoy bringing their dogs along on the trail. It's easy to enjoy a hike with Fido and still leave little impact on the environment. Most trails in this guide welcome dogs as long as they are kept on a leash. For unleashed fun opt for one of the area's growing number of dog parks that have open spaces for dogs to romp. Be aware that some local nature sanctuaries and preserves specifically ban dogs from trails in order to encourage wildlife to inhabit the area.

Here are some tips for hiking with your best friend.

- Pack out everything you pack in—this includes all waste, so be prepared with zip-top bags.
- Stay on the trail. Don't let Fido trample plants by running through the woods.
- Do not let your dog approach other people and their pets unless invited to do so.
- Never let your dog chase wildlife. Some animals may have rabies, and you don't want any run-ins with skunks.
- Keep your dog from barking. Many fellow hikers hit the trail for peace and quiet, so be considerate.
- Step off the trail and wait on the side if other hikers or horses and their riders pass by.
- Be sure to bring water and a bowl so Fido doesn't get dehydrated.
- If hiking in the heat of summer, pay attention to your dog—if he or she is panting profusely, take a break and cut your hike short.
- End the hike with a nice treat, while also checking your dog for any bites, ticks, and fleas.

GREEN TIP

Avoid sensitive ecological areas. Hike, rest, and camp
at least 200 feet from streams, lakes, and rivers.

25 Colleyville Nature Center Trail

This flat, wooded trail begins by a small playground and picnic pavilion and winds along a bubbling creek through a riparian forest, wetlands, and lakes. The ponds are home to an impressive variety of birds including the great blue heron and its smaller relative, the green heron, plus flocks of mallards and the 46-acre park's resident gaggle of geese.

Start: Nature center parking lot
Distance: 1.25-mile balloon
Approximate hiking time: 30 minutes
Difficulty: Easy
Trail surface: Begins with paved path, then becomes dirt path for majority of trail
Seasons: Winter and spring
Other trail users: Mountain bikers, dog walkers
Canine compatibility: Dogs must be on leash
Land status: City park

Fees and permits: None
Schedule: Open daily year-round, 30 minutes before sunrise to 30 minutes after sunset
Map: Detailed trail map available from City of Colleyville Parks and Recreation Department; (817) 656-7275
Trail contact: City of Colleyville Parks and Recreation Department; (817) 656-7275
Special considerations: After a very heavy rain, the creek can turn into a raging river.

Finding the trailhead: From Northeast Loop 820 in North Richland Hills, take the TX 26/Grapevine Highway exit and follow TX 26 northeast for 4.8 miles. Turn left onto Glade Road and proceed 0.6 mile to Mill Creek Drive. Turn left to follow Mill Creek Drive through a subdivision for 0.3 mile. The park's playground and picnic pavilion are located by the intersection of Mill Creek Drive and Mill Wood Drive. Turn into the parking area and look for large sign reading Colleyville Nature Center. GPS: N 32 52.250' / W 97 10.00'

The Hike

The Colleyville Nature Center and its system of 3-plus miles of trails is a relaxing retreat for Mid-Cities residents and birders. Bring your binoculars—more than twenty varieties of warblers have been recorded here, including golden-winged and hooded warblers. Winter is less crowded, and spring is best for birding and wildlife spotting. The trail has several shaded picnic tables and an adjacent playground, making it a great hike for parents with young children or anyone looking to walk off a meal. And you can enjoy catch-and-release fishing from the park's fishing pier.

The nature trail is the main trail in the park, but other short trails join and connect it in various spots, making it easy to shorten or lengthen your hike. While parts of the trail wind close to neighborhood homes, most of it wanders along Little Bear Creek, which joins Big Bear Creek near the Dallas/Fort Worth International Airport then flows into the West Fork of the Trinity River. Several years ago, some residents reported seeing a panther along the creek's banks, but officials never confirmed any of the sightings. Still, local lore did prompt the high school to become the Colleyville Panthers.

PLAYING POSSUM

Possums are solitary, nocturnal animals that are also North America's only marsupial; that is, they have a pouch used to carry their young. Once a baby possum, called a joey, grows too large for the pouch, it often rides on its mother's back during her nighttime search for food. When threatened by a predator, possums "play dead" until the danger is gone. Contrary to popular belief, they do not hang by their prehensile tails, but do use them for balance when climbing.

Begin the hike on a paved trail by the parking lot, then head into a dense forest of post oaks, cottonwoods, American elms, pecans, and sugar hackberry trees. The trail crosses a smaller tributary of Little Bear Creek by an outdoor amphitheater and winds along the creek for 0.25 mile before reaching an open, grassy area by the ponds, where you may spot herons, kingfishers, and flycatchers, as well as flocks of ducks and the park's resident gaggle of noisy geese.

Bird watchers flock to Colleyville Nature Center's ponds.

Colleyville Nature Center Trail

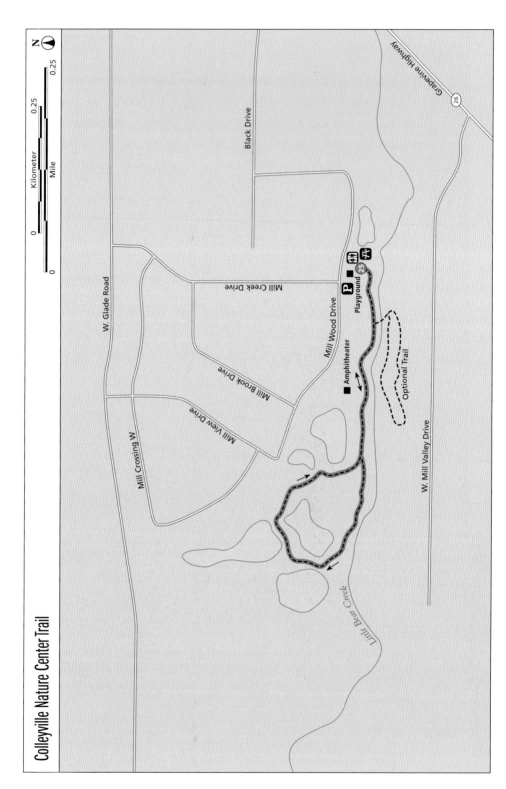

The trail circles around the ponds then reenters the forest where you cross back over the creek and meet the trail back at the amphitheater. From here you can spot the parking lot and return to the trailhead.

Miles and Directions

0.0 Look for marker labeled Colleyville Nature Center and take the paved path into the woods.

0.2 Look for marker with the map of park trails. Follow the paved path toward the woods as it turns into a dirt trail.

0.3 Cross the bridge over Little Bear Creek and go by the outdoor amphitheater.

0.5 Trail enters a grassy meadow by the ponds.

0.8 Trail loops back toward a wooded area.

1.0 Cross over the Little Bear Creek bridge again, and meet the trail back at outdoor amphitheater.

1.25 Arrive back at trailhead.

Hike Information

Local information: Colleyville Chamber of Commerce; (817) 488-7148; www .colleyvillechamber.org

GREEN TIP
If you see someone else littering, muster up the courage to ask them not to.

26 Lake Grapevine Horseshoe Trails

This hike is on a paved street long ago closed to traffic, making it a quiet stroll through a Cross Timbers forest of post oaks and cedar elms to a solitary point with a sheltered picnic table and view of Lake Grapevine. The trail gently winds up and down low hills as it reaches Oak Grove Park, home to multiple soccer fields, baseball diamonds, and picnic pavilions. The trail ends at a lakeside playground. While this hike sticks to paved surfaces, there are multiple points to access unpaved mountain bike trails, but pedestrians must yield to cyclists on these rocky trails.

Start: Dove Road parking lot
Distance: 4.7-mile out-and-back
Approximate hiking time: 2 hours
Difficulty: Easy
Trail surface: Paved
Season: Mar through Oct
Other trail users: Cyclists, joggers, in-line skaters
Canine compatibility: Dogs must be on leash

Land status: City park
Fees and permits: None
Schedule: Open daily 6 a.m. to 9 p.m.
Maps: National Geographic TOPO! Texas; Grapevine Parks and Recreation; www.grapevinetexas.gov
Trail contact: City of Grapevine Parks and Recreation; (817) 410-3450

Finding the trailhead: Take TX 114 west from Dallas to Grapevine and exit at Park Boulevard, bearing right at the fork to stay on Park. Drive about 1 mile to an intersection with Dove Road and turn left onto Dove; the parking lot for the trail is about 0.25 mile down on the right. The trailhead is off Dove Road. GPS: N32 57.345'/W 097 06.308'

The Hike

Located on the south side of Lake Grapevine, which supplies water for Highland Park and University Park as well as portions of Grapevine, this trail is only a few miles from bustling Grapevine Mills, DFW International Airport, and the massive Gaylord Texan and Great Wolf Lodge resorts. Thanks to those developments and others, the city enjoys a healthy tax base and offers first-rate parks including this well-tended trail.

The first part of the hike, about 1.5 miles, is on an old, paved park road, open only to foot and bike traffic now. Off-road cyclists take to side dirt trails that branch off the road. The trail starts from the parking lot off Dove Road, then heads through grassy expanses bounded by post oaks and cedar elms, passing houses on the right. Because the area contains both grasslands and forests, it attracts a great variety of birds, including woodpeckers, bluebirds, and cardinals.

The paved road curves to the right and then another, smaller paved road shoots off to the left, leading to a point with several picnic tables and a small path that leads down to the lake—a perfect place to drop a fishing line and try to catch some of the

Views of Lake Grapevine make this hike special.

lake's bass, catfish, and crappie. It's easy to turn around and retrace the trail back to the main road, where you bear left, passing a side road that leads to a residential neighborhood on the right and following the road's sharp curve to the left as it heads down a hill, showing off another peek at the lake at 0.8 mile.

As the trail meets up with Boathouse Drive, hikers must cross a park road and continue up the trail as it turns from asphalt to concrete, then crosses over Dove Loop Road into a forest of post oak trees. Here the trail heads downhill to cross over a creek. The trail continues into a scrubbier forest of cedar elms as it gets closer to Oak Grove Park. Squirrels frequently cross the trail here in this last stand of woods before the trail reaches the park, a hub of baseball and soccer fields and plenty of picnic tables filled with people on sunny weekends. A dog park and lakeside playground with nearby water fountains and restrooms make a nice resting spot before turning around and heading back to the trailhead.

If you time this hike right, you'll receive a true gift: This hike is gorgeous around sunset.

Miles and Directions

0.0 Begin trail by parking lot off Dove Road, where a trail sign is posted.

0.1 Stay on large, paved street at junction with concrete-paved path.

0.5 Bear left at trail split, heading down a smaller asphalt road lined with tall grasses in the spring, summer, and fall. Proceed to end of the point with picnic tables and a view of the lake, then turn around.

Lake Grapevine Horseshoe Trails

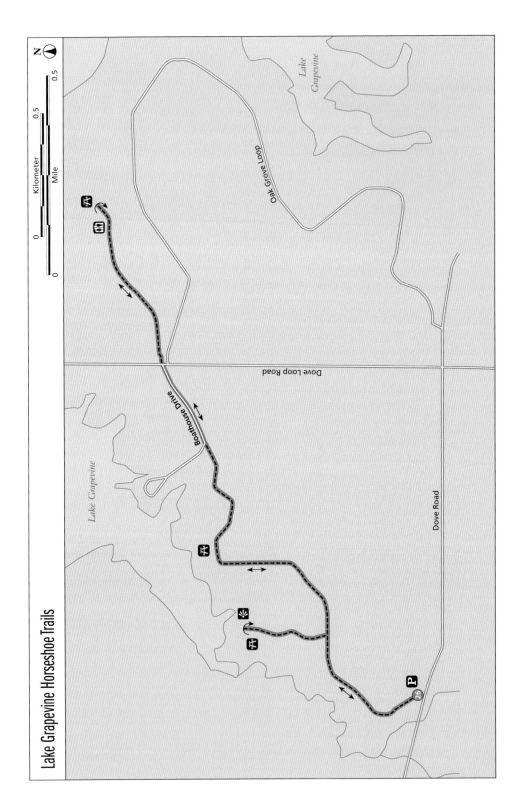

0.8 Rejoin the main trail, bearing left and following the road as it winds downhill with the lake on the left.

1.2 Cross Dove Loop Road, and follow the path as it leads into the woods.

1.8 Stay on the trail as it emerges from woods to an open area with soccer fields overlooking Lake Grapevine.

2.5 Trail reaches a playground. After a break, turn around and retrace steps back to trailhead.

4.7 Arrive back at trailhead.

Hike Information

Local information: Grapevine Convention & Visitors Bureau; (800) 457-6338; www.grapevinetexasusa.com

Good eats: The Main Street Bistro and Bakery serves croissants and other French pastries and sandwiches in historic downtown Grapevine; 316 S. Main St., Grapevine; (817) 424-4333; www.themainbakery.com

Breadhaus offers great post-hike organic treats from cookies to pies to all types of breads; 700 W. Dallas Rd., Grapevine; (817) 488-5223; www.breadhaus.com

Attractions/events: Grapevine has become a destination for wine lovers, and several Texas-based wineries have tasting rooms in and around the city's historic downtown.

A complete list of wineries and operating hours are available at www.grapevine texasusa.com. The city celebrates its growing wine industry with the annual Grape-Fest street festival held in September; www.grapevinetexasusa.com/grapefest.

Other resources: The city has cabins and campsites nearby that are available for rent at The Vineyards Campground, which also offers kayak rentals and a geocaching program; (817) 329-8993; www.vineyardscampground.com.

MUSTANG GRAPES

Texas is home to several types of wild grapes, including mustang grapes, namesake of the Mustang Trail and the city of Grapevine, which was named for the abundant wild grapes that grew in the region. Other common grapes along North Texas trails include sweet mountain grape and the winter grape, but mustangs are the most common. They have a tart flavor, tough skins, and seeds. Mustang grape jelly is available at some local stores and farmers markets. The grapes are also used in winemaking. Grapevine has parlayed its name into a marketing niche, welcoming wine lovers with numerous wineries and wine tasting rooms. For a complete list of wineries, go to www.grapevinetexasusa.com.

27 Bob Jones Nature Center Trail

This short loop through woods, fields, and wetlands is ideal for families with small children. The adjacent nature center features hands-on exhibits, educational programs, and a gift shop. While less than a mile, the trail manages to cover a diverse array of ecosystems including grassy prairie and Cross Timbers woodlands as well as a small pond that draws animals such as wild turkeys, raccoons, coyotes, and white-tailed deer.

Start: Butterfly garden to right of nature center building
Distance: 0.75-mile loop
Approximate hiking time: 30 minutes
Difficulty: Easy
Trail surface: Packed dirt and grass
Seasons: Mar through June; Oct through Dec
Other trail users: Horseback riders on side trails
Canine compatibility: No dogs permitted
Land status: City park and nature preserve
Fees and permits: None
Schedule: Open daily sunrise to sunset; Bob Jones Nature Center open 9 a.m. to 5 p.m. Tues to Sat
Map: National Geographic TOPO! Texas
Trail contact: Bob Jones Nature Center and Preserve; (817) 491-6333; www.bjnc.org

Finding the trailhead: From Dallas take TX 114 west to the White Chapel Boulevard exit. Drive north for 2.5 miles to the intersection with Bob Jones Road (there is another trailhead located in Bob Jones Park, but horseback riders mainly use this trail and its entrance). Turn right onto Bob Jones Road; the nature center is on the right. The trailhead is just to the left of the nature center building. GPS: N 32 59.825' / W 97 09.168'

The Hike

The Bob Jones Nature Center opened in 2008 on land owned by Bob Jones—who was born a slave on a nearby farm in Roanoke and eventually bought this land where he and his wife, Meady Chisum, raised their ten children. Now part of the City of Southlake's parks system, the grounds cover nearly 500 acres of wildlife habitat along the shores of Lake Grapevine. To encourage wildlife, dogs and horses are prohibited on this trail.

Growing in popularity, the center and this hike make a great afternoon family outing. The nature center includes a small gift shop where you can buy butterfly nets, birdcalls, and other kid-friendly gear. There's also a small animal display that includes several snakes and lizards, plus a water fountain and restrooms. On weekends and during summer, the center offers hands-on nature programs for kids. Other activities include periodic guided nature hikes and an annual nature photography competition.

Outside the nature center, just south of the parking lot, there's a butterfly garden and also an interactive composting exhibit. The park's main trail is called the Blue

Bird Trail, but another trail called the Whitetail Deer Loop connects with the network of horse trails in the area for hikers looking for more of a workout. These trails tend to be much easier to hike in late fall, winter, and early spring before the grasses get too tall. In summer, hoards of grasshoppers leap up in waves as hikers pass through. An information center inside the nature center offers a one-page map to the center's trails as well as others in the area along the southern shores of Lake Grapevine.

Texas is home to more than 400 species of butterfly—more any other state. For more information about local butterflies, contact the Dallas County Lepidopterists Society at www.dallasbutterflies.com.

The Blue Bird Trail begins by a picnic shelter south of the Bob Jones Nature Center and circles through native Cross Timbers as well as open prairie. Several large trees and some plants are labeled with identifying markers. At about 0.6 mile there's a small pond with a viewing area that provides a pleasing vantage point to view birds and other wildlife, including wild turkeys and white-tailed deer, commonly spotted here. The trail then heads up a small hill through a field back to the nature center and parking lot.

Storm clouds start to gather over the prairie.

Bob Jones Nature Center Trail

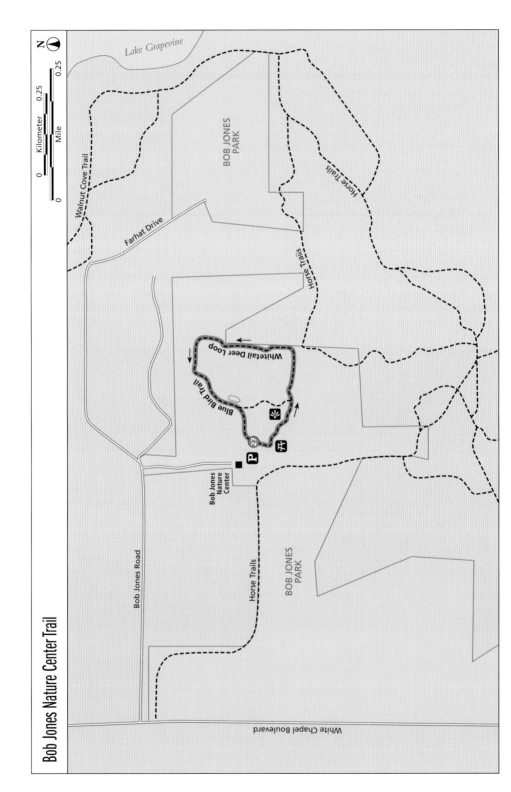

POKEWEED

Every part of the pokeweed, also called poke salad and inkberry, is poisonous. Boiling can reduce the toxins, and its boiled juices have been a folk remedy for all types of ailments from acne to arthritis. In the Civil War, soldiers made ink from the berries to write letters home.

Miles and Directions

0.0   Start from the nature center parking lot and head toward the picnic pavilion.

0.3   Follow the trail as it circles toward the marker that says Prairie View.

0.6   Pass the pond and wildlife observation area, then wind your way back, moving slightly uphill to head back to the nature center.

0.75 Arrive back at trailhead.

Hike Information

Local information: Southlake Chamber of Commerce stages the city's annual Oktoberfest held at Southlake Town Square; (817) 481-8200; www.southlakechamber .com

Bob Jones Nature Center and Preserve; (817) 491-6333; www.bjnc.org

28 Walnut Grove Trail

This 5-mile out-and-back trail hugs the south shore of Lake Grapevine, offering stunning views and surprising solitude. The upper part of the trail runs through woods and the lower part goes along the shoreline. The trail is open to horses and closed to mountain bikers, but they sometimes can't resist, so be prepared to see a few fat tire marks along with tracks of armadillos, possums, and the occasional coyote.

Start: Parking lot at dead end of White Chapel Boulevard
Distance: 5-mile out-and-back
Approximate hiking time: 2 to 3 hours
Difficulty: Moderate to difficult
Trail surface: Packed dirt and sand
Seasons: Mar through May; Nov through Dec
Other trail users: Horseback riders, joggers
Canine compatibility: Dogs must be on leash.
Land status: Watershed managed by US Army Corps of Engineers
Fees and permits: None

Schedule: Day use only
Maps: National Geographic TOPO! Texas; Southlake Parks and Recreation; www.swf-wc .usace.army.mil/grapevine/Recreation/Trails/ Walnut-Grove-trail-2011.pdf
Trail contact: US Army Corps of Engineers; (817) 865-2600
Special considerations: Since this is an equestrian trail, watch for horse droppings and give horseback riders the right-of-way. Shoes can sink in the sand along the beach, so wear older boots.

Finding the trailhead: From Dallas take TX 114 west to the White Chapel Boulevard exit and drive north 3 miles to where the road ends in a parking lot. The trailhead is adjacent to the parking lot's east side. GPS: N33 00.280' / W97 09.419'

The Hike

A series of interconnecting loops makes it easy to shorten or lengthen this hike along the shore of Lake Grapevine. Despite being a few miles west of DFW International Airport, the park feels very remote. For simplicity, this trail simply follows the sandy beach, providing a good workout that can also be somewhat muddy depending on recent rainfall. Hikers who prefer not to navigate the sandy shore can opt for one of the many dirt paths farther inland that also run parallel to the lake's edge, but these trails may be less traveled and have more tree limbs to dodge and, in warmer months, thorny vines that can be treacherous. These trails crisscross each other and can be confusing, but the lake provides an easy navigating point to prevent going in circles.

The trailhead is the low gate entrance to the right side of the parking lot. Here the dirt trail winds through a tall grassy meadow behind a few large homes. At about 0.5 mile the trail comes to another parking lot on the right. For a hike along the sandy lakeshore, hikers can bear left at the trail split, heading by several tall bird boxes toward the beach. The trail simply follows the shoreline, providing a peaceful view

The trail follows the sandy shoreline of Lake Grapevine.

that's likely to include the occasional angler in this remote part of the lake in search of bass, catfish, and crappie.

On the lakeshore, the sand is sprinkled with freshwater oyster shells and driftwood, and it's possible to spot tracks from possums, raccoons, and the band of coyotes known to roam here. Horse riders are another common sight, as it's a popular trail ride at nearby Marshall Creek Ranch. Follow the shoreline to the point that juts out revealing the next cove, about 2.5 miles, then turn around and retrace the shoreline back to the trailhead.

Walnut Grove Trail

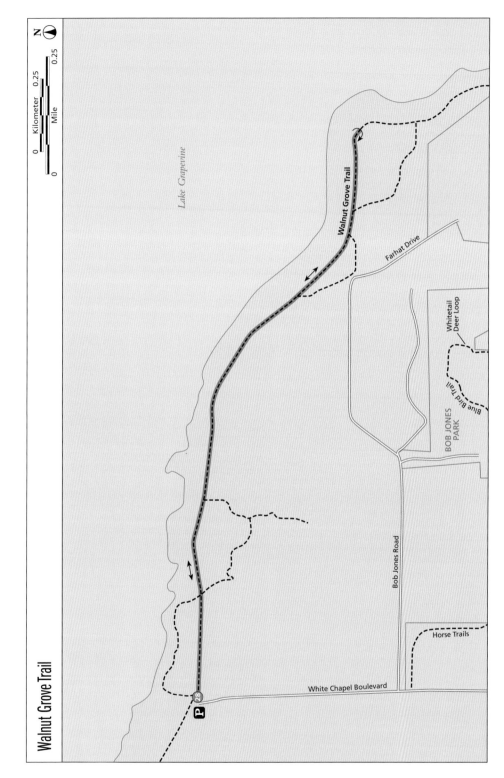

N

Kilometer
0   0.25

Mile
0   0.25

Lake Grapevine

Walnut Grove Trail

Farhat Drive

Whitetail
Deer Loop

Blue Bird Trail

BOB JONES
PARK

Bob Jones Road

Horse Trails

White Chapel Boulevard

28

P

Miles and Directions

0.0   Find the trailhead on the east side of parking lot.

0.5   Pass another parking lot on the right, then bear left and follow trail to the lake's shore.

0.6   Continue on the trail, following the shoreline another 1.5 miles.

2.5   Reach the peninsula jutting into the lake; turn around and retrace your steps to the trailhead.

5.0   Arrive back at trailhead.

Hike Information

Local information: Southlake Chamber of Commerce; (817) 481-8200; www.southlakechamber.com

Attractions/events: The Southlake Chamber of Commerce holds an annual Oktoberfest in nearby Southlake Town Square celebrating all things German, including beer, sausage, and dachshund races.

Good eats: One of the oldest restaurants in town, Feedstore Barbecue is so-named because it was once largely a feed and tack store. But as the number of local farms and ranches gave way to development, the food, once a sideline, took over the business; 530 S. White Chapel Blvd., Southlake; (817) 488-1445

Organizations: Bob Jones Nature Center and Preserve; (817) 491-6333; www.bjnc.org

GREEN TIP

When hiking at the beach, stay off dunes and
away from nesting areas.

THE MONARCH MIGRATION

In autumn, as the days grow shorter and temperatures start to cool, nature signals flora and fauna that it's time to prepare for the coming winter. For ducks, geese, and other species of migratory birds, it's time to begin to move out of the north into areas of more abundant food to the south. Many insects spend the winter as eggs or larvae and dehydrate themselves to keep from freezing. One unique insect has a different survival strategy—the monarch butterfly. Like migratory birds, monarch butterflies have evolved the ability to fly long distances, escaping winter cold and the absence of food. Decreasing day length and cooler temperatures tell the monarchs that emerge in the early fall not to breed. Instead they begin the immense journey across North America, over unfamiliar terrain, moving through Texas as they travel to nine high mountain sites in the fir forests of central Mexico. They typically arrive in Mexico by November and remain there until March of the following spring. Then they return to Texas and the southern United States to lay eggs on freshly sprouted milkweeds. By late spring most from this generation have left the Gulf Coast states and headed farther north to breed. By the beginning of June they have reached the northern United States and Canada where they continue to breed all summer. Texas is an important state in their migration because it is situated between the principal breeding grounds in the north and their winter home in Mexico. Monarchs funnel through Texas both in the fall and the spring. During the fall, monarchs use two main flyways. One traverses Texas in a 300-mile-wide path stretching from Wichita Falls in the west all the way to the edge of the Piney Woods, including all of North Texas. This is called the Central Flyway and is typically most active from early to mid-October. The second flyway is situated along the Texas coast and is most active from late October through November.

During their migrations through Texas, the monarchs feed on flowers such as oxeye and goldenrod that can be found in low-lying areas near streams, especially those with overhanging trees near flower fields. Around dusk, they stop feeding and fly into trees, where they search out each other, sometimes gathering together in the hundreds or thousands to form a night-time roost—few who have ever seen one of these vibrant orange "butterfly trees" ever forget the sight. By morning, the sun warms up the butterflies and their roost breaks apart as they continue their journey. They will remain in the area as long as they can enjoy hot, moist weather and southerly winds, but will leave immediately with a passing cold front.

While the monarch is one of the best-known butterflies in North America, the species is declining and was recently added to the World Wildlife Fund's Top 10 Most Threatened Species. To help boost its numbers, biologists are teaming with parks professionals in Texas and other states where the monarch lives and working to monitor when, where, and how many monarchs are in a given location. The Texas Parks and Wildlife Department operates a Texas Monarch Watch Hotline at (800) 792-1112, ext. 8759, to report large groups of monarchs. The department also has an informative Texas Monarch Watch Monitoring Packet available on its website, www.tpwd.state.tx.us, to encourage participants to help in the research and preservation of this fascinating creature. In spring the volunteers from the Texas Monarch Watch project often offer workshops designed to train volunteers how to mark monarchs with paper tags and examine milkweed for monarch larvae. For more information, including how to build a monarch waystation, go to www.monarchwatch.org.

29 Lake Ray Roberts Johnson Branch Trail

With well-marked paved trails, plenty of picnic tables, and a great swimming beach for a post-hike dip, this 3.5-mile loop is well worth the drive.

Start: Near the boat ramp and the fish-cleaning station
Distance: 3.5-mile balloon
Approximate hiking time: 1.5 hours
Difficulty: Easy
Trail surface: Paved concrete
Season: Mar through Oct
Other trail users: Cyclists
Canine compatibility: Dogs must be on leash

Land status: State park
Fees and permits: Small entrance fee
Schedule: Open daily 8 a.m. to 10 p.m.
Maps: National Geographic TOPO! Texas; park maps available at the front gate or www.tpwd.texas.gov/publications/pwdpubs/media/park_maps/pwd_mp_p4503_0153b.pdf
Trail contact: Texas State Parks, (940) 637-2294

Finding the trailhead: Take I-35 north to exit 483 and head east on FM 3002 for 7 miles. The park's entrance is on the right. From the entrance, continue straight until the road ends at the Oak Point parking lot; the trailhead is by the boat ramp and the fish-cleaning station. GPS: N 33 24.388' / W 97 02.900'

The Hike

Lake Ray Roberts supplies water to the cities of Dallas and Denton and is named after longtime congressman Ray Roberts, who died in 1993. The lake has two state parks—Isle du Bois and Johnson Branch—and a collection of protected wetlands and wildlife management areas. The nearby Lake Roberts Greenbelt offers 20 miles of trails, but this park tends to have fewer hikers, making it feel worlds away from the Metroplex even though it makes an easy day trip.

The trailhead is at the back of the park, all the way down the main road, by the boat ramp and fish-cleaning station. To start, look for the paved concrete trail and bear right, walking away from the parking lot. In about 1,000 feet, you'll see the entrance to the Vanishing Prairie Nature Trail; bear left here and head into the forested area, which has educational markers identifying trees, plants, and area wildlife. The nature trail is a small loop that eventually returns to the same point, rejoins the main trail, and crosses over the park's main road, heading toward a large swimming area by the lake.

The trail follows the shoreline, passing picnic tables on the right. The trail then crosses back over the park road and heads into the woods and away from the lake. The trail winds through the Juniper Cove camping area at 1.1 miles, then meanders back into the woods, passing by a chemical toilet on the right. Cross back over the main park road and head into the woods, looping around until you join the trail back by the beach area. Finish your hike with a refreshing dip in the lake, then hike to the trailhead.

The Texas spiny lizard is typically shy and will crawl away when frightened.

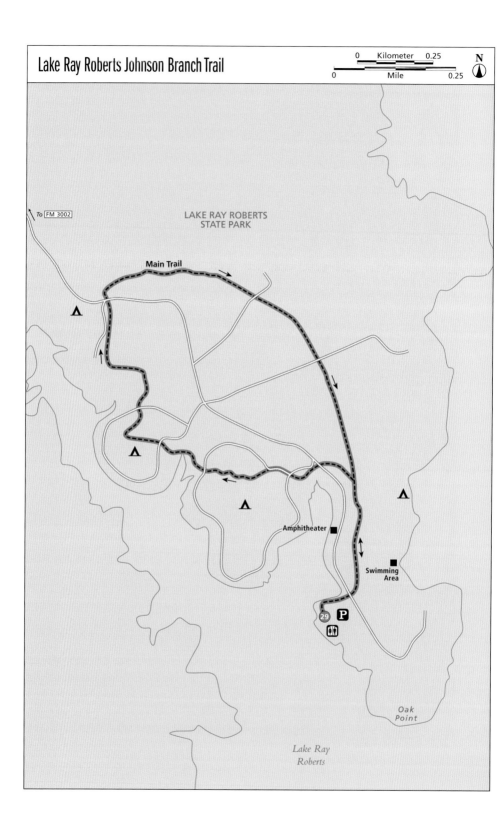

Lake Ray Roberts Johnson Branch Trail

0   Kilometer   0.25

0   Mile   0.25

N

To FM 3002

LAKE RAY ROBERTS
STATE PARK

Main Trail

Amphitheater

Swimming
Area

29   P

*Oak
Point*

*Lake Ray
Roberts*

Miles and Directions

0.0 The trailhead is by the boat ramp and fish-cleaning station adjacent to the parking lot. In about 1,000 feet, bear left, taking Vanishing Prairie Nature Trail as it loops by a small pond.

0.4 The nature trail rejoins the main trail. At the main trail, bear left up a small hill, crossing the park road and heading to the beach area.

0.5 At the next trail split, bear left, heading into the woods and away from the lake.

0.7 The trail crosses back over the main park road.

1.1 Follow the trail through the camping area, bearing left as it rejoins the campground road and follows it clockwise around the loop.

1.5 Cross over the main road again and bear right, heading into the woods as the trail loops around back to the beach.

2.5 Follow the trail as it goes to the lake shoreline, heading back to the parking lot and trailhead.

3.5 Arrive back at trailhead.

Hike Information

Local information: Denton Convention and Visitors Bureau; (940) 382-7895 or (888) 381-1818; www.discoverdenton.com

Attractions/events: The park offers free, guided nature walks on many Saturdays and occasional fireside chats and speakers at the Oak Point Amphitheater. Check for latest schedule; www.tpwd.state.tx.us/newsmedia/calendar/?calpage=s0138

GREEN TIP
Minimize the use and impact of fires. Use designated fire spots or existing fire rings (if permitted). When building fires, use small sticks (less than 1½ inches in diameter) that you find on the ground. Keep your fire small, burn it to ash, put it out completely, and scatter the cool ashes. If you can, it's best to avoid making a fire at all.

30 Lake Ray Roberts Greenbelt Trail

This 5-mile out-and-back hike through dense forest by the banks of the Elm Fork of the Trinity River links Lake Ray Roberts to Lake Lewisville and offers great bird watching and plenty of wildlife, including cottontail rabbits hopping over the trail. Easily accessed off US 380 in Denton, the trail stretches as far as 10 miles, but can easily be shortened or lengthened as needed. While its dense canopy of trees doesn't make for great views, the shade is welcome during the summer months when this trail is still enjoyable. We access the trailhead from US 380, but you can also get there via FM 455 and FM 42.

Start: Back of parking lot behind chemical toilets

Distance: 5-mile out-and-back

Approximate hiking time: 2 to 3 hours

Difficulty: Easy

Trail surface: Crushed gravel, some pavement

Seasons: Year-round

Other trail users: Birders, cyclists, horseback riders, kayakers, canoeists, anglers

Canine compatibility: Dogs must be on leash

Land status: US Army Corps of Engineers; Texas State Parks

Fees and permits: Small entrance fee (cash only) at a numbered drop box

Schedule: Open daily sunrise to sundown

Map: Texas Parks and Wildlife Department, https://tpwd.texas.gov/publications/pwdpubs/media/park_maps/pwd_mp_p4503_0176b.pdf.

Trail contact: Texas Parks and Recreation; (940) 637-2294; for camping reservations, (512) 389-8900

Special considerations: No restrooms other than at trailhead

Finding the trailhead: From Denton take I-35E at Loop 288, then exit at US 380. Head east approximately 6 miles and look for the park entrance on the left. The trail begins at the back of the parking lot behind the chemical toilets. GPS: N 33 14.362' / W 97 02.462'

The Hike

This leafy trail through riparian bottomland by the Elm Fork of the Trinity River can be heavenly on a crisp fall day when the Eastern Cross Timbers forest of oak, sycamore, cedar, American elm, hackberry, and redbud turn vibrant hues of red and gold. Even in the heat of summer, the trail is a pleasant escape for hikers and backpackers who choose to make this a two-day trek with an overnight camping stop at the Lake Ray Roberts–Isle du Bois Unit State Park. The distance from the southern end of the trail by US 380 north to the access point on FM 455 is about 11 miles, making it too long for a day hike for most folks, but the trail can easily be shortened—the distance from US 380 to the underpass of FM 428 is a more manageable 6.5 miles. This hike is even shorter, turning around 2.5 miles into the trail when its leafy canopy gives way to an open expanse of Indian and bluestem grasses, and glimpses of the river appear on the left side of the trail.

TEXAS MASTER NATURALISTS

For Texans eager to share their love of nature, the Texas Master Naturalist program provides a path to greater understanding and involvement in preserving natural habitats and educating others. The all-volunteer program, co-sponsored by Texas Parks and Wildlife and Texas AgriLife Extension Service, helps the agencies by providing additional manpower for projects such as monitoring river waters and wildlife populations. To achieve the title of Master Naturalist, one must complete an approved chapter program with forty hours of classroom and field training, obtain eight hours of advanced training, and then complete forty hours of volunteer service. Currently, more than 9,600 Texas Master Naturalist volunteers are working in forty-six local chapters. For more information and to find a local chapter, go to www.txmn.org.

Because this trail's scenery is pretty consistent, some might say it's monotonous. It's easy to lose track of how far you've traveled despite the mile markers along the trail noting the distance to the major trailheads. On this hike, more than any other in the guide, hikers should be aware of their physical limits, particularly during extreme

The cool shade is welcome on a hot summer day.

ARMADILLOS

Nine-banded armadillos enjoy a habitat that ranges from the southeastern United States through Central and South America. Generally nocturnal, armadillos use their extremely sensitive noses to help them locate invertebrates like grub worms, earthworms, and snails buried deep in the soil. Armadillos in captivity require specialized care because their wild diets are difficult to replicate. Armadillos are unique because they give birth to four identical offspring. In 1995 the Texas legislature named the nine-banded armadillo the official small state mammal of Texas and honored the longhorn as the official large state mammal.

weather, and turn around sooner rather than later. The hike begins by the parking lot, where park-goers must self-pay a small entrance fee, then heads into a forest that breaks up briefly by a major train crossing that goes over the trail at about the 0.3-mile mark.

The trail is shared with cyclists and with horseback riders taking a parallel trail for much of the distance. Hikers and cyclists must yield to horses when they appear on the trail, taking care when passing from behind so as to not spook them. Despite all the human activity on this trail—it's a very popular weekend getaway for local families and fitness buffs—there is still abundant wildlife in and around the trail, including the busy squirrels and cottontail rabbits frequently spotted hopping across the trail. Other animals in the area include Mexican free-tailed bats, beavers, plains pocket gophers, white-tailed deer, armadillos, raccoons, skunks, coyotes, and bobcats. Butterflies commonly flit over the trail, and a variety of birds make their home here, including woodpeckers, ducks, eastern screech-owls, and great horned owls. The lakes occasionally draw wintering bald eagles.

At the 1.5-mile mark, there's a small bench to enjoy a brief rest before continuing along the trail, which now has more occasional openings in the tree canopy. At the 2.5-mile mark, the trail heads into the open grassy area, marking the turnaround point for this hike. For a longer hike, simply continue on the trail, which eventually reaches Lake Ray Roberts.

Miles and Directions

0.0 Trail begins at the back of the parking lot by chemical toilets, which are sometimes closed due to maintenance.

0.3 The trail crosses under a railroad line.

1.5 The trail passes a small bench that provides a resting spot to watch woodland wildlife.

2.5 The trail enters an area of intermittent forest with some open grassy areas where the river can be spotted to the left. This marks the turnaround for this hike.

5.0 Arrive back at trailhead.

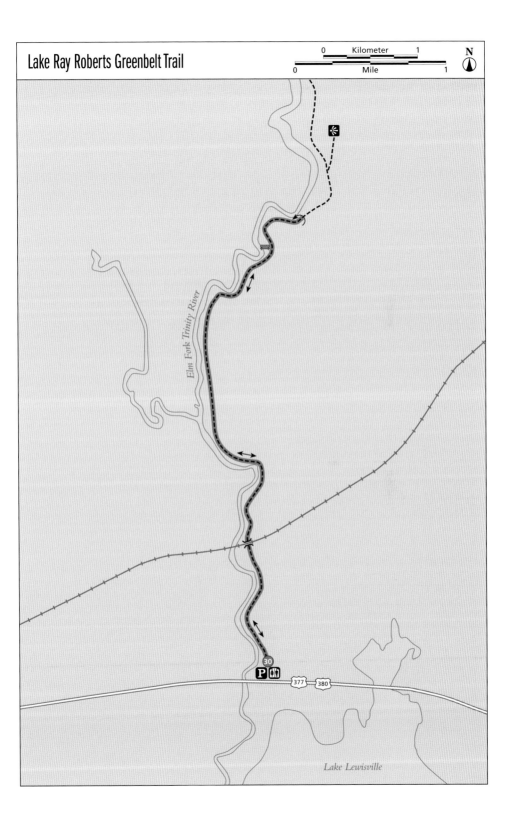

Elm Fork Trinity River

377 380

Lake Lewisville

0   Kilometer   1
0   Mile   1

N

Hike Information

Local information: Denton Convention and Visitors Bureau; (940) 382-7895 or (888) 381-1818; www.discoverdenton.com

Good eats: Beth Marie's Old Fashioned Ice Cream and Soda Fountain lives up to its name with homemade ice cream served up in historic downtown Denton; 117 W. Hickory St., Denton; (940) 384-1818; www.bethmaries.com

Organizations: The Elm Fork Chapter of the Texas Master Naturalists maintains an informative website offering the latest news on county hiking trails and apps with multimedia-guided tours of local nature centers and parks.

GREEN TIP

Don't take souvenirs home with you. This means natural materials such as plants, rocks, shells, and driftwood, as well as historic artifacts, such as fossils and arrowheads.

31 Lake Ray Roberts Elm Fork Trail

The 3.6-mile out-and-back trail begins with a legendary haunted bridge then winds through woods to reach the shores of Lake Lewisville.

Start: Old Alton Bridge
Distance: 3.6-mile out-and-back
Approximate hiking time: 2 hours
Difficulty: Moderate
Trail surface: Packed dirt, grass, and rocks
Season: Oct through May
Other trail users: Birders, horseback riders, ghost hunters
Canine compatibility: Dogs must be on leash
Land status: US Army Corps of Engineers property managed by the City of Copper Canyon
Fees and permits: None
Schedule: Open daily sunrise to sundown

Map: Texas Parks and Wildlife Department, https://tpwd.texas.gov/publications/pwdpubs/media/park_maps/pwd_mp_p4503_0176b.pdf.
Trail contact: Texas Parks and Recreation, (940) 637-2294; for camping reservations, (512) 389-8900
Other: Hikers must yield to horses. Some parts of the trail may be under construction due to roadwork. The trail is affected by water levels of Lake Lewisville and, during times of heavy rains, some parts of the trail may be impassable.

Finding the trailhead: From Dallas take I-35E north to Swisher Road, then exit and head west. Turn onto Old Alton Road; the park is approximately 100 yards down Old Alton Road on the left. The trailhead is just south of the bridge. GPS: N 33 07.781' / W 97 06.233'

The Hike

This hike begins at Old Alton Bridge, named for the small community of Alton, a town created around 1848 when settlers, looking for a steady supply of water, built the community on the banks of Hickory Creek. The town grew to include several homes, a blacksmith, a salon, and a hotel and bar, but eventually the county seat was moved to the more central location of Denton. When the area's water table dropped, making it difficult to build new wells, Alton literally dried up and now little is left of the settlement. What remains is the historic one-lane iron bridge, built in 1884, and the local legend of "Goatman's Bridge" that draws paranormal investigators and would-be ghost hunters eager to encounter the Goatman Ghost.

While there are several versions of the tale, most agree that a man who was murdered on the bridge still haunts it today in the form of a human with a goat's head (see sidebar). Signs on the bridge note that it's under investigation by local paranormal groups. The bridge crosses over the muddy waters of Hickory Creek where it connects with the Pine Knoll Trail, which, combined with the Elm Fork Trail, offers more than 14 miles of trails around Lake Lewisville.

For this hike on the Elm Fork Trail, the trailhead is located to the east of the parking lot, where a wide path heads into a grassy field and where some side trails

THE LEGEND OF GOATMAN'S BRIDGE

Just east of the trailhead for the Elm Fork Trail is the historic, and reportedly haunted, Old Alton Bridge, sometimes called Goatman's Bridge. Built in 1884, the iron bridge was a crucial link over Hickory Creek, connecting the town of Alton, the original county seat of Denton County, to Denton. Alton doesn't exist today—its falling water table made water scarce—but the bridge was included in the National Register of Historic Places in 1988. It was deemed unsafe for car traffic in the 1970s, and a new bridge was constructed to replace it. It remains a local landmark in large part because of the local legend of the "Goatman." Legend has it that an African American goat farmer named Oscar Washburn used to live by the bridge and once placed a sign on it that read "This Way to the Goatman." The sign drew the ire of white locals, and on an August night in 1938, the Ku Klux Klan drove over the bridge, their car headlights off, to Washburn's home, and dragged him to the bridge where Klansmen made a noose and hanged him from the bridge. When they looked over the side, the noose was empty. In anger, they went to his home and murdered his family. Now his spirit reportedly haunts the bridge. Some people have claimed to see a man

with a goat's head peering at them with glowing eyes; others have reported hearing the beat of hooves, maniacal laughter, and growling coming from the woods.

It's an interesting story, but historians have never been able to verify that any man named Oscar Washburn had ever lived in the area, and there is also no historical report of a lynching at that time in the area. Still, the bridge remains under surveillance by the Paranormal Investigators of North Texas and the Denton County Paranormal Investigators, and it has proved to be a popular location for haunted tours.

Lake Ray Roberts Elm Fork Trail

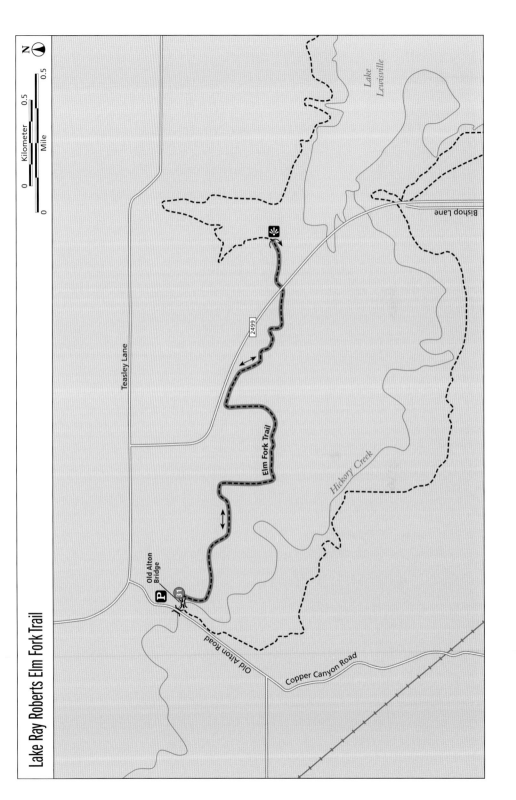

branch off to the right. They lead to fishing spots along the creek where anglers cast for sand bass. The trail enters the woods, part of the Eastern Cross Timbers, and winds through intermittent areas of prairie grasslands and trees before crossing two small creeks. After the second creek at 1 mile, bear right as the trail winds by a suburban neighborhood. The trail continues along the creek, and the rolling hills become a bit steeper as the trail gets closer to Lake Lewisville.

At 1.8 miles, the trail offers a nice view of the lake, a good place to rest before returning to the trailhead. At press time, some parts of the trail were affected by construction of FM 2499. This section of the trail is still a work in progress, with some sections closed to horses, but hikers should have access to the full 6 miles of the trail, which will eventually stretch to east Sycamore Bend Park in the town of Hickory Creek.

Miles and Directions

0.0 Elm Fork Trail begins on the east side of Old Alton Bridge; the connecting Pine Knoll Trail heads west from this point.

0.8 Trail passes by FM 2499.

1.0 Bear right as the trail splits, following path alongside the creek.

1.8 Reach overlook of the lake and the turnaround point.

3.6 Arrive back at trailhead.

Hike Information

Local information: Denton Convention and Visitors Bureau; (940) 382-7895 or (888) 381-1818; www.discoverdenton.com

Honorable Mentions

Here are some other great hikes in this region:

E. Fish Creek Linear Park

This 3-mile paved trail winds by Fish Creek Linear Park, passing under TX 360, through woods along Fish Creek. Surprisingly bucolic given its urban location, the trail is popular with cyclists and in-line skaters. Take I-20 toward Grand Prairie exit, Great Southwest Parkway, going south. Turn right onto Claremont Drive, then exit onto Largo Drive. Go to the parking lot at the end of the road to find the trailhead. Grand Prairie Parks and Recreation; www.grandfungp.com.

F. Pine Knoll Trail

This 8-mile trail connects to the Elm Fork Trail (see hike 31) and can be added for a longer hike. This trail passes largely through forested areas, making it a great option for spotting woodland birds. It's shared with horseback riders, who enjoy the right-of-way. The trail is located on US Army Corps of Engineers property managed by the town of Copper Canyon. The trail begins at the historic, and supposedly haunted, Old Alton Bridge, or it can be accessed at the other end at Pilot Knoll Park. To get to the trailhead from Dallas, take I-35E north to Swisher Road, then exit and head west. Once you turn onto Old Alton Road, the park is approximately 100 yards on the left. The trail begins on the other side of the bridge. To get to Pilot Knoll Park, from I-35E take the FM 407/Justin Road exit and head west. Turn right onto Chinn Chapel Road, which dead-ends at Orchid Hill Road. Turn right on Orchid Hill Road, which dead-ends at Pilot Knoll Park. US Army Corps of Engineers; (469) 645-9100; www.swf-wc.usace.army.mil/lewisville/Recreation/Trails/Horse.asp.

G. Sansom Park Trail

Rocky in parts, this 3-mile trail along the shoreline of Lake Worth winds up and down a bluff, offering some steep climbs and descents before moving into flatter terrain. Popular with mountain bikers, the park has 7 miles of interconnecting loops and a main rim loop. To get to the trail, take Jacksboro Highway, also called TX 199 west, from downtown Fort Worth. Turn left onto Biway Street, then turn right onto Roberts Cut Off Road and into Marion Sansom Park. City of Fort Worth Parks and Recreation; (817) 392-2255.

Fort Worth and Points West

I n this region the Cross Timbers provide shady trails, such as the Elm Fork and Greenbelt Trails, easily hiked even in the heat of summer.

In this region—which includes Eagle Mountain Lake, Lake Worth, and Possum Kingdom Lake—there are multiple trails with gorgeous vistas and ample birding opportunities.

For city dwellers, the region has one of the nation's largest systems of trails in the Trinity Trails—paved walkways that line the Trinity River. Sections such as the one through downtown Fort Worth are heavily traveled, but other areas, including the section near the Joint Air Force Reserve base, have yet to be discovered.

For hikers eager to get out of town, state parks, such as Dinosaur Valley State Park and the less-populated Cleburne State Park, offer great trails for a weekend getaway.

Hike up the hill to enjoy the view of Dinosaur Valley (Dinosaur Valley Trail).

32 Fort Worth Nature Center Canyon Ridge Trail

This challenging 6.5-mile out-and-back trail climbs through shaded canyons and patches of yucca to a panoramic ridgetop view of Lake Worth. The Fort Worth Nature Center's diverse 3,600 acres include native tallgrass prairie and deciduous forest of oaks, cottonwoods, and pecans. The hike passes projects created by 1930s-era workers for the Civilian Conservation Corps and offers abundant wildlife, including white-tailed deer and coyotes.

Start: Southwest side of the parking lot

Distance: 6.5-mile out-and-back

Approximate hiking time: 2 to 3 hours

Difficulty: Moderate with some challenging climbs

Trail surface: Packed dirt, road, and rocky trail

Seasons: Mar through May; Oct through Nov

Other trail users: Birders

Canine compatibility: Dogs permitted if on leash no longer than 6 feet. Solid animal waste must be removed.

Land status: Wildlife refuge and city park

Fees and permits: Small entrance fee

Schedule: Oct through Apr, 8 a.m. to 5 p.m. daily; May through Sept, 7 a.m. to 5 p.m. Mon to Fri, 7 a.m. to 7 p.m. Sat and Sun. Check website for latest information.

Maps: National Geographic TOPO! Texas; Fort Worth Nature Center; www.fwnaturecenter.org

Trail contact: Fort Worth Nature Center; (817) 392-7410, www.fwnaturecenter.org

Other: Facilities are limited so bring your own food and water. Binoculars and a camera are suggested for wildlife viewing and photos.

Finding the trailhead: From Loop I-820, exit onto TX 199 (Jacksboro Highway) and go west 4 miles. Exit Confederate Park Road to the right and stay on service road. At the stop sign, turn right into the nature center entrance. Stop by the gatehouse to pay fee and obtain a day pass and trail map. From the entrance, take a right on Broadview Drive and another right on Shoreline Road. Follow Shoreline until it dead-ends. The trailhead is on the southwest side of the parking lot. GPS: N 32 49.438' / W 97 27.547'

The Hike

This hike begins by the Fort Worth Nature Center's canoe launch area by Greer Island on Lake Worth. The trailhead is marked with the Canyon Ridge Trail marker, and, true to its name, the trail moves uphill through the wooded canyon to the top of a ridge that overlooks the lake. Because the nature center trails don't allow cyclists, horses, or any vehicles, the trails here are blissfully quiet and free of the heavy weekend traffic that plagues many multiuse trails in the Metroplex.

To help in its mission as a wildlife preserve, the center has strict rules and regulations that limit the impact of human visitors to the area's wildlife. Hikers must stay on marked trails only and park only in designated parking lots. Picnicking is allowed

Yucca is an iconic drought-tolerant plant that bears gorgeous stalks of flowers in the spring.

in designated areas only, and no fires or overnight camping are permitted. It's wise to check with the guard at the gatehouse on what time the park will be closing. Hours are seasonal, and hikers on the grounds after hours will be locked in and forced to call the Fort Worth Police Department at (817) 335-4222 to get out of the center.

In the beginning, the Canyon Ridge Trail follows Shoreline Road as it gradually heads uphill. Rock stairs built by 1930s-era workers in the Civilian Conservation Corps (CCC) ease the climb. Part of President Franklin Roosevelt's New Deal

Native Americans used yucca plants in a great variety of ways, including as a shampoo, to treat arthritis, and to weave ropes, baskets, and sandals.

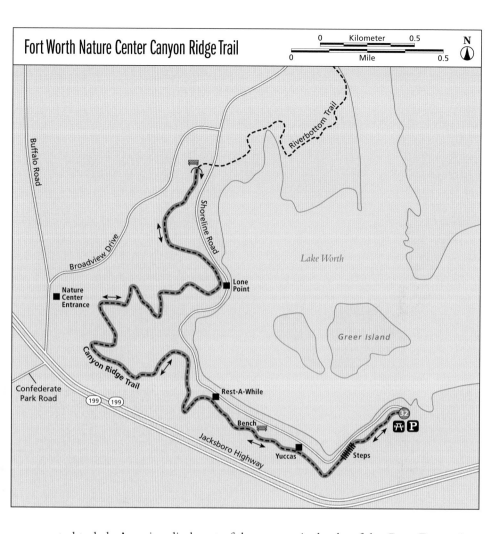

Fort Worth Nature Center Canyon Ridge Trail

0 Kilometer 0.5
0 Mile 0.5

N

Buffalo Road

Riverbottom Trail

Shoreline Road

Broadview Drive

Lake Worth

Nature Center Entrance

Lone Point

Greer Island

Canyon Ridge Trail

Confederate Park Road

199 199

Rest-A-While

Bench

Jacksboro Highway

Yuccas

Steps

32

enacted to help America climb out of the economic depths of the Great Depression, the CCC was active in developing many parks projects. About 200 members and staff personnel of CCC Camp No. 1816 were located south of the nature center across the Jacksboro Highway on the shore of Lake Worth near Sunset Park. They worked to build recreation facilities for a new state park, but the park didn't materialize. The City of Fort Worth eventually took over management of the area, working with the Audubon Society, and made it a wildlife sanctuary and preserve in 1964. Today the remnants of the CCC's work, including the rock steps of the Caprock and Canyon Ridge Trails are solidly in place, as are the rock shelters they built. Dubbed "Lone Point," "Rest Awhile," and "Broadview," all are easily accessible from this trail and worth taking a few minutes to explore—just be wary of the orb-spinning spiders and their webs commonly found here much of the year.

As the trail climbs, views of Lake Worth begin to peek through the trees on the right side of the trail. The trail continues up and down small hills interspersed with meadows of yucca plants. Eventually, the trail reaches a bench that overlooks the canyon, a nice picnicking spot. The trail continues through some small meadows where white-tailed deer can be spotted and wildflowers bloom spring though summer. It then descends back toward the lake, reaching another bench at 3.25 miles where you turn around. **(Option:** The trail soon crosses Shoreline Road and connects with the nature center's Riverbottom Trail, which follows the shores of Lake Worth and the West Fork of the Trinity River for more than 2.5 miles.) Retrace the up-and-down, winding route back to the trailhead. For a shorter, less rigorous return, simply take Shoreline Road south back to the trailhead.

Miles and Directions

0.0   Start by the sign marked Canyon Ridge with the picture of a flowering yucca, on the southwest side of the parking lot. Follow the trail as it runs alongside Shoreline Road.

0.75   Reach a long staircase as the trail heads uphill toward a scenic overlook with views of Lake Worth and Greer Island.

1.4   The trail reaches a small bench that provides a scenic resting spot before continuing through a series of meadows.

2.6   Trail passes remains of CCC "Lone Point" and other structures.

3.25   Trail reaches a small bench. Retrace your steps on the trail to return the way you came.

6.5   Arrive back at trailhead.

Hike Information

Local information: Fort Worth Convention and Visitors Bureau; (817) 336-8791; www.fortworth.com

Attractions/events: Don't miss the center's herd of bison or Prairie Dog Town, where hundreds of these once ubiquitous creatures roam their native habitat. The center's Hardwicke Interpretive Center offers interactive, educational exhibits and is the gathering point for many guided hikes.

Organizations: Friends of the Fort Worth Nature Center; (817) 392-7410; www .naturecenterfriends.org

33 Fort Worth Nature Center Shoreline and Forked Creek Trails

Hiking with buffalo? The herd here is fenced off, but getting an occasional glimpse of these iconic creatures of the American West adds allure and a photo op to this trail. With more than 3,600 acres of forests, prairies, and wetlands, the Fort Worth Nature Center is one of the largest city-owned nature centers in the United States. Thankfully all that space and the park's entrance fee keep it relatively sparsely populated much of the time. Even on busy weekends, only one or two hikers may be spotted along this 1.8-mile trail by the shores of the West Fork of the Trinity River and through a forested river bottom.

Start: Parking lot on Shoreline Road
Distance: 1.8-mile figure eight
Approximate hiking time: 1 hour
Difficulty: Easy
Trail surface: Packed dirt, with portions on wooden boardwalk
Seasons: Mar through May; Oct through Nov
Other trail users: Birders
Canine compatibility: Dogs permitted on leash no longer than 6 feet. Solid animal waste must be removed.
Land status: City park
Fees and permits: Small entrance fee

Schedule: Oct through Apr, 8 a.m. to 5 p.m. daily; May through Sept, 8 a.m. to 7 p.m. Mon to Fri, 7 a.m. to 7 p.m. Sat and Sun; closed Thanksgiving, Christmas, and other major holidays; check website for latest schedule information
Maps: National Geographic TOPO! Texas; Fort Worth Nature Center; www.fwnaturecenter.org
Trail contact: Fort Worth Nature Center; (817) 392-7410; www.fwnaturecenter.org
Special considerations: Facilities are limited here so bring your own food and water.

Finding the trailhead: From Loop I-820, exit onto TX 199 (Jacksboro Highway) and go west 4 miles. Exit Confederate Park Road to the right and stay on service road. At the stop sign, turn right into the nature center entrance. Stop at the gatehouse to pay entrance fee and obtain a day pass and trail map. Bear right onto Broadview Drive, then turn left onto Shoreline Road and follow it all the way to the end. The trailhead is by the parking lot. GPS: N 32 59.955' / W 97 29.395'

The Hike

The Fort Worth Nature Center stretches over several ecosystems of prairie, forest, and wetlands. The center is home to more than 300 species of flowering plants and more than 200 species of birds. Wild turkeys, armadillos, coyotes, raccoons, skunks, bobcats, possums, beavers, and white-tailed deer are commonly spotted along the center's network of trails that wind through various habitats. Education is a key part of the center's mission, and there are ample opportunities to participate in a variety of educational programs including naturalist-led hikes and wildlife photography

Featured guests along this trail are the bison, a true "wild west moment."

workshops—just be sure to sign up in advance. The center also actively recruits volunteers to help with wildlife surveys and native plant restoration.

To help in its mission as wildlife preserve, the center has strict rules and regulations that limit human activity. Visitors must stay on marked trails only and must park only in designated parking areas. Picnicking is allowed only in designated areas, and no fires or overnight camping are permitted. It's wise to check with the guard at the gatehouse on what time the park will be closing. Hours are seasonal, and hikers on the grounds after hours will be locked in and forced to call the Fort Worth Police Department at (817) 335-4222 to get out of the center.

The park's most famous residents, celebrated with the annual Buffalo Boogie race held each May, are the bison, easily viewable from several spots along the park's main drive—the aptly named Buffalo Road. The park's Hardwicke Interpretive Center has educational exhibits on the park's ecosystems and provides the park's only bathrooms

GETTING BUFFALOED

Buffalo, more properly called American bison, typically mate in late summer to early fall. Males, called bulls, attract the attention of the females, or cows, by wallowing in the dirt and grunting. The cows have their calves in spring, typically May. A calf normally weighs about 50 pounds at birth and sports a cinnamon-colored coat that it sheds in about two months, growing a new coat that's the familiar dark-brown color of adult bison. A fully grown adult male buffalo weighs around 2,000 pounds. Female buffalo average around 1,000 pounds.

with plumbing. It's open Monday to Saturday 9:00 a.m. to 4:30 p.m., and Sunday noon to 4:30 p.m. Portable toilets are placed around major parking areas, but water fountains aren't, so be sure to pack plenty of liquids before heading out. Free trail maps are available at the main entrance gatehouse. Pull over to peruse the varied choices among the center's 20-plus miles of trails. Be sure to bring binoculars and a camera to see and record your experiences.

The Canyon Ridge Trail is the most challenging, connecting a series of ridges in an up-and-down 6.5-mile round-trip trek. The 1.5-mile Greer Island Trail travels over a narrow levee to the small island in the middle of Lake Worth, and 1.13-mile Prairie Trail leads to the park's Prairie Dog Town. This hike combines three of the park's trails—the Marsh Boardwalk, Riverbottom, and Forked Creek Trails—for a 1.8-mile trek.

From the parking lot and the end of Shoreline Road, the trailhead is by a picnic table and two portable restrooms. Look for the path leading to the Trinity River and down to a boardwalk. Here the trail goes over a large marsh and, depending on water levels, it's possible to view animal tracks on the sandy shoreline. The boardwalk loops over the water and provides a great viewing spot for birds including the occasional hawk. As the boardwalk meets the shore, bear left onto the Riverbottom Trail and continue along the river as the trail winds alongside Shoreline Road. When the trail crosses over the road, stay straight and enter the woods. The trail splits just inside the forest, go right to get on Forked Creek Trail as it moves deeper into the woods, and the path becomes a boardwalk above the mucky soil.

The trail surface alternates between packed dirt and boardwalk, and a small stream joins up with the trail. This part of the trail is not as well marked, so be careful to look for signs you haven't wandered off. The Forked Creek Trail eventually loops back to join the Riverbottom Trail and at this junction, veer left. The trail makes a right-angle turn and returns to the intersection with Shoreline Road, where you can retrace your steps along the river, this time on your right side, back to the parking lot.

Miles and Directions

0.0   Locate trailhead by a picnic table and head down to the river and boardwalk.

0.1   Bear left onto the boardwalk, being careful to watch for tall reeds that push through the wooden boards.

0.2   As the boardwalk connects back to shore, bear left onto Riverbottom Trail, with the river on your left side.

0.6   The trail crosses over Shoreline Road. Bear right at the trail junction and head into the forest to reach a small creek (the creek may be dry).

1.1   The trail meets the Riverbottom Trail; bear left on the Riverbottom Trail and follow it until the junction with the Forked Creek Trail

1.3   Both trails merge. Bear right and cross over Shoreline Drive then the trail goes by the lake.

1.6   Bear left at the trail split by the marsh boardwalk to return to the parking lot.

1.8   Arrive back at trailhead.

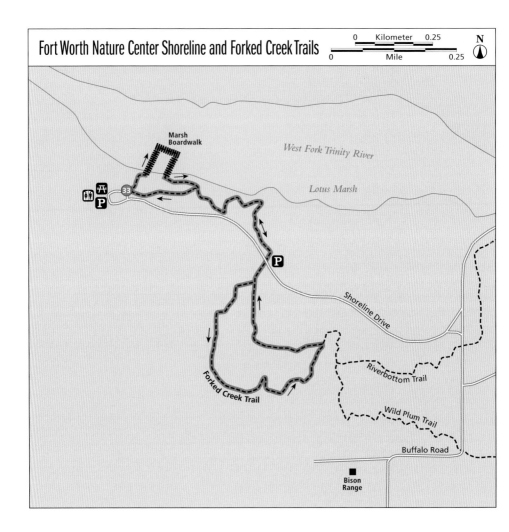

Fort Worth Nature Center Shoreline and Forked Creek Trails

Hike Information

Local information: Fort Worth Convention and Visitors Bureau; (817) 336-8791; www.fortworth.com

Attractions/events: Don't miss the Prairie Dog Town, where hundreds of these once ubiquitous creatures roam their native habitat.

Good eats: Bosses' Brick Oven Pizza and Sandwiches is a great place for a post-hike calzone; 6059 Lake Worth Blvd., Lake Worth; (817) 238-9899; www.bossespizza.com

Organizations: Friends of the Fort Worth Nature Center; (817) 392-7410; www .naturecenterfriends.org

34 Trinity Trails

Fort Worth's Trinity Trails offer easy access and scenic views that attract runners, walkers, and bicyclists who make them part of their daily workout regime. The scenic network of more than 40 miles of paved pathways connect many city parks and attractions as they meander along greenbelts of the Trinity River and its tributaries. The trails are in the midst of a massive upgrade. With more links coming online, it has become the place to see and be seen by Cowtown hipsters. This 4.4-mile out-and-back hike follows one of the most popular segments of the trail—from University Drive through Trinity Park to the Zero Mile Marker, located near the Main Street Bridge just north of downtown Fort Worth. The trail is rarely empty and can get packed on weekends as runners, cyclists, dog walkers, and others get in their workouts, but this being friendly Fort Worth, be ready to wave and say howdy to passersby.

Start: Trinity River Park trails map
Distance: 4.4-mile out-and-back
Approximate hiking time: 1 to 2 hours
Difficulty: Easy
Trail surface: Concrete and crushed packed gravel
Season: Oct through May
Other trail users: Cyclists, joggers, kayakers
Canine compatibility: Dogs must be on leash
Land status: City park and protected watershed
Fees and permits: None

Schedule: Open daily 5 a.m. to 10 p.m.
Map: www.trwd.com/wp-content/uploads/trinity-river-trail-map.pdf
Trail contact: Trinity River Vision Authority oversees planning and development for the river and surrounding areas; (817) 698-0700; www.trinityrivervision.org
Other: Boating, fishing, and swimming are allowed on the Trinity, unless specifically posted, but swimming in the river is dangerous due to strong currents.

Finding the trailhead: From Dallas or downtown Fort Worth, take I-30 west to the University Drive exit. From the exit ramp, wind to the right to the light on University Drive and turn left. From University Drive, take a right into Trinity River Park and look for parking either in lots to the left or along the street that runs by the trail and Trinity River. The trailhead begins at the large Trinity Trails map and information sign. GPS: N 32 44.198' / W 97 21.631'

The Hike

San Antonio may have the Lone Star State's most famous Riverwalk, but Fort Worth is making a run, so to speak, to make the most of its own riverside locale by pumping millions of dollars into the 40-plus-mile network of paved trails along the Trinity River. There are many places to hit the trail, but one of the easiest and most popular is Trinity River Park, just east of University Drive. This spot is where the Tarrant Regional Water District, the government agency that manages the river, stocks the

This trail along the Trinity Rivers provides a lovely stroll—or pick up the pace to make it a cardio buster.

Trinity with hundreds of trout each spring. It's also the home of Mayfest, a Fort Worth tradition held the first weekend in May featuring food, arts, and live performances.

From here, the trail passes by park benches, including a special one with a bronze statue of Mark Twain, as it winds closer to the downtown Fort Worth skyline. The statue of the famous writer has him holding a copy of one of his works. A small plaque notes the statue was given to the families of Fort Worth for the pleasure of reading together by the Red Oak Foundation and dedicated back in 2007.

Humorist Will Rogers once said, "Fort Worth is where the West begins. Dallas is where the East peters out."

For most of this hike, there are actually two parallel trails—one paved, the other crushed shale. While it's not a hard-and-fast rule, cyclists generally stick to the paved trail while joggers and walkers stay on the gravel one.

The trail crosses under the Lancaster Avenue Bridge, also crossing the path taken by an F-2 tornado that swept through downtown Fort Worth on March 28, 2000, killing five people and causing a half-billion dollars in property damage, including hundreds of blown-out windows on the city's skyscrapers. There aren't many reminders of the twister today except for specially marked tornado-logo street signs in the Lindale neighborhood west of downtown. Since the storm, the area has enjoyed a retail and residential renaissance that included the transformation of the Montgomery Ward warehouse into an upscale residential and retail development.

HELL'S HALF ACRE

As Fort Worth grew as a frontier cattle town in the later part of the nineteenth century, a growing number of brothels, saloons, and other rowdy establishments popped up on the south side of downtown where they were the first thing trail drivers saw as they approached town. By the 1890s, the district had grown to almost 3 acres, sprawling from Union Station to the south up to Seventh Street, and had become a hangout for train and stagecoach robbers—a duo dubbed Butch Cassidy and the Sundance Kid were among the reported revelers. The wild scene drove away some more-pious institutions including a young men's Bible college that left downtown Fort Worth for the small town of Thorp Spring. The school would eventually become known as Texas Christian University and returned to Fort Worth in 1910 after a fire destroyed much of its campus, and city leaders won a bidding war against Waco and Dallas. While some Cowtown leaders periodically tried to shut down the illicit activities of "the Acre" with cleanup campaigns, they didn't stick until the early twentieth century when Fort Worth began courting a lucrative government training camp. After Camp Bowie was built on the city's far west side, martial law was brought to the Acre, driving out its bars and bordellos. Today the only reminders of "the Acre" are a historical marker noting its past and the name of the upscale retail and residential complex that includes the world-class Bass Performance Hall—Sundance Square.

As the trail winds around the riverbend just north of downtown, there's a small duck pond where mallards swim in the shadows of gleaming office buildings. At the Zero Mile Marker, the point from which all distances on all the Trinity Trails are measured, it's possible to either head east to Gateway Park, or travel north to the city's historic Fort Worth Stockyards, where millions of cattle were once slaughtered as they came off the famed Chisholm Trail. Today the city celebrates its Cowtown heritage with two daily cattle drives in the historic stockyards at 11:30 a.m. and 4:00 p.m. The drives may be canceled due to inclement weather or if the trail boss on duty decides the longhorns aren't up to it (check updated schedules at www.fortworth.com).

Miles and Directions

0.0 Begin the trail at an information sign in Trinity River Park.

0.3 Trail passes a statue of Mark Twain sitting on a bench.

1.0 Pass under Lancaster Avenue Bridge by the basketball courts.

2.2 Trail reaches the Zero Mile Marker and the bridge over the Trinity River. Turn around and retrace your steps to the trailhead.

4.4 Arrive back at trailhead.

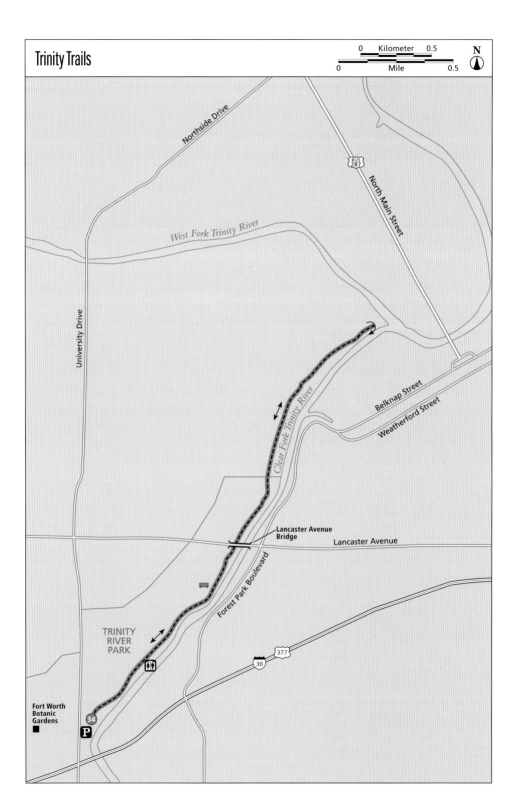

Hike Information

Local information: Fort Worth Convention and Visitors Bureau; (800) 433-5747; www.fortworth.com

Richard F. Selcer, *Hell's Half Acre: The Life and Legend of a Red Light District* (Fort Worth: Texas Christian University Press, 1991).

Attractions/events: Mayfest is an annual spring festival that raises funds and awareness of the Trinity River and surrounding parks; www.mayfest.org

The Fort Worth Botanic Garden is the oldest botanic garden in Texas and is home to more than 2,500 species of native and exotic plants. Located just north of I-30 on University Drive; (817) 871-7686; www.fwbg.org

Good eats: Fred's Texas Café is a one-of-a-kind bar and burgers joint that's been featured on the Food Network show *Diners, Drive-Ins and Dives*; 915 Currie St., Fort Worth; (817) 332-0083; www.fredstexascafe.com

Woodshed Smokehouse serves up smoked meat goodness with a dog-friendly outdoor patio on the banks of the Trinity River; 3201 Riverfront Dr., Fort Worth; (817) 877-4545; www.woodshedsmokehouse.com

Organizations: Streams and Valleys Inc. plans and coordinates beautification and recreational development of the Trinity River in Fort Worth; www.streamsandvalleys .org

GREEN TIP

Especially for day hikes, use a camp stove for cooking
so there's no need to make a fire.

35 Airfield Falls Trail

Situated only a few miles west of downtown Fort Worth, this trail feels more like a rural ramble as it winds by a goat farm before meeting up with a tributary of the Trinity River. The trail and the adjacent park are a relatively new addition to the 40 miles that make up the Trinity Trails system and is less traveled than popular sections closer to downtown. The trail includes a scenic waterfall where hikers can easily cool their heels in the bubbling waters of the east fork of the Trinity River, after tackling the expansive, flat hike along the river's greenbelt as it meanders through the leafy neighborhoods of the city's west side.

Start: Parking lot just off Pumphrey Drive
Distance: 5-mile out-and-back
Approximate hiking time: 2 hours
Difficulty: Easy
Trail surface: Concrete and crushed packed gravel
Season: Oct through May
Other trail users: Cyclists, joggers
Canine compatibility: Dogs must be on leash
Land status: City park and watershed

Fees and permits: None
Schedule: Open daily 5 a.m. to 10 p.m. (violation constitutes trespassing)
Map: Visit www.trwd.org/Libraries/Maps/Trinity_Trails_Map_West.sflb.ashx for a detailed map of the western side of the trails
Trail contact: Trinity River Vision Authority oversees planning and development for the river and surrounding areas; (817) 698-0700; www.trinityrivervision.org

Finding the trailhead: From Fort Worth take White Settlement Road west toward the Naval Air Station Joint Reserve Base. Turn right on Pumphrey Drive and look for a small parking lot on the right (if you reach the entrance to the base, you've gone too far). The trailhead begins at the large Trinity Trails map and information sign. GPS: N 32 45.822' / W 97 25.238'

The Hike

Originally part of Carswell Air Force Base, the land near the trailhead has been largely left in its natural state, and the Tarrant Regional Water District has constructed Airfield Falls Conservation Park as part of an extensive erosion control project to reinforce the Trinity's riverbanks. Former TRWD president George Shannon persuaded the district to extend the Trinity Trails to the waterfalls so others could enjoy them. The trail's close proximity to the military base makes it an ideal escape for members of the armed forces stationed there, and a new parking lot has made it even more accessible.

The trailhead is located just east of the parking lot. The trail moves into the forest and crosses a bridge over Farmers Branch Creek then bears left. The trail winds around the creek to where it meets the river and, at around 0.3 mile, comes to a wide waterfall that spans the river's limestone bottom. There are plenty of rocks for turtles to sun themselves, and the spot is a popular rest stop for walkers, joggers, and cyclists who have finished their workout or others who simply want to enjoy the soothing sounds of the falling water. It's also possible to spot the occasional snake on a riverside rock. From the waterfall, the trail winds down a small hill, moving to the larger Trinity River. The trail continues in the open greenbelt that lines the river, sometimes splitting into two trails—one paved, one crushed gravel. While it's possible to cross the river in various places along the trail by hiking up to a road and walking across the bridge, this hike focuses on staying on the south side of the river as it winds toward downtown Fort Worth.

The trail crosses under River Oaks Boulevard at the 1.2 mile mark, then continues to wind along the riverside. At about 2.5 miles, a water fountain with a small shaded bench provides a great resting spot. The bench marks the turnaround point for this hike. (**Options:** For a longer hike, bear right and join the trail leading to the Riverbend Nature Area or continue along the Trinity Trail as it winds through the city's western neighborhoods toward downtown, eventually reaching the central Zero Mile Marker downtown in about 6 miles.)

The limestone ledges and small pools of Airfield Falls make it a perfect spot to make a splash.

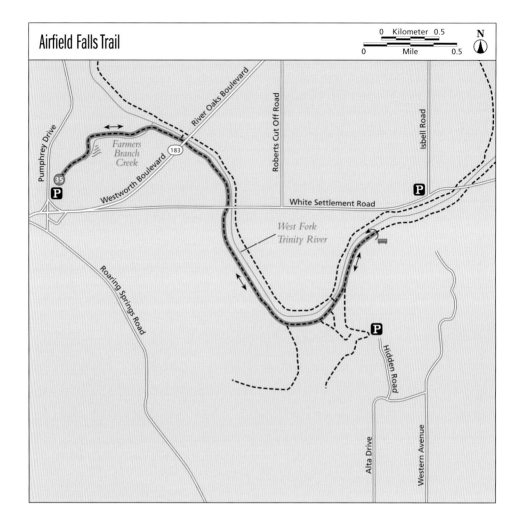

Airfield Falls Trail

Miles and Directions

0.0 Trail begins by Airfield Falls Conservation Park just off Pumphrey Drive.

0.2 Trail crosses over a bridge; bear left as trail follows Farmers Branch Creek.

0.3 Trail reaches waterfalls where turtles sun themselves on the rocks.

1.2 Trail crosses under River Oaks Boulevard.

2.5 Trail connects with trail to Riverbend Nature Area by a protected bench and water fountain. Turn around and retrace steps back to trailhead.

5.0 Arrive back at trailhead.

Hike Information

Local information: Fort Worth Convention and Visitors Bureau; (800) 433-5747; www.fortworth.com

Good eats: The Bluebonnet Bakery is a great place to grab a picnic to go. Located at 4705 Camp Bowie Blvd., Fort Worth; (817) 731-4233; www.bluebonnetbakery.com

Organizations: Streams and Valleys Inc. plans and coordinates beautification and recreational development of the Trinity River in Fort Worth; www.streamsandvalleys .org

GREEN TIP

Even if it says it's biodegradable, don't put soap into streams or lakes. If you need to use soap, bring the water with you.

36 Eagle Mountain Park Trails

This new 400-acre park on the shores of Eagle Mountain Lake offers nearly 7 miles of trails through forests and grassy bluffs overlooking the lake. While there are nearby gas pad sites tapping into the Barnett Shale underground reservoir of natural gas, the park feels remote and has remained in a largely natural state. The park's sandy trail provides a great place to spot animal tracks, particularly after moderate to heavy rains.

Start: Information kiosks
Distance: 5.4-mile out-and-back
Approximate hiking time: 2 hours
Difficulty: Easy
Trail surface: Packed dirt, grass, and rocks
Season: Oct through May
Other trail users: Birders
Canine compatibility: No dogs permitted
Land status: County park and watershed

Fees and permits: None
Schedule: Open daily sunrise to 30 minutes after sunset when the gate is closed
Map: http://www.trwd.com/recreation/activites/hiking/
Trail contact: Tarrant Regional Water District, (817) 444-3221; https://www.trwd.com/recreation/locations/eagle-mountain/eagle-mountain-park/.

Finding the trailhead: From Fort Worth take I-35 north to Loop 820; head west on Loop 820 to Business 287 (Main Street). Turn left onto Peden Road. The park is at the intersection of Peden Road and FM 1220. The trail begins by the information kiosks detailing the flora and fauna found in the park, by an old barn and windmill. GPS: N 32 56.098' / W 97 28.809'

The Hike

Preserving this 400-acre patch of forests and grasslands along the shores of Eagle Mountain Lake was the work of dedicated conservationists who fought a three-year battle to keep the State of Texas from selling the land to developers. Thanks to their efforts, and local benefactors, residents have a pristine park with almost 7 miles of trails, some with bluff-top views that can be enjoyed in relative peace and quiet. No bikes or motorized vehicles are permitted on the trails, and even dogs aren't allowed so the area can remain as close as possible to its natural state. As a trade-off, the state retained mineral rights from natural gas wells on about 12 acres of the property, with the proceeds going to fund future parkland purchases. The wells are huddled on one side of the park, so they don't really intrude on the remote feel of the park, which can feel empty during most weekdays.

The park is home to several trails, two large overlooks, and two picnic pavilions and is a great destination for families looking for a fun 2- to 3-hour outing. The hike begins at the park entrance where there's a series of information signs explaining the geology, history, and ecosystems of the area, plus profiles of common plants and animals. From here, the hike heads straight ahead to take in the 0.25-mile Overlook

Watch for animal tracks on the sandy paths.

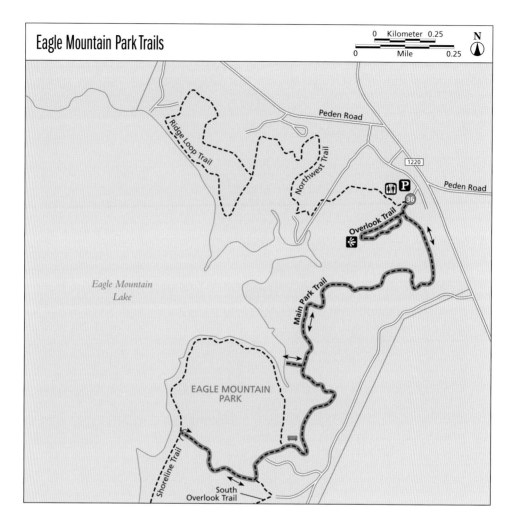

0   Kilometer 0.25

0   Mile   0.25

N

Peden Road

1220

Peden Road

Ridge Loop Trail

Northwest Trail

Overlook Trail

36

P

Main Park Trail

Eagle Mountain Lake

EAGLE MOUNTAIN PARK

Shoreline Trail

South Overlook Trail

Trail, a flat trail that's easy to navigate with a wheelchair or stroller and leads to a scenic overlook of the lake. The trail also includes shaded picnic tables. After taking in the view and/or enjoying an outdoor repast, return to Main Park Trail, bearing right (southeast) and following it into the woods.

From here, the trail winds through the upland savanna filled with tall prairie grasses, yucca, lantana, prickly pear cacti, and seasonal wildflowers. The trail takes a sharp drop at 0.85 mile, winding downhill toward the lake. At about 1.1 miles, the trail splits; bear right to go down a short path to the lake, where anglers like to cast for sand bass and catfish. Return to the Main Trail, this time bearing right (south) and heading up a hill. At 1.7 miles, a small bench provides a quiet resting place. From this trail junction it's possible to take a longer trek along the park's Shoreline Trail, but this hike continues straight ahead on the Main Park Trail, entering a dense forest where a herd of white-tailed deer (also called a mob) makes their home. The dank smell of the lake signals that the trail is approaching the shore, and at about 2.9 miles, the trail connects with the Shoreline Trail. (**Options:** From here, hikers can bear left to take a 1.25-mile trek along the Shoreline and South Overlook Trails, or bear right for the 0.7-mile hike on the Shoreline Trail—both reconnect with the Main Park Trail.)

For this hike, simply retrace your steps back to the trailhead on the Main Trail.

Miles and Directions

0.0   Trail begins by information kiosks at the park entrance next to an old barn and windmill.

0.1   At the first trail junction, go straight and take in the scenic view of Eagle Mountain Lake on the Overlook Trail, which also offers a couple of picnic tables.

0.5   Return to the main junction; this time bear right (southeast) on the Main Park Trail, following it as it winds into the woods.

0.85 Trail winds downhill, making its way to the lake.

1.1   At a trail junction, bear right, taking the small side trail to view the lake and a popular fishing spot.

1.7   Pass a small bench and continue uphill toward the woods. Pass the Shoreline Trail that goes to the right down to the lake.

2.2   Enter forest area.

2.9   Reach the second junction with Shoreline Trail and the end of the Main Trail. Turn around and retrace your steps back to the trailhead.

5.4   Arrive back at trailhead.

Hike Information

Local information: Northwest Tarrant Chamber of Commerce; (817) 237-0060; www.nwtcc.org

Organizations: Save Eagle Mountain Lake Inc. was organized to preserve and protect the lake and lands around it. Periodic park and trail cleanup efforts are conducted; 8551 Boat Club Rd., Ste, 121, #115; Fort Worth; (817) 236-1466; www.seml.org

37 Possum Kingdom Lake Trail

Part of the popular Possum Kingdom Hike and Bike Trail, this hike offers gorgeous views of Possum Kingdom Lake as it winds through a scrubby forest of cedar and juniper trees. The hike includes a trek through a meadow of wildflowers where lizards dart across the trail. There's also the option of enjoying a picnic and/or swim at Sandy Beach.

Start: Left of Sandy Beach parking lot
Distance: 3.2-mile out-and-back
Approximate hiking time: 1 to 2 hours
Difficulty: Moderate due to elevation gain. The sandy trail surface can also be a real workout.
Trail surface: Packed dirt in forested areas, sand in open spaces
Seasons: Mar through May; Sept through Nov
Other trail users: Mountain bikers
Canine compatibility: Dogs must be on leash
Land status: Managed by Brazos River Authority

Fees and permits: None
Schedule: Open daily sunrise to sunset
Maps: National Geographic TOPO! Texas; www.brazos.org/Portals/0/generalPdf/pkHikeBik-eTrail.pdf
Trail contact: Brazos River Authority, (888) 922-6272
Other: Free trail access, but small fee to enter beach area. Trails may be closed after heavy rains.
Special consideratons: Limited cell phone coverage

Finding the trailhead: From Fort Worth take I-30 west; merge onto I-20 then exit onto US 180 in Weatherford. Go through town and continue west to about 2 miles past Mineral Wells. Turn right onto TX 337 and head north for about 7 miles. At Graford turn left onto TX 254. After about 8 miles, bear left onto TX 16 and head south for 4 miles. Turn right onto Park Road (P) 36 and then bear to the right onto FM 2951. Follow the road to the end of the lake's main peninsula. The trailhead is to the left of the small parking lot near Sandy Beach. GPS: N 32 52.925' / W 98 30.314'

The Hike

For generations, the 17,000-acre Possum Kingdom Lake nestled in the Palo Pinto Mountains has been a weekend getaway for folks from Dallas/Fort Worth who enjoy boating, waterskiing, swimming, fishing, and scuba diving. In recent years, the lake, often simply called "PK," has become a hiking destination thanks to development of Possum Kingdom Hike and Bike Trail, a network of more than 16 miles of trails in and around the lake's main peninsula. Despite devastating fires that swept through the lake area in 2011, it continues to draw abundant wildlife, including white-tailed deer, foxes, wild turkeys, cranes, bobcats, and endangered species such as golden-cheeked warblers and black-capped vireos. Bald eagles are occasionally spotted here, along with more common red-tailed hawks. Signs caution hikers to stay on the marked trails and not to disturb any wildlife encountered, which may also include copperheads and rattlesnakes. Of course it's also possible to see the occasional possum. The lake got its name thanks to a fur trader named Sablosky who settled in the area in the early 1900s and called his cadre of fur providers the "boys from Possum Kingdom." The name became official when a dam was built on the Brazos River in 1941, creating the lake.

Possum Kingdom State Park lies on the southern side of the lake and offers several trails as well as cabins and campsites, but the trails of the lake's eastern peninsula are more easily accessible for Dallas/Fort Worth residents looking for a weekend getaway. The peninsula also offers great views, since there is water on both sides of the trails.

The first phase of the trail opened in 2007 and is located just off LaVilla Road. In the last two years, more trails have been completed and, thanks to grant funds from Texas Wildlife and Development, there are now 16 miles of trail linking the five Brazos River Authority parks. Most of the trails average a gentle 5 to 12 degree slope, but the climb up Johnson Peak is much steeper—about a 20 percent grade. Here hikers are rewarded with a sweeping view of the lake including the landmark Hell's Gate rock formation. The hike up Johnson Peak can be accessed from the trailhead off P36 or on FM 2951 in the D&D Park just after Harris Drive. The Possum Kingdom Hike and Bike Trail offers ample entry points and well-marked parking areas and maps at many trail entrances. There are also well-placed restrooms and plenty of resting spots, including cedar benches placed at scenic overlooks.

The lake's trails offer abundant wildflowers that attract butterflies.

The lake's system of trails has well-marked trailheads.

This hike begins at Sandy Beach, which offers picnic shelters with grills, a new children's playground, and a popular swimming area. From the trailhead, the trail winds eastward through a meadow of wildflowers where it's common to see lizards darting across the trail. The hike then moves up into the treed forest of ash, juniper, and cedar trees, providing a welcome canopy of shade, particularly in summer when temperatures routinely hit 100-plus degrees. At about 1.2 miles, the trail reaches the Longhorn Trailhead. Bear left to take the Longhorn Trail as it crosses over Frontier Unit Road. (**Option:** For a longer, more challenging hike it's possible to go straight at this junction and take in scenic views of the lake.)

In another mile, Longhorn Trail crosses over Frontier Unit Road, where it's possible to sneak a peek at the lake over some housetops, then it reaches the junction for the trail that goes to Bug Beach. From here, the trail splits, with both trails leading to the next major junction, located near the intersection of Hamilton Drive and FM 2951. This spot makes a nice turn-around for those seeking a relatively easy 1- to 2-hour hike. (**Option:** For a longer hike, continue east and tackle more challenging climbs including Johnson Peak.)

Miles and Directions

0.0 Begin hike at trailhead just to the left of Sandy Beach Park and follow it eastward through a meadow, which has ample wildflowers that attract butterflies including monarchs and swallowtails.

GOLDEN-CHEEKED WARBLERS

The endangered golden-cheeked warbler is the only bird known to breed and raise its young entirely in the state of Texas. They make their home in the scrubby "Cedar Brakes" of the Edwards Plateau and make their nest from the bark of the ash juniper tree. These birds have been found as far north as Possum Kingdom Lake in Palo Pinto County. They have a bright yellow face framed by a black crown, bib, and back and like many other bird species, the males are more brightly colored than the females.

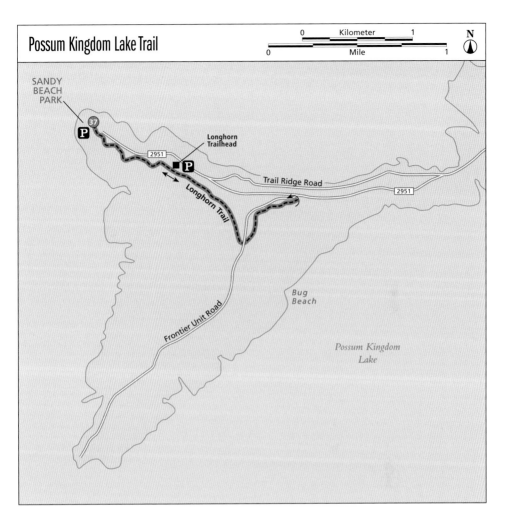

Possum Kingdom Lake Trail

1.2 The trail reaches the five-point junction with the Longhorn Trail; bear left and cross over Frontier Unit Road.

1.6 Trail meets the Hamilton Trailhead, which marks the turnaround spot.

3.2 Arrive back at trailhead by Sandy Beach.

Hike Information

Local information: Possum Kingdom Lake Chamber of Commerce, 362 North FM 2353, Graford; (940) 779-2424

Attractions/events: Possum Kingdom Lake Chamber of Commerce hosts the annual PossumFest each fall, and July Fourth brings the famous Fireworks at Hell's Gate; (940) 779-2424; www.possumkingdomlake.com

38 Lake Mineral Wells Trailway

This 3-mile out-and-back hike begins in Lake Mineral Wells State Park by the park's amphitheater and descends downhill on a 5 percent grade past a pasture of longhorn cattle and open prairie. Here, the trail moves through a prairie filled with wildflowers much of the year as it winds down to the site of an old railway bed that now serves as a hike and bike trail linking Mineral Wells and Weatherford. The hike heads west toward Mineral Wells, crossing a bridge over US 180 with an optional stop at a museum dedicated to the Vietnam War.

Start: Park amphitheater
Distance: 3-mile out-and-back
Approximate hiking time: 1 to 2 hours
Difficulty: Moderate due to elevation changes
Trail surface: Paved concrete to crushed gravel with some sand
Seasons: Mar through May; Sept through Nov
Other trail users: Cyclists
Canine compatibility: Dogs must be on leash
Land status: State park
Fees and permits: Fee per entry or purchase annual pass

Schedule: Open daily year-round 6 a.m. to 10 p.m.; trails open sunrise to sunset
Maps: National Geographic TOPO! Texas; Texas State Parks maps
Trail contact: Lake Mineral Wells State Park and Trailway; (940) 328-1171; www.tpwd.texas .gov/state-parks/lake-mineral-wells
Other: The park is also a popular rock-climbing site; climbers must sign a waiver at the park's entrance.

Finding the trailhead: From downtown Fort Worth, take I-30 west and merge onto I-20. Exit onto US 180 west and travel about 21 miles through Weatherford and the small crossroads of Cool. Look for the park's entrance on the right. Once in the park, take the park road as it bears to the right, winding up a hill about a mile to reach the parking lot for the amphitheater and Mineral Wells Trailway. The well-marked trailhead is to the left of the amphitheater. GPS: N 32 48.828' / W 98 1.828'

The Hike

Lake Mineral Wells is well worth the drive west from Fort Worth, offering a scenic lake, plenty of picnic spots, and multiple hiking trails. One of the park's main attractions is its steep rock canyons, which draw scores of rock climbers on the weekends. Originally created to be the city of Mineral Wells' water source, the lake now appeals to anglers. There's also a swimming beach that's perfect for post-hike cooldowns. The park offers extensive cultural and nature education programs and has a resident naturalist who gives guided nature hikes (call or check the park's website for upcoming treks).

The park has multiple trails, and one of the more popular is the Cross Timbers Back Country Trail, a 5-mile out-and-back hike through a forest of post oaks—the

A herd of longhorn cattle rests along the trail.

park lies in the Western Cross Timbers. Other shorter hikes are great options for families with small children. A complete map of all the trails is available at the ranger's station or on the large sign posted at the entrance of the park.

This hike combines trails inside the park with a narrow greenbelt that was once the location of a 20-mile rail line linking Mineral Wells and Weatherford. The trail begins by the Mineral Wells Trailway parking lot, near the park's Lone Star Amphitheater, with some chemical toilets to the left. The trail has a relatively steep descent in the beginning, before its paved section gives way to crushed gravel, then levels off a bit as it passes by the pasture that is home to a herd of longhorns on the left. They are a reminder that the lush grasslands of this part of the Western Cross Timbers attracted ranchers to the region back in the 1850s, including the famous Oliver Loving and C. C. Slaughter, who ran large herds of longhorn through the area.

In 1877 the area around Mineral Wells was settled by James Alvis Lynch, who found the water here to have miracle healing properties that cured his rheumatism. Others reported similar healing effects including a woman who said the water cured her epilepsy, which was mistaken for insanity in those times. Sensing a profitable economic niche, local leaders embraced the so-called "Crazy Water," and Mineral Wells became a mecca for those seeking to cure their ills. The city's famous Baker Hotel drew Hollywood celebrities such as Clark Gable, Judy Garland, and Marlene Dietrich in its heyday back in the 1930s, but the water tourism eventually dried up after the federal government told local authorities to stop making claims they couldn't back up with scientific evidence.

At 0.4 mile, there is a bench overlooking the valley with a guide to local wild-flowers that bloom in the fields here from spring through fall. The famed Texas blue-bonnets blanket the field in March through early April along with Indian paintbrush.

The trail continues down a series of switchbacks as it descends, past an informative sign about the red-tailed hawk, the most common bird of prey in North Texas. At 0.6 mile, the trail connects with the Mineral Wells Trailway, which travels 14 miles east to the city of Weatherford and 6 miles west to Mineral Wells. This hike continues to the right, toward Mineral Wells, and enters the portion of the trail that's off-limits to horseback riders. (**Option:** The hike toward Weatherford is a bit more isolated as it winds 3.4 miles to the small town of Garner, past the entrance to Clark Gardens, for those looking for a longer trek.) The trail heads straight up a gradually rising hill as it reaches the pedestrian bridge over US 180, the turnaround spot.

Miles and Directions

0.0 Start from the Mineral Wells Trailway and Lone Star Amphitheater parking lot where you'll see the well-marked trail map and guide.

0.1 Pass by Lone Star Amphitheater on the right and continue downhill as the paved trail gives way to crushed rock and sand.

0.4 Trail passes by a bench overlooking the valley with an informative sign on native flowers.

0.6 Trail connects with Lake Mineral Wells Trailway; bear right and head up a small hill as the trail travels alongside a two-lane highway.

1.5 Trail reaches the bridge over US 180, and this marks the turnaround point. (**Option:** To reach the National Vietnam War Museum, cross over the bridge and bear right. It's about 100 yards.)

3.0 Arrive back at trailhead.

Options

The bridge crosses over the four-lane highway to reach the National Vietnam War Museum, which celebrates the 5 million men and women who served in Vietnam as well as the Vietnamese culture and even those who protested the war. The site for the museum was chosen in part because many of the war's helicopter pilots were trained at nearby Fort Wolters. While the main museum building hasn't been built, there are meditation gardens and a replica of the Vietnam War Memorial in Washington DC. For more information see www.nationalvnwar museum.org. The museum is 100 yards past the bridge, making it a good turnaround spot for hikers looking to tackle an easy 1- to 2-hour trek. For a longer hike, the trail continues about 4.5 miles to reach downtown Mineral Wells.

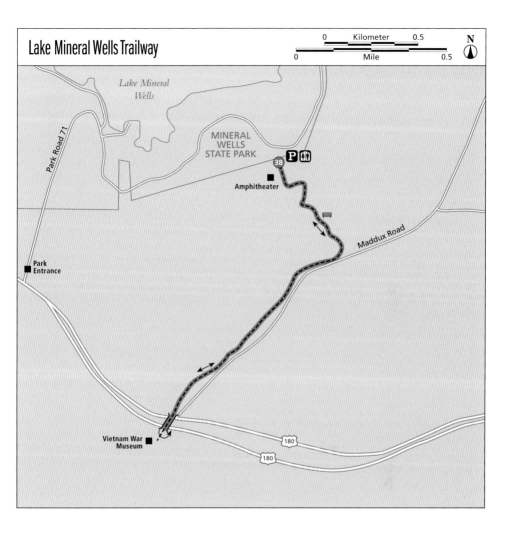

Lake Mineral Wells Trailway

Lake Mineral Wells

MINERAL WELLS STATE PARK

Amphitheater

Park Road 71

Maddux Road

Park Entrance

Vietnam War Museum

180

180

▶ **KID APPEAL**

At the new Mineral Wells Fossil Park, amateur and professional paleontologists can hunt for fossils of ancient sea creatures. Visitors may bring small plastic bags to collect specimens and don kneepads for crawling around the sandy soils in search of ancient treasures.

The best time to hunt for exposed fossils is after a hard rain. Because the park has little or no shade, it's best to visit during cooler times of year or get there early morning in the summer.

The park is open Monday through Friday from 8 a.m. to sunset. From Mineral Wells, head west on US 180. Turn north on Indian Creek Road and drive approximately 2 miles to the park's entrance. For more information go to www.mineralwellsfossilpark.com.

CLARK GARDENS

Located just east of Lake Mineral Wells State Park on Maddux Road, the world-famous Clark Gardens began as the small private garden of Billie and Max Clark, but it has now grown into a 50-plus-acre educational facility and tourist destination featured in *Southern Living* magazine and on HGTV. The gardens showcase sustainable landscapes, including an English-style garden that utilizes Texas-tough plants that thrive in the region's red-clay and rocky soils and that tolerate drought conditions. The garden also features an elaborate model train track through the gardens, as well as a flock of peacocks and guinea fowl. www.clarkgardens.org.

Hike Information

Local information: Mineral Wells Chamber of Commerce, Mineral Wells; (940) 325-2557; www.mineralwellstx.com

Attractions/events: Mineral Wells' annual Crazy Water Festival, celebrating the region's famous mineral water, is held the second Saturday in October; www.crazywaterfestival.org

The park's Lone Star Amphitheater often holds educational programs on cowboy history and poetry, astronomy, and local wildlife. Events are posted on the park's website, www.tpwd.state.tx.us/spdest/findadest/parks/lake_mineral_wells/.

Good eats: Woody's is an old-school Texas roadhouse whose sign boasts "Best Hamburger in Texas" along with the fact they offer pool and shuffleboard; 6105 US 180 E., Mineral Wells; (940) 325-9817

Other resources: Fowler, Gene. *Crazy Water: The Story of Mineral Wells and Other Texas Health Resorts* (Fort Worth: Texas Christian University Press, 1991).

39 Cleburne State Park Spillway Trail

This 2-mile hike crosses over a spillway area before heading uphill on a rocky, at times steep, trek that leads to a panoramic overlook of the park's 528 acres, including Cedar Lake on the west fork of Camp Creek. The hike continues through a forest of ash and juniper trees to a peaceful resting spot with the option of taking a dip in the lake before heading back to the trailhead. There's also an adjacent 1-mile trail along Camp Creek that offers prime birding opportunities.

Start: Back of parking lot
Distance: 2-mile out-and-back
Approximate hiking time: 1 to 2 hours
Difficulty: Moderately difficult due to some steep stretches that require climbing over rocky outcrops
Trail surface: Packed dirt, grass, and rocks
Season: Oct through May
Other trail users: Birders, swimmers

Canine compatibility: Dogs must be on leash
Land status: State park
Fees and permits: Small entrance fee or Texas State Parks Pass
Schedule: Open daily 7 a.m. to 10 p.m.
Map: National Geographic TOPO! Texas
Trail contact: Texas State Parks; (817) 645-4215; www.tpwd.texas.gov/state-parks/cleburne

Finding the trailhead: The park is located 10 miles southwest of Cleburne. Take TX 67 south out of Cleburne, then turn left on Park Road (P) 21. The park is another 6 miles on the right. Once inside the park, pass the restroom facilities and look for a small parking lot on the left. The trailhead is on the backside of the lot. GPS: N 32 15.459'/W 97 33.183'

The Hike

Cleburne State Park makes a great day trip for Metroplex residents looking to escape for a few hours because it's relatively easy to get to and not that crowded compared to other parks in the region. The only downside is a noisy quarry operation located next to the park, which creates a constant hum in the distance. The park includes a small, spring-fed reservoir, Cedar Lake, that's surrounded by rocky hills ridged with juniper, cedar elm, mesquite, and redbud trees. In the area around the creek, hardwoods, such as bur oak, hackberry, willow, and sycamore, provide habitat for woodland birds, including the northern bobwhite, red-bellied woodpecker, eastern bluebird, and American robin. A guide listing the various varieties of birds that have been spotted in the park is available at the park's entrance or on the park's website.

Pole and line fishing are allowed on the lake, home to crappie, bass, and catfish. A family of white-tailed deer makes their home near the park's entrance, so drivers are urged to use caution on the park's roads. Other wildlife here includes gray foxes, wild turkeys, cottontail rabbits, raccoons, skunks, and armadillos.

This panoramic view of Cedar Lake is a highlight of this hike.

This hike begins in the wooded forest, then at about 0.3 mile, crosses over the rocky spillway of the lake's dam before heading uphill. The trail curves to the left, then heads up a ridgeline to the top of a hill overlooking the park. The closer the trail gets to the top, the steeper it becomes, providing a good workout near the end when it requires climbing over some rocky outcrops to reach a panoramic view. From there, the trail evens out, but does require a few more up–and–down climbs as it winds through a forest of juniper trees. When the trail splits at 0.8 mile, bear left to take a side trail that leads down to a sandy beach where it's possible to enjoy a swim in the lake, then retrace your steps back to the trailhead.

Miles and Directions

0.0 Trail begins in back of a small parking lot off the main park road. Look for the marker then follow the trail into a riparian forest of oaks, elms, hackberries, and redbuds.

0.3 Trail crosses over the rocky spillway. During times of heavy rains, this area could be inaccessible. After crossing, the trail heads uphill and curves to the left.

0.7 Trail reaches panoramic view of the lake and surrounding area.

0.8 Bear left as the trail splits to head down to the lake. (**Option:** For a longer hike, continue straight to join Coyote Run Nature Trail.)

1.0 Reach the lake to enjoy a rest or take a dip in the spring-fed waters, then retrace your steps back to the trailhead.

2.0 Arrive back at trailhead.

Cleburne State Park Spillway Trail

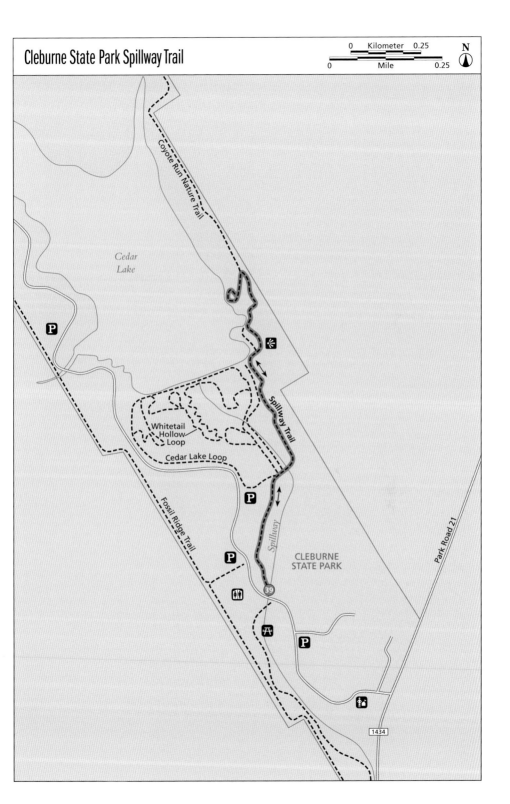

Coyote Run Nature Trail

Cedar Lake

Whitetail
Hollow
Loop

Cedar Lake Loop

Fossil Ridge Trail

Spillway Trail

Spillway

CLEBURNE
STATE PARK

Park Road 21

39

1434

0   Kilometer   0.25

0   Mile   0.25

N

DEER FEAR

White-tailed deer communicate through sounds, smells, and body language. This animal will raise its tail to signal danger to others in the herd. A mother deer may also raise her tail to help her fawn follow her.

Options

For those seeking a longer hike, continue on the main trail, which connects with the park's Coyote Run Nature Trail and follows a fence line through a forest of juniper and oak trees. The park's other 5-plus miles of trails include the 1.7-mile Whispering Meadow Trail, the 3.5-mile Fossil Ridge Trail, and the 1.3-mile Camp Creek Loop, all of which are flatter than the Spillway Trail and may be easier for small children. Two more options include a 1-mile loop along the creek and a 3.2-mile trek on the Whitetail Hollow Trail nestled in the low-lying wooded area of the park.

Hike Information

Local information: Cleburne Chamber of Commerce; (817) 645-2455; www .cleburnechamber.com

WATERING HOLE

Cleburne State Park's unique landscape, its dense woods in a region that was largely open prairie, and its natural springs made the area a favorite hunting ground for Native American tribes. The Comanche also used the dense forests here as a base for raiding pioneer settlements, including Kimbell, the first incorporated town in Johnson County and now called Kimbell Bend. Located about 8 miles south of the park, the town was where the Chisholm Trail crossed the Brazos River. Cowboys also used the springs and woods here as a resting place for their huge herds of cattle on the trail that stretched from the massive ranches of South Texas up to railheads in Texas and Kansas.

In the 1870s the Chisholm Trail was in its heyday, with cattle herds driven north on this famous trail from South Texas through Oklahoma to the stockyards and railroads of Kansas, to be shipped back east. From its beginnings in 1863 until it died out in 1886, as many as 5 million head of cattle, many of them Texas longhorns, were driven along this trail that stretched north to Abilene, Kansas.

The end of the trail came in the 1880s with the invention of barbed wire, which prevented the large herds from crossing vast tracts of land, and a Kansas quarantine law designed to prevent the spread of Texas fever in cattle.

40 Dinosaur Valley Trail

This hike crosses over the Paluxy River and through a bottomland forest before winding uphill through stands of scrubby cedars for a panoramic view of Dinosaur Valley State Park, home to some of the best-preserved dinosaur tracks in the world. There's also a couple of kitschy dinosaur replicas, created by Sinclair Oil Company for the 1964 World's Fair, that provide a dino-mite photo opportunity.

Start: Parking lot just before North Primitive Camping Area
Distance: 5.2-mile balloon
Approximate hiking time: 2 to 3 hours
Difficulty: Moderately difficult due to change in elevation
Trail surface: Packed dirt, grass, and rocks
Season: Oct through May
Other trail users: Birders, swimmers, campers
Canine compatibility: Dogs must be on leash

Land status: State park
Fees and permits: Entrance fee or Texas State Parks Pass
Schedule: Open daily year-round 7 a.m. to 10 p.m.
Map: National Geographic TOPO! Texas
Trail contact: Texas State Parks; (254) 897-4588; www.tpwd.texas.gov/state-parks/dinosaur-valley

Finding the trailhead: From Fort Worth take US 67 southwest to Glen Rose, then take FM 205 right, heading west for 2.7 miles to Park Road (P) 59. Turn right on the park road and go 0.6 mile to the entrance. From there, take the park road and bear right at the junction to the hiking trailhead, the first right after the entrance. The trail begins on the southwest side of the parking lot. GPS: N 32 14.974' / W 97 48.747'

The Hike

The hike is a trip with all lizards great and small. The park's fiberglass replica dinosaurs—a 70-foot Apatosaurus and a 45-foot *Tyrannosaurus rex*—were originally made by the Sinclair Oil Company for the 1964 World's Fair, but were donated to the park after it opened in 1972. Located in the park's central circle, they provide a perfect photo opportunity, and kids love seeing these prehistoric creatures up-close and personal. But prehistoric reptiles aside, the park is also home to multitudes of modern-day lizards, which are likely to scamper ahead on the trail as they hear footsteps. The laid-back Texas spiny lizard can also be easily spotted hanging out on tree trunks and on the plentiful rocks found here.

The unique geology of the park includes limestone, sandstone, and mudstone deposited about 113 million years ago along an ancient shoreline. In the last million or so years, the layered formations have been worn away by the Paluxy River. The river and its tributaries have also served to protect and preserve the dinosaur tracks located just beneath the water surface. In popular swimming spots, such as the eerily

Picture yourself next to one of these replicas from eons past.

beautiful Blue Hole, it's possible to actually swim in the tracks of the dinosaurs—a feature few other places can offer.

The 1,525-acre park also offers extensive hiking trails that wander through both bottomland forests and the upland forest of juniper and cedar trees that are home to golden-cheeked warblers and black-capped vireos, as well as the more common great-crested flycatcher and blue-gray flycatcher.

T REX

The *Tyrannosaurus rex*, often simply called T rex and Latin for "king tyrant lizard," was the largest carnivore to ever walk the earth, with some recorded specimens reaching 50-feet long and weighing 8 tons. Its 33-foot jaws had some sixty serrated teeth, each up to 7 inches long. Too large for quick chases, they sought easy prey like young sauropods or duckbills and likely bullied other predators away from their meals. They stalked the American West 67 to 65.5 million years ago.

THE PALUXY RIVER

Local legend has it that the Paluxy River got its name from the Biloxi Choctaw tribe that once lived along its banks—the name "Paluxy" is derived from "Biloxi." Other tribes that made the region their home include the Comanche, Wichita, Kiowa, Apache, Tonkawa, and Caddo.

From the parking lot just north of the main junction and site of the dinosaur replicas, the hike begins on the Cedar Brake Trail, crosses the river, and joins the White Trail as it winds through the dense forest of oaks, sycamores, and cedar elms. The river is only viewable in small patches through the dense forest canopy as the hike reaches and bears left onto the Blue Trail at 0.8 mile.

A few steps into the Blue Trail, it splits—offering the option of taking the high road or the low road to the top. This hike goes with the low road bearing left, as the trail continues to roughly follow the river's edge. The trail then crosses over a wooden bridge and hits another major junction, this time bearing right and following the Blue Trail as it climbs a rocky incline up the hill and into a more shrubby, upland forest. As the trail climbs, it's possible to catch glimpses of the valley and the dinosaur replicas below before eventually reaching the crest of the rocky hill. From here the trail begins a steeper descent, eventually reaching the split with the "low road" option at 4.2 miles, and crossing back over the bridge and the river and returning to the trailhead.

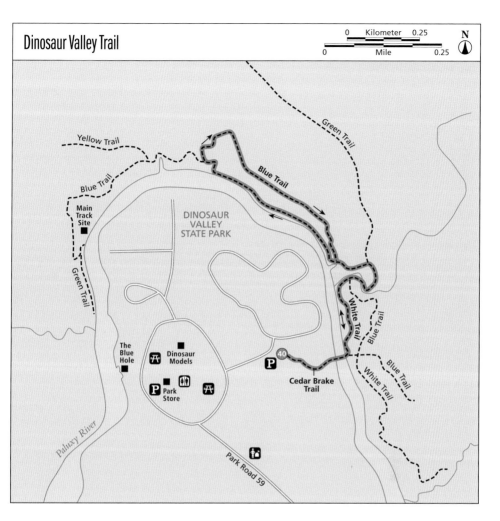

Dinosaur Valley Trail

Miles and Directions

0.0 The trail begins by the parking lot that leads to the North Primitive Camping Area. Follow the trail around a corner and into the woods as it leads to the Paluxy River.

0.3 Cross over the river, easily managed by walking rock-to-rock or simply wading through the ankle-deep water—of course that won't be true after heavy rains, so plan an alternate hike if that's the case. After crossing, look for the sign marking the White Trail and bear left entering the White Trail. (**FYI:** The trail is well marked by white-paint blazes on trees.)

0.8 The white trail joins the Blue Trail; at this junction, bear left and enter the Blue Trail as it follows along the river and winds through the hardwood forest.

1.5 The trail crosses a bridge; bear right and follow the Blue Trail as it begins to climb the rocky hill and enter a scrubby cedar forest.

2.8 The trail passes several overlooks that offer nice views of the river and valley below, including the large dinosaur models, which look tiny from this vantage point.

4.2 The trail rejoins the White Trail; this time take a hard left, retracing your steps on the White Trail and re-crossing the river.

5.2 Arrive back at trailhead.

Hike Information

Local information: Glen Rose Convention and Visitors Bureau; (888) 326-6282; www.glenrosetexas.net

Attractions/events: Fossil Rim Wildlife Center welcomes visitors to drive through the park and enjoy scenery that includes giraffes, rhinos, and antelopes; 2155 CR 2008, Glen Rose; (254) 897-2960; www.fossilrim.com

Big Rocks Park is a free park with plenty of large rocks perfect for climbing and exploring, located in Glen Rose about 5 miles from Dinosaur Valley State Park on the Paluxy River.

Dinosaur World offers more than 100 life-size dinosaur statues, a museum, and fossil digging. There's a picnic area, and coolers are encouraged; (254) 898-1782; https://dinosaurworld.com/texas/

The Promise is an outdoor theatrical event staged in the state's largest permanent amphitheater, telling the story of Jesus Christ and his disciples; (254) 897-3926; www .thepromiseglenrose.com

Good eats: Hammond's BBQ offers classic chopped brisket, sausage, ribs, and an array of homemade pies from coconut meringue to peanut butter cream; 1106 Northeast Big Bend Trail, Glen Rose; (254) 897-3008; www.hammondsbbq.com

Honorable Mentions

Here are some other great hikes in this region:

H. Lost Creek Reservoir State Trailway

This biking, hiking, and equestrian trail, located in Fort Richardson State Park, follows Lost Creek on the east side of Lake Jacksboro by an old airport runway and Lost Creek Reservoir, then crosses over the dam until it reaches a campground on the west side of the lake. The trail offers abundant wildflowers in the spring, and the area's creeks and lakes draw wildlife year-round. There's a large swimming beach on the west side of the reservoir for post-hike dips. Accessible from two trailheads—one in Fort Richardson State Park, the other in Lost Creek Reservoir by the swimming beach—the wide and flat trail is a great choice for combining a hike with overnight camping. Small fee per entry or use the Texas State Parks Pass (available from Texas Parks and Recreation, 940-567-3506). To reach Fort Richardson State Park, take TX 114 to Jacksboro then travel 0.5 mile south of Jacksboro on US 281.

I. Lake Mineral Wells Back Country Trail

This 5-mile out-and-back trail is open only to hikers, while the longer Cross Timbers Back Country Trail is open to cyclists and horseback riders. This hike through the Western Cross Timbers forests of post oaks and blackjack oaks by the waters of Rock Creek leads to a primitive camping area, making it a great overnight hike. There are steep grades the first half of the trail before it evens out for a more leisurely trek. Thanks to its position in the Western Cross Timbers, the park is a place where east meets west and several species of birds reach their easternmost or westernmost habitats. A complete guide to the park's 262 known bird species is available for download on the park's website or upon request at the front gate. To find the trailhead, from downtown Fort Worth, take I-30 west and merge onto I-20. Exit onto US 180 west and go through Weatherford. Travel about 15 miles west through the small crossroads of Cool and look for the park's entrance on the right. From the gate, take a left and follow the park road to the Cross Timbers Camping Area. The trail is by the restrooms and shower facilities. Lake Mineral Wells State Park and Trailway; (940) 328-1171; www.tpwd.texas.gov/state-parks/lake-mineral-wells

J. Black Creek Trail

Just getting to this sandy trail that winds through the remote LBJ National Grasslands is an adventure. The trail is remote, but draws campers, picnickers, and those seeking an escape from the urban grind. Part of the National Park Service system, the grasslands are also used for cattle grazing and, in certain seasons, by hunters. Named after former president and Texas native Lyndon Baines Johnson, the area draws a multitude of wildlife including deer, red-tailed fox, coyote, and wild turkey. The Dallas Lepidopterists' Society organizes butterfly hikes in the grasslands' protected prairie, whose wildflowers draw eastern tiger swallowtails and silver spotted skippers. Spring is the best time of year to take in the bluebonnets and other wildflowers here and enjoy the trail, which is largely open, before the heat of summer sets in. There's a nice swimming beach by the trailhead for those who need a post-hike swim to cool down. The hike links the two major parks of the grasslands—Black Creek and Cottonwood Creek Recreation Areas. The trailhead is well marked by Black Creek, as it crosses over the creek on a wooden bridge and enters the grasslands, but the pavement turns to a sandy, sometimes rocky trail that can be difficult for some to hike. Depending on recent trail maintenance, it may be difficult to follow the trail in places. Black Creek Recreation Area levies a small user fee, cash only, which is collected using an envelope and box system.

From Fort Worth, take US 287 north toward Decatur, then after going through Decatur and its historic square, go north on US 287 for 9.7 miles to FM 1655 in Alvord. Turn right and go 0.7 mile through Alvord to East Pine Road. Turn right on Pine Road and go 5 miles to CR 2372 and turn left, then go 1.4 miles to CR 2461. Turn left onto CR 2461 and go 0.4 mile to FS 902. Turn left on FS 902 and continue 0.4 mile to the recreation area; (940) 627-5475.

The swimming beach is inviting after a good hike.

The Art of Hiking

When standing nose to nose with a bobcat, you're probably not too concerned with the issue of ethical behavior in the wild. No doubt you're just terrified. But let's be honest. How often are you nose to nose with a bobcat? For most of us, a hike into the "wild" means loading up the SUV with expensive gear and driving to a toileted trailhead. Sure, you can mourn how civilized we've become—how GPS units have replaced natural instinct and Gore-Tex, true grit—but the silly gadgets of civilization aside, we have plenty of reasons to take pride in how we've matured. With survival now on the back burner, we've begun to realize—and it's about time—that we have a responsibility to protect, no longer just conquer, our wild places; that they, not we, are at risk. So please, do what you can. The following section will help you understand better what it means to "do what you can" while still making the most of your hiking experience. Anyone can take a hike, but hiking safely and well is an art requiring preparation and proper equipment.

Trail Etiquette

Leave no trace. Always leave an area just like you found it—if not better than you found it. Avoid camping in fragile grasslands and along the banks of streams and lakes. Use a camp stove versus building a wood fire. Pack out all of your trash and extra food. Bury human waste at least 100 feet from water sources under 6 to 8 inches of topsoil. Don't bathe with soap in a lake or stream—use prepackaged moistened towels to wipe off sweat and dirt, or bathe in the water without soap.

Stay on the trail. It's true, a path anywhere leads nowhere new, but purists will just have to get over it. Paths serve an important purpose: They limit impact on natural areas. Straying from a designated trail may seem innocent, but it can cause damage to sensitive areas—damage that may take years to recover, if it can recover at all. Even simple shortcuts can be destructive. So, please, stay on the trail.

Leave no weeds. Noxious weeds tend to overtake other plants, which in turn affects animals and birds that depend on them for food. To minimize the spread of noxious weeds, hikers should regularly clean their boots, tents, packs, and hiking poles of mud and seeds. Also brush your dog to remove any weed seeds before heading off into a new area.

Keep your dog under control. You can buy a flexi-lead that allows your dog to go exploring along the trail, while allowing you the ability to reel him in should another hiker approach or should he decide to chase a rabbit. Always obey leash laws, and be sure to bury your dog's waste or pack it out in resealable plastic bags.

Respect other trail users. Often you're not the only one on the trail. With the rise in popularity of multiuse trails, you'll have to learn a new kind of respect beyond the nod and "hello" approach you may be used to. First investigate whether you're on a multiuse trail and assume the appropriate precautions. When you encounter motorized vehicles (ATVs, motorcycles, and 4WDs), be alert. Though they should always yield to the hiker, often they're going too fast or are too lost in the buzz of their engine to react to your presence. If you hear activity ahead, step off the trail just to be safe. Note that you're not likely to hear a mountain biker coming, so be prepared and know ahead of time whether you share the trail with them. Cyclists should always yield to hikers, but that's little comfort to the hiker. Be aware. When you approach horses or pack animals on the trail, always step quietly off the trail, preferably on the downhill side, and let them pass. If you're wearing a large backpack, it's often a good idea to sit down. To some animals, a hiker wearing a large backpack might appear threatening. Many national forests allow domesticated grazing, usually for sheep and cattle. Make sure your dog doesn't harass these animals, and respect ranchers' rights while you're enjoying yours.

Getting Into Shape

Unless you want to be sore—and possibly have to shorten your trip or vacation—be sure to get in shape before a big hike. If you're terribly out of shape, start a walking program early, preferably eight weeks in advance. Start with a 15-minute walk during your lunch hour or after work and gradually increase your walking time to an hour. You should also increase your elevation gain. Walking briskly up hills really strengthens your leg muscles and gets your heart rate up. If you work in a storied office building, take the stairs instead of the elevator. If you prefer going to a gym, walk the treadmill or use a stair machine. You can further increase your strength and endurance by walking with a loaded backpack. Stationary exercises you might consider are squats, leg lifts, sit-ups, and push-ups. Other good ways to get in shape include biking, running, aerobics, and, of course, short hikes. Stretching before and after a hike keeps muscles flexible and helps avoid injuries.

Preparedness

It's been said that failing to plan means planning to fail. So do take the necessary time to plan your trip. Whether going on a short day hike or an extended backpack trip, always prepare for the worst. Simply remembering to pack a copy of the U.S. Army Survival Manual is not preparedness. Although it's not a bad idea if you plan on entering truly wild places, it's merely the tourniquet answer to a problem. You need to do your best to prevent the problem from arising in the first place. In order to survive—and to stay reasonably comfortable—you need to concern yourself with the basics: water, food, and shelter. Don't go on a hike without having these bases covered. And don't go on a hike expecting to find these items in the woods.

Water. Even in cool conditions, you need at least two quarts of water a day to function efficiently. Add Texas's heat and taxing terrain and you can bump that figure up to one gallon. That's simply a base to work from—your metabolism and your level of conditioning can raise or lower that amount. Unless you know your level, assume that you need one gallon of water a day. Now, where do you plan on getting the water?

Preferably not from natural water sources. These sources can be loaded with intestinal disturbers, such as bacteria, viruses, and fertilizers. *Giardia lamblia,* the most common of these disturbers, is a protozoan parasite that lives part of its life cycle as a cyst in water sources. The parasite spreads when mammals defecate in water sources. Once ingested, *Giardia* can induce cramping, diarrhea, vomiting, and fatigue within two days to two weeks after ingestion. Giardiasis is treatable with prescription drugs. If you believe you've contracted giardiasis, see a doctor immediately.

Treating water. The best and easiest solution to avoid polluted water is to carry your water with you. Yet, depending on the nature of your hike and the duration, this may not be an option—one gallon of water weighs 8.5 pounds. In that case, you'll need to look into treating water. Regardless of which method you choose, you should always carry some water with you in case of an emergency. Save this reserve until you absolutely need it.

There are three methods of treating water: boiling, chemical treatment, and filtering. If you boil water, it's recommended that you do so for 10 to 15 minutes. This is often impractical because you're forced to exhaust a great deal of your fuel supply. You can opt for chemical treatment, which will kill *Giardia* but will not take care of other chemical pollutants. Another drawback to chemical treatments is the unpleasant taste of the water after it's treated. You can remedy this by adding powdered drink mix to the water. Filters are the preferred method for treating water. Many filters remove *Giardia,* organic and inorganic contaminants, and don't leave an aftertaste. Water filters are far from perfect as they can easily become clogged or leak if a gasket wears out. It's always a good idea to carry a backup supply of chemical treatment tablets in case your filter decides to quit on you.

Food. If we're talking about survival, you can go days without food, as long as you have water. But we're also talking about comfort. Try to avoid foods that are high in sugar and fat like candy bars and potato chips. These food types are harder to digest and are low in nutritional value. Instead, bring along foods that are easy to pack, nutritious, and high in energy (e.g., whole-grain bagels, nutrition bars, dehydrated fruit, gorp, and jerky). If you are on an overnight trip, easy-to-fix dinners include rice mixes with dehydrated potatoes, corn, pasta with cheese sauce, and soup mixes. For a tasty breakfast, you can fix hot oatmeal with brown sugar and reconstituted milk powder topped off with banana chips. If you like a hot drink in the morning, bring along herbal tea bags or hot chocolate. If you are a coffee junkie, you can purchase coffee that is packaged like tea bags or individually packaged instant coffee. You can prepackage all of your meals in heavy-duty resealable plastic bags to keep food from spilling in your pack. These bags can be reused to pack out trash.

Shelter. The type of shelter you choose depends less on the conditions than on your tolerance for discomfort. Shelter comes in many forms—tent, tarp, lean-to, bivy sack, cabin, cave, and so on. If you're camping in the desert, a bivy sack may suffice, but if you're above the tree line and a storm is approaching, a better choice is a three- or four-season tent. Tents are the logical and most popular choice for most backpackers as they're lightweight and packable—and you can rest assured that you always have shelter from the elements. Before you leave on your trip, anticipate what the weather and terrain will be like and plan for the type of shelter that will work best for your comfort level (see Equipment later in this section).

Finding a campsite. If there are established campsites, stick to those. If not, start looking for a campsite early—around 3:30 or 4 p.m. Stop at the first decent site you see. Depending on the area, it could be a long time before you find another suitable location. Pitch your camp in an area that's level. Make sure the site is at least 200 feet from fragile areas like lakeshores, meadows, and stream banks. And try to avoid areas thick in underbrush, as they can harbor insects and provide cover for approaching animals.

If you are camping in stormy, rainy weather, look for a rock outcrop or a shelter in the trees to keep the wind from blowing your tent all night. Be sure that you don't camp under trees with dead limbs that might break off on top of you. Also, try to find an area that has an absorbent surface, such as sandy soil or forest duff. This, in addition to camping on a surface with a slight angle, will provide better drainage. By all means, don't dig trenches to provide drainage around your tent—remember you're practicing zero-impact camping.

If you're in bear country, steer clear of creek beds or animal paths. If you see any signs of a bear's presence (i.e., scat, footprints), relocate. You'll need to find a campsite near a tall tree where you can hang your food and other items that may attract bears such as deodorant, toothpaste, or soap. Carry a lightweight nylon rope with which to hang your food. As a rule, you should hang your food at least 20 feet from the ground and 5 feet away from the tree trunk. You can put food and other items in a waterproof stuff sack and tie one end of the rope to the stuff sack. To get the other end of the rope over the tree branch, tie a good-size rock to it and gently toss the rock over the tree branch. Pull the stuff sack up until it reaches the top of the branch and tie it off securely. Don't hang your food near your tent! If possible, hang your food at least 100 feet away from your campsite. Alternatives to hanging your food are bear-proof canisters and metal bear boxes.

Lastly, think of comfort. Lie down on the ground where you intend to sleep and see if it's a good fit. For morning warmth (and a nice view to wake up to), have your tent face east.

First Aid

I know you're tough, but get 10 miles into the woods and develop a blister and you'll wish you had carried that first-aid kit. Face it, it's just plain good sense. Many companies produce lightweight, compact first-aid kits. Just make sure yours contains at least the following:

- ❏ adhesive bandages
- ❏ moleskin or duct tape
- ❏ various sterile gauze and dressings
- ❏ white surgical tape
- ❏ Ace bandage
- ❏ antihistamine
- ❏ aspirin
- ❏ Betadine solution
- ❏ first-aid book
- ❏ antacid tablets
- ❏ tweezers
- ❏ scissors
- ❏ antibacterial wipes
- ❏ triple-antibiotic ointment
- ❏ plastic gloves
- ❏ sterile cotton tip applicators
- ❏ syrup of ipecac (to induce vomiting)
- ❏ thermometer
- ❏ wire splint

Here are a few tips for dealing with and hopefully preventing certain ailments.

Sunburn. Take along sunscreen or sunblock, protective clothing, and a wide-brimmed hat. If you do get a sunburn, treat the area with aloe vera gel, and protect it from further sun exposure. At higher elevations, the sun's radiation can be particularly damaging to skin. Remember that your eyes are vulnerable to this radiation as well. Sunglasses can be a good way to prevent headaches and permanent eye damage from the sun, especially in places where light-colored rock or patches of snow reflect light up in your face.

Blisters. Be prepared to take care of these hike-spoilers by carrying moleskin (a lightly padded adhesive), gauze and tape, or adhesive bandages. An effective way to apply moleskin is to cut out a circle of moleskin and remove the center—like a doughnut—and place it over the blistered area. Cutting the center out will reduce the pressure applied to the sensitive skin. Other products can help you combat blisters. Some are applied to suspicious hot spots before a blister forms to help decrease friction to that area, while others are applied to the blister after it has popped to help prevent further irritation.

Insect bites and stings. You can treat most insect bites and stings by applying 1% hydrocortisone cream topically and taking a pain medication such as ibuprofen or acetaminophen to reduce swelling. If you forgot to pack these items, a cold compress or a paste of mud and ashes can sometimes assuage the itching and discomfort. Remove any stingers by using tweezers or scraping the area with your fingernail or a knife blade. Don't pinch the area as you'll only spread the venom.

Some hikers are highly sensitive to bites and stings and may have a serious allergic reaction that can be life threatening. Symptoms of a serious allergic reaction can include wheezing, an asthma attack, and shock. The treatment for this severe type of reaction is epinephrine. If you know that you are sensitive to bites and stings, carry a prepackaged kit of epinephrine, which can be obtained only by prescription from your doctor.

Ticks. While ticks aren't as much of a problem in Texas as in other parts of the country because fire ants here feed on them, ticks can carry diseases such as Rocky Mountain spotted fever and Lyme disease. The best defense is, of course, prevention. If you know you're going to be hiking through an area littered with ticks, wear long pants and a long-sleeved shirt. You can apply a permethrin repellent to your clothing and a Deet repellent to exposed skin. At the end of your hike, do a spot check for ticks (and insects in general). If you do find a tick, grab the head of the tick firmly—with a pair of tweezers if you have them—and gently pull it away from the skin with a twisting motion. Sometimes the mouth parts linger, embedded in your skin. If this happens, try to remove them with a disinfected needle. Clean the affected area with an antibacterial cleanser and then apply triple antibiotic ointment. Monitor the area for a few days. If irritation persists or a white spot develops, see a doctor for possible infection.

Poison ivy, oak, and sumac. These skin irritants can be found most anywhere in North America and come in the form of a bush or a vine, having leaflets in groups of three, five, seven, or nine. Learn how to spot the plants. The oil they secrete can cause an allergic reaction in the form of blisters, usually about 12 hours after exposure. The itchy rash can last from ten days to several weeks. The best defense against these irritants is to wear clothing that covers the arms, legs, and torso. For summer, zip-off cargo pants come in handy. There are also nonprescription lotions you can apply to exposed skin that guard against the effects of poison ivy/oak/sumac and can be washed off with soap and water. If you think you were in contact with the plants, after hiking (or even on the trail during longer hikes) wash with soap and water. Taking a hot shower with soap after you return home from your hike will also help to remove any lingering oil from your skin. Should you contract a rash from any of these plants, use an antihistamine to reduce the itching. If the rash is localized, create a light bleach/water wash to dry up the area. If the rash has spread, either tough it out or see your doctor about getting a dose of cortisone (available both orally and by injection).

Snakebites. Snakebites are rare in North America. Unless startled or provoked, the majority of snakes will not bite. If you are wise to their habitats and keep a careful eye on the trail, you should be just fine. When stepping over logs, first step on the log, making sure you can see what's on the other side before stepping down. Though your chances of being struck are slim, it's wise to know what to do in the event you are.

If a *nonpoisonous* snake bites you, allow the wound to bleed a small amount and then cleanse the wounded area with a Betadine solution (10% povidone iodine). Rinse the wound with clean water (preferably) or fresh urine (it might sound ugly, but it's sterile). Once the area is clean, cover it with triple antibiotic ointment and a clean bandage. Remember, most residual damage from snakebites, poisonous or otherwise, comes from infection, not the snake's venom. Keep the area as clean as possible and get medical attention immediately.

If you are bitten by a poisonous snake, remove the toxin with a suctioning device, found in a snakebite kit. If you do not have such a device, squeeze the wound—*do not* use your mouth for suction, as the venom will enter your bloodstream through the vessels under the tongue and head straight for your heart. Then clean the wound just as you would a nonpoisonous bite. Tie a clean band of cloth snugly around the afflicted appendage, about an inch or so above the bite (or the rim of the swelling). This is *not* a tourniquet—you want to simply slow the blood flow, not cut it off. Loosen the band if numbness ensues. Remove the band for a minute and reapply a little higher every 10 minutes.

If it is your friend who's been bitten, treat him or her for shock—make the person comfortable, have him or her lie down, elevate the legs, and keep him or her warm. Avoid applying anything cold to the bite wound. Immobilize the affected area and remove any constricting items such as rings, watches, or restrictive clothing as swelling may occur. Once your friend is stable and relatively calm, hike out to get help. The victim should get treatment, ideally within 12 hours, which usually consists of a tetanus shot, antivenin, and antibiotics.

If you are alone and struck by a poisonous snake, stay calm. Hysteria will only quicken the venom's spread. Follow the procedure above, and do your best to reach help. When hiking out, don't run—you'll only increase the flow of blood throughout your system. Instead, walk calmly.

Dehydration. Have you ever hiked in hot weather and had a roaring headache and felt fatigued after only a few miles? More than likely you were dehydrated. Symptoms of dehydration include fatigue, headache, and decreased coordination and judgment. When you are hiking, your body's rate of fluid loss depends on the outside temperature, humidity, altitude, and your activity level. On average, a hiker walking in warm weather will lose 4 liters of fluid a day. That fluid loss is easily replaced by normal consumption of liquids and food. However, if a hiker is walking briskly in hot, dry weather and hauling a heavy pack, he or she can lose 1 to 3 liters of water an hour. It's important to always carry plenty of water and to stop often and drink fluids regularly, even if you aren't thirsty.

Heat exhaustion is the result of a loss of large amounts of electrolytes and often occurs if a hiker is dehydrated and has been under heavy exertion. Common symptoms of heat exhaustion include cramping, exhaustion, fatigue, lightheadedness, and nausea. You can treat heat exhaustion by getting out of the sun and drinking an electrolyte solution made up of one teaspoon of salt and one tablespoon of sugar dissolved in a liter of water. Drink this solution slowly over a period of 1 hour. Drinking plenty of fluids (preferably an electrolyte solution/sports drink) can prevent heat exhaustion. Avoid hiking during the hottest parts of the day, and wear breathable clothing, a wide-brimmed hat, and sunglasses.

Hypothermia is one of the biggest dangers in the backcountry, especially for day hikers in the summertime. That may sound strange, but imagine starting out on a hike in midsummer when it's sunny and 80 degrees out. You're clad in nylon shorts and a cotton T-shirt. About halfway through your hike, the sky begins to cloud up, and in the next hour a light drizzle begins to fall and the wind starts to pick up. Before you know it, you are soaking wet and shivering—the perfect recipe for hypothermia. More advanced signs include decreased coordination, slurred speech, and blurred vision. When a victim's temperature falls below 92 degrees F, the blood pressure and pulse plummet, possibly leading to coma and death.

To avoid hypothermia, always bring a windproof/rainproof shell, a fleece jacket, tights made of a breathable, synthetic fiber, gloves, and hat when you are hiking in the mountains. Learn to adjust your clothing layers based on the temperature. If you are climbing uphill at a moderate pace you will stay warm, but when you stop for a break you'll become cold quickly, unless you add more layers of clothing.

If a hiker is showing advanced signs of hypothermia, dress the victim in dry clothes and make sure he or she is wearing a hat and gloves. Place the person in a sleeping bag in a tent or shelter that will provide protection from the wind and other elements. Give the person warm fluids to drink and keep him awake.

Frostbite. When the mercury dips below 32 degrees F, your extremities begin to chill. If a persistent chill attacks a localized area, say, your hands or your toes, the circulatory system reacts by cutting off blood flow to the affected area—the idea being to protect and preserve the body's overall temperature. And so it's death by attrition for the affected area. Ice crystals start to form from the water in the cells of the neglected tissue. Deprived of heat, nourishment, and now water, the tissue literally starves. This is frostbite.

Prevention is your best defense against this situation. Most prone to frostbite are your face, hands, and feet, so protect these areas well. Wool is the material of choice because it provides ample air space for insulation and draws moisture away from the skin. Synthetic fabrics, however, have recently made great strides in the cold-weather clothing market. Do your research. A pair of light silk liners under your regular gloves is a good trick for keeping warm. They afford some additional warmth, but more important they'll allow you to remove your mitts for tedious work without exposing the skin.

If your feet or hands start to feel cold or numb due to the elements, warm them as quickly as possible. Place cold hands under your armpits or bury them in your crotch. If your feet are cold, change your socks. If there's plenty of room in your boots, add another pair of socks. Do remember, though, that constricting your feet in tight boots can restrict blood flow and actually make your feet colder more quickly. Your socks need to have breathing room if they're going to be effective. Dead air provides insulation. If your face is cold, place your warm hands over your face, or simply wear a head stocking.

Should your skin go numb and start to appear white and waxy, chances are you've got or are developing frostbite. Don't try to thaw the area unless you can maintain the warmth. In other words, don't stop to warm up your frostbitten feet only to head back on the trail. You'll do more damage than good. Tests have shown that hikers who walked on thawed feet did more harm, and endured more pain, than hikers who left the affected areas alone. Do your best to get out of the cold entirely and seek medical attention—which usually consists of performing a rapid rewarming in water for 20 to 30 minutes.

The overall objective in preventing both hypothermia and frostbite is to keep the body's core warm. Protect key areas where heat escapes, like the top of the head, and maintain the proper nutrition level. Foods that are high in calories aid the body in producing heat. Never smoke or drink when you're in situations where the cold is threatening. By affecting blood flow, these activities ultimately cool the body's core temperature.

Hantavirus Pulmonary Syndrome (HPS). Deer mice spread the virus that causes HPS, and humans contract it from breathing it in, usually when they've disturbed an area with dust and mice feces from nests or surfaces with mice droppings or urine. Exposure to large numbers of rodents and their feces or urine presents the greatest risk. As hikers, we sometimes enter old buildings, and often deer mice live in these places. We may not be around long enough to be exposed, but do be aware of this disease. About half the people who develop HPS die. Symptoms are flu-like and appear about two to three weeks after exposure. After initial symptoms, a dry cough and shortness of breath follow. Breathing is difficult. If you even think you might have HPS, see a doctor immediately!

Natural Hazards

Besides tripping over a rock or tree root on the trail, there are some real hazards to be aware of while hiking. Even if where you're hiking doesn't have the plethora of poisonous snakes and plants, insects, and grizzly bears found in other parts of the United States, there are a few weather conditions and predators you may need to take into account.

Lightning. Thunderstorms build over the mountains almost every day during the summer. Lightning is generated by thunderheads and can strike without warning, even several miles away from the nearest overhead cloud. The best rule of thumb is to start leaving exposed peaks, ridges, and canyon rims by about noon. This time can vary a little depending on storm buildup. Keep an eye on cloud formation and don't underestimate how fast a storm can build. The bigger they get, the more likely a thunderstorm will happen. Lightning takes the path of least resistance, so if you're the high point, it might choose you. Ducking under a rock overhang is dangerous, as you form the shortest path between the rock and ground. If you dash below tree line, avoid standing under the only or the tallest tree. If you are caught above tree line, stay away from anything metal you might be carrying. Move down off the ridge slightly to a low, treeless point and squat until the storm passes. If you have an insulating pad, squat on it. Avoid having both your hands and feet touching the ground at once and never lie flat. If you hear a buzzing sound or feel your hair standing on end, move quickly because an electrical charge is building up.

Tornadoes. Don't hike if there is a tornado watch, which means conditions are right for tornado formation, or a warning, which means one or more have already been spotted on the ground. Much of the area is equipped with high-pitched sirens that sound an alarm when dangerous weather is approaching. If you hear the sirens, take cover in a nearby building, preferably in a windowless room on the lowest floor. (As an aside, remember that cities also periodically test their sirens.) If you are out in the open and cannot make it to a building, find a low-lying area, but avoid culverts or streambeds. Because tornadoes are typically followed or accompanied by heavy rains, creeks can quickly fill with water and result in flash flooding.

Flash floods. While hiking or driving, keep an eye on the weather. In heavy rains the region's thick clay soils become muddy quagmires, and bubbling streams turn into raging rivers, so consider trail conditions before heading out. Flash floods can subside quickly, so be patient and don't cross a swollen stream.

Some dirt trails may be closed a day or two after a heavy rain. If you are hiking a trail that's also used by mountain bikers, check the Dallas Off-Road Bicycle Association website, www.dorba.org/trails, to see if the trail is open or closed. You can also contact state and local park contacts before heading out. Trails that are maintained by equestrian groups are also typically closed after heavy rains, particularly the Trinity Trails at Lake Lavon, which has black quagmire soils that can stay muddy for several days after a downpour.

Feral hogs. An estimated 2 million feral hogs call Texas home, and they are increasingly making their home in the urban landscape of Dallas/Fort Worth, where they are multiplying along the Trinity River and have been known to startle early morning hikers in Arlington's River Legacy Park and on Southlake's Bob Jones Nature Center and Walnut Grove Trails. During times of heavy rains, these animals move out of the Trinity River's floodplains and into suburban neighborhoods, tearing up lawns and other landscaping. While they are generally not considered dangerous and will typically run away from humans, their knife-like tusks can cause serious injury.

Coyotes have also acclimated to city living and have even been spotted around White Rock Lake, the Park Cities, and Colleyville during the winter mating season, mid-January through March. In February 2010, Governor Rick Perry shot a coyote he said was threatening his daughter's Labrador puppy during an early morning jog in an undeveloped area near Austin. But wildlife experts say in most cases all it takes is raising your voice and raising your hands to make a skittish coyote head the other direction.

Bobcats are more elusive and are rarely seen due to their reclusive nature and nocturnal hunting habits, but the urban population of these cats is increasing, and they have been spotted in Arlington, Fort Worth, and even downtown Dallas in the early morning and around sunset. Although some people may mistake a bobcat for either a domestic cat or mountain lion, the bobcat has a distinct shape—with its shortened, bobbed tall and back legs that are disproportionately larger than its front legs. Bobcats weigh anywhere from between 15 to 40 pounds and have large, tufted ears. Trees bearing deep scratch marks from bobcats using the bark to sharpen their claws could be evidence that bobcats are in the area. The DFW Wildlife Coalition, a nonprofit group that protects native wildlife in the Metroplex, notes that bobcat attacks on humans are virtually unknown, but cautions not to attempt to touch or handle a bobcat. It's especially important to stay away from female bobcats and their young kittens.

Bears. Black bears are rarely sighted in North Texas; neertheless, here are some tips in case you and a bear scare each other. Most of all, avoid scaring a bear. Watch for bear tracks (five toes) and droppings (sizable with leaves, partly digested berries, seeds, and/or animal fur). Talk or sing where visibility or hearing are limited. Keep a clean camp, hang food and toiletries, and don't sleep in the clothes you wore while cooking. Be especially careful in spring to avoid getting between a mother and her cubs. In late summer and fall, bears are busy eating berries and acorns to fatten up for winter, so be extra careful around berry bushes and oakbrush. If you do encounter a bear, move away slowly while facing the bear, talk softly, and avoid direct eye contact. Give the bear room to escape. Since bears are very curious, it might stand upright to get a better whiff of you, and it may even charge you to try to intimidate you. Try to stay calm. If a bear does attack, fight back with anything you have handy. Unleashed dogs have been known to come running back to their owners with a bear close behind. Keep your dog on a leash or leave it at home.

Other considerations. Hunting is a popular sport in Texas, especially during rifle season in October and November. While the hikes featured in this book are not in hunting areas, it's still good to take precautions. First, learn when the different hunting seasons start and end in the area in which you'll be hiking. During this time frame, be sure to wear at least a blaze orange hat, and possibly put an orange vest over your pack. Don't be surprised to see hunters in camo outfits carrying bows or muzzleloading rifles during their season. If you would feel more comfortable without hunters around, hike where hunting is not allowed.

Navigation

Whether you are going on a short hike in a familiar area or planning a weeklong backpack trip, you should always be equipped with the proper navigational equipment—at the very least a detailed map and a sturdy compass.

Maps. There are many different types of maps available to help you find your way on the trail. Easiest to find are US Forest Service maps and BLM (Bureau of

Land Management) maps. These maps tend to cover large areas, so be sure they are detailed enough for your particular trip. You can also obtain national park maps as well as high-quality maps from private companies and trail groups. These maps can be obtained either from outdoor stores or ranger stations.

U.S. Geological Survey (USGS) topographic maps are particularly popular with hikers—especially serious backcountry hikers. These maps contain the standard map symbols such as roads, lakes, and rivers, as well as contour lines that show the details of the trail terrain like ridges, valleys, passes, and mountain peaks. The 7.5-minute quadrangle series (1 inch on the map equals approximately 0.4 mile on the ground) provides the closest inspection available. USGS maps are available by mail (U.S. Geological Survey, Map Distribution Branch, P.O. Box 25286, Denver, CO 80225) or at www.usgs.gov/pubprod.

If you want to check out the high-tech world of maps, you can purchase topographic maps on CD-ROM. These software-mapping programs let you select a route on your computer, print it out, then take it with you on the trail. Some software mapping programs let you insert symbols and labels, download waypoints from a GPS unit, and export the maps to other software programs.

The art of map reading is a skill that you can develop by first practicing in an area you are familiar with. To begin, orient the map so it is lined up in the correct direction (i.e., north on the map is lined up with true north). Next, familiarize yourself with the map symbols and try to match them up with terrain features around you such as a high ridge, mountain peak, river, or lake. If you are practicing with a USGS map, notice the contour lines. On gentler terrain these contour lines are spaced farther apart, and on steeper terrain they are closer together. Pick a short loop trail, and stop frequently to check your position on the map. As you practice map reading, you'll learn how to anticipate a steep section on the trail or a good place to take a rest break, and so on.

Compasses. First off, the sun is not a substitute for a compass. So, what kind of compass should you have? Here are some characteristics you should look for: a rectangular base with detailed scales, a liquid-filled protective housing, a sighting line on the mirror, luminous alignment and back-bearing arrows, a luminous north-seeking arrow, and a well-defined bezel ring.

You can learn compass basics by reading the detailed instructions included with your compass. If you want to fine-tune your compass skills, sign up for an orienteering class or purchase a book on compass reading. Once you've learned the basic skills of using a compass, remember to practice these skills before you head into the backcountry.

If you are a klutz at using a compass, you may be interested in checking out the technical wizardry of the GPS (Global Positioning System) device. The GPS was developed by the Pentagon and works off twenty-four NAVSTAR satellites, which were designed to guide missiles to their targets. A GPS device is a handheld unit that calculates your latitude and longitude with the easy press of a button. The Department of Defense used to scramble the satellite signals a bit to prevent civilians (and spies!)

from getting extremely accurate readings, but that practice was discontinued in May 2000, and GPS units now provide nearly pinpoint accuracy (within 30 to 60 feet).

There are many different types of GPS units available, and they range in price from $100 to $400. In general, all GPS units have a display screen and keypad where you input information. In addition to acting as a compass, the unit allows you to plot your route, easily retrace your path, track your traveling speed, find the mileage between waypoints, and calculate the total mileage of your route.

Before you purchase a GPS unit, keep in mind that these devices don't pick up signals indoors, in heavily wooded areas, on mountain peaks, or in deep valleys.

Pedometers. A pedometer is a small, clip-on unit with a digital display that calculates your hiking distance in miles or kilometers based on your walking stride. Some units also calculate the calories you burn and your total hiking time. Pedometers are available at most large outdoor stores and range in price from $20 to $40.

Trip Planning

Planning your hiking adventure begins with letting a friend or relative know your trip itinerary so they can call for help if you don't return at your scheduled time. Your next task is to make sure you are outfitted to experience the risks and rewards of the trail. This section highlights gear and clothing you may want to take with you to get the most out of your hike.

Day Hikes

- ❏ camera/film
- ❏ compass/GPS unit
- ❏ pedometer
- ❏ daypack
- ❏ first-aid kit
- ❏ food
- ❏ guidebook
- ❏ headlamp/flashlight with extra batteries and bulbs
- ❏ hat
- ❏ insect repellent
- ❏ knife/multipurpose tool
- ❏ map
- ❏ matches in waterproof container and fire starter
- ❏ fleece jacket
- ❏ rain gear
- ❏ space blanket
- ❏ sunglasses

- ❑ sunscreen
- ❑ swimsuit
- ❑ watch
- ❑ water
- ❑ water bottles/water hydration system

Overnight Trips

- ❑ backpack and waterproof rain cover
- ❑ backpacker's trowel
- ❑ bandanna
- ❑ bear repellent spray
- ❑ bear bell
- ❑ biodegradable soap
- ❑ collapsible water container (2–3 gallon capacity)
- ❑ clothing—extra wool socks, shirt, and shorts
- ❑ cook set/utensils
- ❑ ditty bags to store gear
- ❑ extra plastic resealable bags
- ❑ gaiters
- ❑ garbage bag
- ❑ ground cloth
- ❑ journal/pen
- ❑ nylon rope to hang food
- ❑ long underwear
- ❑ permit (if required)
- ❑ pot scrubber
- ❑ rain jacket and pants
- ❑ sandals to wear around camp and to ford streams
- ❑ sleeping bag and waterproof stuff sack
- ❑ sleeping pad
- ❑ small bath towel
- ❑ stove and fuel
- ❑ tent
- ❑ toiletry items
- ❑ water filter
- ❑ whistle

Equipment

With the outdoor market currently flooded with products, many of which are pure gimmickry, it seems impossible to both differentiate and choose. Do I really need a tropical-fish-lined collapsible shower? (No, you don't.) The only defense against the maddening quantity of items thrust in your face is to think practically—and to do so before you go shopping. The worst buys are impulse buys. Since most name brands will differ only slightly in quality, it's best to know what you're looking for in terms of function. Buy only what you need. You will, don't forget, be carrying what you've bought on your back. Here are some things to keep in mind before you go shopping.

Clothes. Clothing is your armor against Mother Nature's little surprises. Hikers should be prepared for any possibility, especially when hiking in mountainous areas. Adequate rain protection and extra layers of clothing are a good idea. In summer, a wide-brimmed hat can help keep the sun at bay. In the winter months the first layer you'll want to wear is a "wicking" layer of long underwear that keeps perspiration away from your skin. Wear long underwear made from synthetic fibers that wick moisture away from the skin and draw it toward the next layer of clothing, where it then evaporates. Avoid wearing long underwear made of cotton, as it is slow to dry and keeps moisture next to your skin.

The second layer you'll wear is the "insulating" layer. Aside from keeping you warm, this layer needs to "breathe" so you stay dry while hiking. A fabric that provides insulation and dries quickly is fleece. It's interesting to note that this one-of-a-kind fabric is made out of recycled plastic. Purchasing a zip-up jacket made of this material is highly recommended.

The last line of layering defense is the "shell" layer. You'll need some type of waterproof, windproof, breathable jacket that will fit over all of your other layers. It should have a large hood that fits over a hat. You'll also need a good pair of rain pants made from a similar waterproof, breathable fabric. Some Gore-Tex jackets cost as much as $500, but you should know that there are more affordable fabrics out there that work just as well.

Now that you've learned the basics of layering, don't forget to protect your hands and face. In cold, windy, or rainy weather you'll need a hat made of wool or fleece and insulated, waterproof gloves that will keep your hands warm and toasty. As mentioned earlier, buying an additional pair of light silk liners to wear under your regular gloves is a good idea.

Footwear. If you have any extra money to spend on your trip, put that money into boots or trail shoes. Poor shoes will bring a hike to a halt faster than anything else. To avoid this annoyance, buy shoes that provide support and are lightweight and flexible. A lightweight hiking boot is better than a heavy, leather mountaineering boot for most day hikes and backpacking. Trail running shoes provide a little extra cushion and are made in a high-top style that many people wear for hiking. These running shoes are lighter, more flexible, and more breathable than hiking boots. If you know you'll be hiking in wet weather often, purchase boots or shoes with a Gore-Tex liner, which will help keep your feet dry.

When buying boots or trail shoes, be sure to wear the same type of socks you'll be wearing on the trail. If the boots you're buying are for cold-weather hiking, try them on while wearing two pairs of socks. Speaking of socks, a good cold-weather sock combination is to wear a thinner sock made of wool or polypropylene covered by a heavier outer sock made of wool. The inner sock protects the foot from the rubbing effects of the outer sock and prevents blisters. Many outdoor stores have some type of ramp to simulate hiking uphill and downhill. Be sure to take advantage of this test, as toe-jamming shoe fronts can be painful and debilitating on the downhill trek.

Once you've purchased your footwear, be sure to break them in before you hit the trail. New footwear is often stiff and needs to be stretched and molded to your foot.

Hiking poles. Hiking poles help with balance and, more important, take pressure off your knees. The ones with shock absorbers are easier on your elbows and knees. Some poles even come with a camera attachment to use as a monopod. And heaven forbid you meet a mountain lion, bear, or unfriendly dog, the poles can make you look a lot bigger.

Daypacks and backpacks. No matter what type of hiking you do, you'll need a pack of some sort to carry the basic trail essentials. There are a variety of packs on the market, but let's first discuss what you intend to use it for: day hikes or overnight trips.

If you plan on doing a day hike, a daypack should have some of the following characteristics: a padded hip belt that's at least 2 inches in diameter (avoid packs with only a small piece of nylon webbing for a hip belt); a chest strap (which helps stabilize the pack against your body); external pockets to carry water and other items that you want easy access to; an internal pocket to hold keys, a knife, a wallet, and other miscellaneous items; an external lashing system to hold a jacket; and a hydration pocket for carrying a hydration system (which consists of a water bladder with an attachable drinking hose).

For short hikes, some hikers like to use a fanny pack to store just a camera, food, a compass, a map, and other trail essentials. Most fanny packs have pockets for two water bottles and a padded hip belt.

If you intend to do an extended, overnight trip, there are multiple considerations. First off, you need to decide what kind of framed pack you want. There are two backpack types for backpacking: the internal frame and the external frame. An internal frame pack rests closer to your body, making it more stable and easier to balance when hiking over rough terrain. An external frame pack is just that, an aluminum frame attached to the exterior of the pack. An external frame pack is better for long backpack trips because it distributes the pack weight better and you can carry heavier loads. It's easier to pack, and your gear is more accessible. It also offers better back ventilation in hot weather.

The most critical measurement for fitting a pack is torso length. The pack needs to rest evenly on your hips without sagging. A good pack will come in two or three sizes and have straps and hip belts that are adjustable according to your body size and characteristics.

When you purchase a backpack, go to an outdoor store with salespeople who are knowledgeable in how to properly fit a pack. Once the pack is fitted for you, load the pack with the amount of weight you plan on taking on the trail. The weight of the pack should be distributed evenly and you should be able to swing your arms and walk briskly without feeling out of balance. Another good technique for evaluating a pack is to walk up and down stairs and make quick turns to the right and to the left to be sure the pack doesn't feel out of balance. Other features that are nice to have on a backpack include a removable daypack or fanny pack, external pockets for extra water, and extra lash points to attach a jacket or other items.

Sleeping bags and pads. Sleeping bags are rated by temperature. You can purchase a bag made of synthetic fiber, or you can buy a goose down bag. Goose down bags are more expensive, but they have a higher insulating capacity by weight and will keep their loft longer. You'll want to purchase a bag with a temperature rating that fits the time of year and conditions you are most likely to camp in. One caveat: The techno-standard for temperature ratings is far from perfect. Ratings vary from manufacturer to manufacturer, so to protect yourself you should purchase a bag rated 10 to 15 degrees below the temperature you expect to be camping in. Synthetic bags are more resistant to water than down bags, but many down bags are now made with a Gore-Tex shell that helps to repel water. Down bags are also more compressible than synthetic bags and take up less room in your pack, which is an important consideration if you are planning a multiday backpack trip. Features to look for in a sleeping bag include a mummy-style bag, a hood you can cinch down around your head in cold weather, and draft tubes along the zippers that help keep heat in and drafts out.

You'll also want a sleeping pad to provide insulation and padding from the cold ground. There are different types of sleeping pads available, from the more expensive self-inflating air mattresses to the less expensive closed-cell foam pads. Self-inflating air mattresses are usually heavier than closed-cell foam mattresses and are prone to punctures.

Tents. The tent is your home away from home while on the trail. It provides protection from wind, snow, rain, and insects. A three-season tent is a good choice for backpacking and can range in price from $100 to $500. These lightweight and versatile tents provide protection in all types of weather, except heavy snowstorms or high winds, and range in weight from 4 to 8 pounds. Look for a tent that's easy to set up and will easily fit two people with gear. Dome-type tents usually offer more headroom and places to store gear. Other tent designs include a vestibule where you can store wet boots and backpacks. Some nice-to-have items in a tent include interior pockets to store small items and lashing points to hang a clothesline. Most three-season tents also come with stakes so you can secure the tent in high winds.

Before you purchase a tent, set it up and take it down a few times to be sure it is easy to handle. Also, sit inside the tent and make sure it has enough room for you and your gear.

Cell phones. Many hikers carry their cell phones into the backcountry these days in case of emergency. That's fine and good, but please know that cell phone coverage is often poor to nonexistent in valleys, canyons, and thick forest. More problematic, people have started to call for help because they're tired or lost. Let's go back to being prepared. You are responsible for yourself in the backcountry. Use your brain to avoid problems, and if you do encounter one, first use your brain to try to correct the situation. Only use your cell phone, if it works, in true emergencies.

Hiking With Children

Hiking with children isn't a matter of how many miles you can cover or how much elevation gain you make in a day; it's about seeing and experiencing nature through their eyes.

Kids like to explore and have fun. They like to stop and point out bugs and plants, look under rocks, jump in puddles, and throw sticks. If you're taking a toddler or young child on a hike, start with a trail that you're familiar with. Trails that have interesting things for kids, like piles of leaves to play in or a small stream to wade through during the summer, will make the hike much more enjoyable for them and will keep them from getting bored.

You can keep your child's attention if you have a strategy before starting on the trail. Using games is not only an effective way to keep a child's attention, it's also a great way to teach him or her about nature. Quiz children on the names of plants and animals. Pick up a family-friendly outdoor hobby like geocaching (www .geocaching.com) or letterboxing (www.atlasquest.com), both of which combine the outdoors, clue-solving, and treasure hunting. If your children are old enough, let them carry their own daypack filled with snacks and water. So that you are sure to go at their pace and not yours, let them lead the way. Playing follow the leader works particularly well when you have a group of children. Have each child take a turn at being the leader.

With children, a lot of clothing is key. The only thing predictable about weather is that it will change. Especially in mountainous areas, weather can change dramatically in a very short time. Always bring extra clothing for children, regardless of the season. In the winter, have your children wear wool socks and warm layers such as long underwear, a fleece jacket and hat, wool mittens, and good rain gear. It's not a bad idea to have these along in late fall and early spring as well. Good footwear is also important. A sturdy pair of high-top tennis shoes or lightweight hiking boots are the best bet for little ones. If you're hiking in the summer near a lake or stream, bring along a pair of old sneakers that your child can put on when he or she wants to go exploring in the water. Remember when you're near any type of water, always watch your child at all times. Also, keep a close eye on teething toddlers who may decide a rock or leaf of poison oak is an interesting item to put in their mouth.

From spring through fall, you'll want your kids to wear a wide-brimmed hat to keep their face, head, and ears protected from the hot sun. Also, make sure your children wear sunscreen at all times. Choose a brand without PABA—children have sensitive skin and may have an allergic reaction to sunscreen that contains PABA. If you are hiking with children younger than six months, don't use sunscreen or insect repellent. Instead, be sure that their head, face, neck, and ears are protected from the sun with a wide-brimmed hat, and that all other skin exposed to the sun is protected with the appropriate clothing.

Remember that food is fun. Kids like snacks, so it's important to bring a lot of munchies for the trail. Stopping often for snack breaks is a fun way to keep the trail interesting. Raisins, apples, granola bars, crackers and cheese, cereal, and trail mix all make great snacks. If your children are old enough to carry their own backpack, fill it with treats before you leave. If your kids don't like drinking water, you can bring boxes of fruit juice.

Avoid poorly designed child-carrying packs—you don't want to break your back carrying your child. Most child-carrying backpacks designed to hold a 40-pound child will contain a large carrying pocket to hold diapers and other items. Some have an optional rain/sun hood.

Hiking With Your Dog

Bringing your furry friend with you is always more fun than leaving him behind. Our canine pals make great trail buddies because they never complain and always make good company. Hiking with your dog can be a rewarding experience, especially if you plan ahead.

Getting your dog in shape. Before you plan outdoor adventures with your dog, make sure he's in shape for the trail. Getting your dog into shape takes the same discipline as getting yourself into shape, but luckily, your dog can get in shape with you. Take your dog with you on your daily runs or walks. If there is a park near your house, hit a tennis ball or play Frisbee with your dog.

Swimming is also an excellent way to get your dog into shape. If there is a lake or river near where you live and your dog likes the water, have him retrieve a tennis ball or stick. Gradually build your dog's stamina up over a two- to three-month period. A good rule of thumb is to assume that your dog will travel twice as far as you will on the trail. If you plan on doing a 5-mile hike, be sure your dog is in shape for a 10-mile hike.

Training your dog for the trail. Before you go on your first hiking adventure with your dog, be sure he has a firm grasp of the basics of canine etiquette and behavior. Make sure he can sit, lie down, stay, and come. One of the most important commands you can teach your canine pal is to "come" under any situation. It's easy for your friend's nose to lead him astray or possibly lost. Another helpful command is the "get behind" command. When you're on a hiking trail that's narrow, you can have your dog follow behind you when other trail users approach. Nothing is more bothersome than an enthusiastic dog that runs back and forth on the trail and disrupts the peace of the trail for others. When you see other trail users approaching on the trail, give them the right-of-way by quietly stepping off the trail and making your dog lie down and stay until they pass.

Equipment. The most critical pieces of equipment you can invest in for your dog are proper identification and a sturdy leash. Flexi-leads work well for hiking because they give your dog more freedom to explore but still leave you in control. Make sure your dog has identification that includes your name and address and a number for your veterinarian. Other forms of identification for your dog include a tattoo or a microchip. You should consult your veterinarian for more information on these last two options.

The next piece of equipment you'll want to consider is a pack for your dog. By no means should you hold all of your dog's essentials in your pack—let him carry his own gear! Dogs that are in good shape can carry 30 to 40 percent of their own weight.

Most packs are fitted by a dog's weight and girth measurement. Companies that make dog packs generally include guidelines to help you pick out the size that's right for your dog. Some characteristics to look for when purchasing a pack for your dog include a harness that contains two padded girth straps, a padded chest strap, leash attachments, removable saddle bags, internal water bladders, and external gear cords.

You can introduce your dog to the pack by first placing the empty pack on his back and letting him wear it around the yard. Keep an eye on him during this first introduction. He may decide to chew through the straps if you aren't watching him closely. Once he learns to treat the pack as an object of fun and not a foreign enemy, fill the pack evenly on both sides with a few ounces of dog food in resealable plastic bags. Have your dog wear his pack on your daily walks for a period of two to three weeks. Each week add a little more weight to the pack until your dog will accept carrying the maximum amount of weight he can carry.

You can also purchase collapsible water and dog food bowls for your dog. These bowls are lightweight and can easily be stashed into your pack or your dog's. If you are hiking on rocky terrain or in the snow, you can purchase footwear for your dog that will protect his feet from cuts and bruises.

Always carry plastic bags to remove feces from the trail. It is a courtesy to other trail users and helps protect local wildlife.

The following is a list of items to bring when you take your dog hiking: collapsible water bowls, a comb, a collar and leash, dog food, plastic bags for feces, a dog pack, flea/tick powder, paw protection, water, and a first-aid kit that contains eye ointment, tweezers, scissors, stretchy foot wrap, gauze, antibacterial wash, sterile cotton tip applicators, antibiotic ointment, and cotton wrap.

First aid for your dog. Your dog is just as prone—if not more prone—to getting in trouble on the trail as you are, so be prepared. Here's a rundown of the more likely misfortunes that might befall your little friend.

Bees and wasps. If a bee or wasp stings your dog, remove the stinger with a pair of tweezers and place a mudpack or a cloth dipped in cold water over the affected area.

Porcupines. One good reason to keep your dog on a leash is to prevent it from getting a nose full of porcupine quills. You may be able to remove the quills with pliers, but a veterinarian is the best person to do this nasty job because most dogs need to be sedated.

Heat stroke. Avoid hiking with your dog in really hot weather. Dogs with heat stroke will pant excessively, lie down and refuse to get up, and become lethargic and disoriented. If your dog shows any of these signs on the trail, have him lie down in the shade. If you are near a stream, pour cool water over your dog's entire body to help bring his body temperature back to normal.

Heartworm. Dogs get heartworms from mosquitoes that carry the disease in the prime mosquito months of July and August. Giving your dog a monthly pill prescribed by your veterinarian easily prevents this condition.

Plant pitfalls. One of the biggest plant hazards for dogs on the trail are foxtails. Foxtails are pointed grass seed heads that bury themselves in your friend's fur and between his toes, and even get in his ear canal. If left unattended, these nasty seeds can work their way under the skin and cause abscesses and other problems. If you have a long-haired dog, consider trimming the hair between his toes and giving him a summer haircut to help prevent foxtails from attaching to his fur. After every hike, always look over your dog for these seeds—especially between his toes and his ears.

Other plant hazards include burrs, thorns, thistles, and poison oak. If you find any burrs or thistles on your dog, remove them as soon as possible before they become an unmanageable mat. Thorns can pierce a dog's foot and cause a great deal of pain. If you see that your dog is lame, stop and check his feet for thorns. Dogs are immune to poison oak, but they can pick up the sticky, oily substance from the plant and transfer it to you.

Protect those paws. Be sure to keep your dog's nails trimmed so he avoids getting soft tissue or joint injuries. If your dog slows and refuses to go on, check to see that his paws aren't torn or worn. You can protect your dog's paws from trail hazards such as sharp gravel, foxtails, lava scree, and thorns by purchasing dog boots.

Sunburn. If your dog has light skin he is an easy target for sunburn on his nose and other exposed skin areas. You can apply a nontoxic sunscreen to exposed skin areas that will help protect him from overexposure to the sun.

Ticks and fleas. Ticks can easily give your dog Lyme disease, as well as other diseases. Before you hit the trail, treat your dog with a flea and tick spray or powder. You can also ask your veterinarian about a once-a-month pour-on treatment that repels fleas and ticks.

Mosquitoes and deer flies. These little flying machines can do a job on your dog's snout and ears. Best bet is to spray your dog with fly repellent for horses to discourage both pests.

Giardia. Dogs can get giardiasis, which results in diarrhea. It is usually not debilitating, but it's definitely messy. A vaccine against *Giardia* is available.

Mushrooms. Make sure your dog doesn't sample mushrooms along the trail. They could be poisonous to him, but he doesn't know that.

When you are finally ready to hit the trail with your dog, keep in mind that national parks and many wilderness areas do not allow dogs on trails. Your best bet is to hike in national forests, Bureau of Land Management (BLM) lands, and state parks. Always call ahead to see what the restrictions are.

Hike Index

About the Author

Kathryn Hopper is the author of *Best Easy Day Hikes Dallas/Fort Worth* (FalconGuides) as well as *Fort Worth: Where the Best Begins* and *Family Fun Travel Southwest*. A mother of four who lives in Southlake, she works as a writer and multimedia producer at Texas Christian University.